INSIGHT GUIDES

HONG KONG

DISCOVERY CHANNEL

APA PUBLICATIONS L
Part of the Langenscheidt Publishing Group

INSIGHT GUIDE
HONG KONG

ABOUT THIS BOOK

Editorial

Project Editor
Scott Rutherford
Editorial Director
Brian Bell

Distribution

UK & Ireland
GeoCenter International Ltd
The Viables Centre, Harrow Way
Basingstoke, Hants RG22 4BJ
Fax: (44) 1256 817988

United States
Langenscheidt Publishers, Inc.
46–35 54th Road, Maspeth, NY 11378
Fax: 1 (718) 784 0640

Canada
Thomas Allen & Son Ltd
390 Steelcase Road East
Markham, Ontario L3R 1G2
Fax: (1) 905 475 6747

Australia
Universal Publishers
1 Waterloo Road
Macquarie Park, NSW 2113
Fax: (61) 2 9888 9074

New Zealand
Hema Maps New Zealand Ltd (HNZ)
Unit D, 24 Ra ORA Drive
East Tamaki, Auckland
Fax: (64) 9 273 6479

Worldwide
Apa Publications GmbH & Co.
Verlag KG (Singapore branch)
38 Joo Koon Road, Singapore 628990
Tel: (65) 6865 1600. Fax: (65) 6861 6438

Printing

Insight Print Services (Pte) Ltd
38 Joo Koon Road, Singapore 628990
Tel: (65) 6865 1600. Fax: (65) 6861 6438

© 2004 Apa Publications GmbH & Co.
Verlag KG (Singapore branch)
All Rights Reserved
First Edition 1980
Ninth Edition 1998
Updated 2004

CONTACTING THE EDITORS
We would appreciate it if readers
would alert us to errors or out-
dated information by writing to:
Insight Guides, P.O. Box 7910,
London SE1 1WE, England.
Fax: (44) 20 7403 0290.
insight@apaguide.co.uk

www.insightguides.com

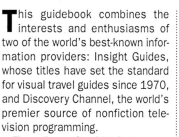

Tthis guidebook combines the
interests and enthusiasms of
two of the world's best-known information providers: Insight Guides,
whose titles have set the standard
for visual travel guides since 1970,
and Discovery Channel, the world's
premier source of nonfiction television programming.

The editors of Insight Guides provide both practical advice and
general understanding about a
destination's history, culture,
institutions, politics and
people. Discovery Chan-
nel and its Web site,
www.discovery.com,
help millions of view-
ers explore their world
from the comfort of
their own home and
also encourage them
to explore it first hand.

How to use this book

The book is carefully structured to
convey an understanding of the territory and its energy, and to guide
you through its sights and activities:
◆ To understand Hong Kong in all
its possibilities, one needs to know
something of its past. The first section covers Hong Kong's history and
culture in lively, authoritative essays.
◆ The main Places section provides
a full run-down of all the destinations worth seeing, covering
not only Hong Kong, but
also both Macau and
Guangzhou. The essential
places of interest are coordinated by number with
full-colour maps.
◆ The Travel Tips listings
section provides a conve-
nient point of reference
for information on travel,

Map Legend

– · – ·	International Boundary
– – – –	Province
⊖	Border Crossing
— · — ·	National Park
– – – –	Ferry Route
Ⓜ	Metro
✈ ✈	Airport
🚌	Bus Station
Ⓟ	Parking
❶	Tourist Information
✉	Post Office
♦ ♦ ♂	Church/Ruins
♀ ♠	Mosque
✿ ✿	Synagogue
♦ ♂	Castle/Ruins
∴	Archaeological Site
∩	Cave
★	Place of Interest

The main places of interest in the Places section are coordinated by number with a full-colour map (e.g. ❶), and a symbol at the top of every right-hand page tells you where to find the map.

hotels, restaurants, and shops in Hong Kong, Macau, and Guangzhou. ◆ Photographs are chosen not only to illustrate geography and locations, but also to convey the many moods of the area.

The contributors

The handover to China in 1997 made 1998 a fine year for the original publication of this new edition, supervised by **Scott Rutherford**, who worked on many of Apa's Asian and Pacific titles. The guide's foundations extend back to 1980, when the first edition of *Insight Guide: Hong Kong* was published. Producing that book were Hong Kong-based **Saul Lockhart**, who still calls Hong Kong home, and long-time Asia resident **Leonard Lueras**.

Ed Peters has lived in Hong Kong's New Territories for over a decade, which prepared him well for updating the New Territories chapters. Peters also wrote the architecture essay. **Paul Hicks** had one of this book's more dashing assignments: updating the chapters for Hong Kong island; and one of the most thankless tasks: overhauling the Travel Tips section.

Suzanne Lidster finds her hometown of Hong Kong well-suited for her interests in both art and Buddhism. She has worked as a translator, copywriter, and travel writer, and updated the Kowloon section. Beijing-born **Angelica Cheung** lives in Hong Kong and works as a freelance writer. She worked on the history and feature chapters. Updating Lamma and Lantau islands was **John Haseman**, a retired US Foreign Service officer.

New to this edition are chapters covering Guangzhou. **Angie Ching Yuan**, who wrote the Guangzhou and Outside Guangzhou chapters, lives in Shanghai. **Bill Williams**, based in Osaka, travelled to Macau to update the details on that small enclave.

Contributing photographers to the guide include San Francisco-based **Catherine Karnow**, who has contributed to Apa books on China, Vietnam, and the Philippines. **Jack Hollingsworth** has photographed Bali, Singapore, China, and Hong Kong for Insight Guides.

Contributors to earlier editions of *Insight Guide: Hong Kong* included **Harry Rolnick**, **Roger Boschman**, **Derek Maitland**, **Alan Chalkey**, **Frena Bloomfield**, **Veronica Huang**, **Lesley Nelson**, **Linda Wong** and **Dinah Gardner**. The guide was brought up to date in 2004 by **Philippa Conway**, a journalist and writer based in Hong Kong.

Insight Guide
HONG KONG

CONTENTS

Maps

Travel Tips

Places

A CHINESE CITY?

*Few cities ignite the senses as does Hong Kong, and the appeal
is as strong as ever following the return to Chinese sovereignty*

In the years that followed the handover on 30 June 1997, Hong Kong has adopted some cosmetic changes – new flags, coins and the royal cypher has been chiselled off some post boxes – but the essential credo of the one-time crown colony, making money, has altered not a whit. The transfer of sovereignty was peaceful, smooth and historic, and Hong Kong is now forging into the new Millennium.

The final years of British rule were not without incident though. When Britain went into negotiations with China in the early 1980s, it was hoping for an extension of the 99-year lease on the New Territories, which comprises 90 percent of Hong Kong's land area. Without claim to the New Territories, which not only buffers Kowloon Peninsula, Victoria Harbour and the island of Hong Kong from the mainland, but also houses many of those who make Hong Kong tick, the rest of Hong Kong was strategically exposed.

In the end, Chinese patience retrieved not only the New Territories, but all of the British Crown Colony, including the two areas of Hong Kong Island and Kowloon that were "ceded in perpetuity" in 1841 and 1856. Britain had legal right to keep Kowloon and Hong Kong Island, but perhaps it had finally realised that the British Empire was indeed history. (During negotiations, Deng Xiaoping had bluntly said that legally he could, and perhaps would, send in his army to the New Territories the moment the lease expired.)

Britain clearly came out second best after two years of negotiations, managing to extract a 50-year guarantee from China beginning in 1997 that on paper ensures Hong Kong's basic freedoms as a Special Administrative Region (SAR) of China. That arrangement is conveniently accommodated by the official Beijing stance of "one country, two systems". In refugee-minded Hong Kong, where almost half the 6 million population had earlier fled from turbulent upheavals in China, the idea of trusting China for the 50 years after 1997 made every year of the 1980s and 1990s a year of heartburn.

It's all history now. Hong Kong is part of China. Still, streets and most public places will retain their colonial names for the foreseeable future, although one day, no doubt, the Chinese will replace the lingering colonial residue.

With the handover came other changes. Perhaps most important was the opening of a new airport. Until 1998, arrival in Hong Kong by air was exciting by contemporary standards: swooping in low over the harbour, a quick turn or two as the pilot lined up with the runway at Kai Tak on Kowloon Peninsula's eastern side, swooshing in low over the infamous Walled City. Then you were on ground right in the

PRECEDING PAGES: Victoria Harbour boat traffic; Tsim Sha Tsui nightlife; festival colours, Kowloon; New Year decorations, Central District, Hong Kong Island.
LEFT: the bright lights of Wan Chai.

middle of Hong Kong. Kai Tak Airport's presence, however, limited the heights of buildings in Kowloon, one of the world's most densely populated places, and it restricted the use of flashing lights on outdoor signs. It was a convenient airport, but awkward in its location. The new international airport on Lantau, Hong Kong's largest island and west of Hong Kong Island, permits more spacious facilities. A high-speed rail link puts the city only 20 minutes away.

Whether on Hong Kong Island or Kowloon, for the most part Hong Kong is an excellent city for walking. Indeed, walking is essential to uncover Hong Kong's musty olden days amidst its small back alleys and obscure little shops forgotten by time. Still, should walking prove impractical, Hong Kong's transport infrastructure of taxis, metro, trams, buses and ferries makes few places inaccessible. It would be a shame, though, not to get out and feel the city.

The peninsula of Kowloon, which juts south from the New Territories into Victoria Harbour, is where most visitors feel they've really jumped into Hong Kong. From Kowloon, three tunnels burrow beneath Victoria Harbour to surface on Hong Kong Island. More enjoyable, however, is the seven-minute cruise of the Star Ferry from Kowloon's Tsim Sha Tsui to Central or Wan Chai. Hong Kong Island's northern shore, which fronts Victoria Harbour, is a forest of skyscrapers buttressed by Victoria Peak, or simply, The Peak. It is truly one of the finest skylines in the world. However, with Kai Tak Airport's closing, height restrictions on Kowloon have eased, and in another decade or two, Kowloon's skyline may rival that of Hong Kong Island's Central and Wan Chai districts.

How is this entrepôt of the Pacific and Asia faring under Chinese rule? The initial worry was that Hong Kong would be dragged into the stultifying Chinese Communist way of doing things. It hasn't happened, and the reality is that Hong Kong may be the engine that drags China into the 21st century and beyond. There is no way that the people of Hong Kong are going to change their motivations, ambitions and lifestyles, especially as they had no voice in the decision to hand over Hong Kong to China.

"Borrowed time, borrowed place" is the perfect description, coined by novelist Han Su-yin, of Hong Kong. Historically, the former colony's citizens tried to ignore the perpetual uncertainty of their future – their "borrowed time" – and preferred to make their fortunes quickly in the fervent hope that destiny would unfold without severe or permanent disruptions. Hong Kong is now reassuming the very real Chinese self that always lay just below the modern urbane façade. It knows that its destiny is in the hands of fate, influenced perhaps by hefty doses of good luck.

China recovered the city that it signed away 156 years before and used the event as a propaganda coup. Now officially part of the PRC, Hong Kong is still markedly different from the mainland. And while it may be a Special Administrative Region, it maintains its own identity, a blend of Chinese with a strong cosmopolitan flavour, an eye for the main chance and a stolid imperturbability when economic times get tough. ❏

RIGHT: morning exercise on the harbour promenade, Tsim Sha Tsui.

Decisive Dates

EARLY HISTORY

1685 Emperor Kangxi allows limited trade in Guangzhou (Canton). Ships begin arriving from the British East India Company.

1773 British traders unload 1,000 chests of opium in Guangzhou.

1800 China's opium consumption reaches 2,000 chests a year, forcing Beijing to ban the drug, which then drives the opium trade underground.

1834 The British East India Company loses its monopoly on the opium trade to other European nations.

1839 China appoints the anti-opium viceroy, Lin Xizu, to clean up drugs in Guangzhou. He confiscates some 20,000 chests of opium from the British. Hostilities mount until November, when British ships blow up four Chinese junks, sparking the first Anglo-Chinese war, known as the Opium War.

1841 Negotiations between China and Britain break down, and on 7 January the British fleet attacks Guangzhou and occupies the city's forts. Three days later, the British envoy and the Chinese representative agree on a preliminary resolution known as the Convention of Chuen Pi, which cedes the island of Hong Kong to the British. But neither government is happy with the terms of the Convention and both refuse to ratify it.

1842 The Opium War ends and British possession of Hong Kong is confirmed by the Treaty of Nanjing, which cedes Hong Kong Island to Britain "in perpetuity". Sir Henry Pottinger becomes the first British governor of Hong Kong.

COLONIAL PERIOD

1856 In March, the Chinese cede Kowloon (Tsim Sha Tsui) and Stonecutter's Island "in perpetuity" to Britain. But outbreaks of hostility continue, culminating in the Second Opium War, also known as the Arrow War.

1862 A Sino-Portuguese treaty is signed, granting Macau a colonial status similar to Hong Kong's.

1898 Britain forces China to lease it the New Territories, which includes 233 outlying islands, for 99 years, beginning 1 July 1898. The lease expires on 27 June 1997.

1911 Dr Sun Yatsen overthrows the Qing dynasty and establishes the Republic of China.

1912 The emperor Puyi officially abdicates.

1922 The first seamen's strike breaks out in Hong Kong.

1931 The Japanese occupy Dongbei, or Manchuria.

1932 The Chinese Communists declare war on Japan.

1945 World War II ends, but China's ongoing civil war between the Communists and the Nationalists (Guomintang) resumes.

1949 The Nationalists are defeated and flee to Taiwan. The Communists found the People's Republic of China.

1966 Rioting flares up in Hong Kong over a price increase in the first-class Star Ferry fare. China begins the disastrous Cultural Revolution.

1971 The People's Republic of China replaces Taiwan in the United Nations General Assembly (Taiwan had become the sole representative of China in the United Nations after the People's Republic of China was founded in 1949). Sir Murray MacLehose becomes the first Hong Kong governor to be appointed from the British diplomatic corps.

1972 U.S. President Richard Nixon visits China.

1973 The first New Town, Tuen Mun, opens.

1974 The Independent Commission Against Corruption (ICAC) is set up to stamp out crime and corruption.

1978 China starts to reform its economy and open its doors to the world.

1979 Hong Kong's US$1 billion Mass Transit Railway (MTR) opens.

1982 British Prime Minister Margaret Thatcher visits Beijing and Hong Kong in September and begins discussion on Hong Kong's future. China decides to develop Shenzhen, a small town on Hong Kong's northern border, into a Special Economic Zone.

HANDOVER COUNTDOWN

1983 China reveals its plan for Hong Kong to become a Special Administrative Region (SAR) after the territory is returned in 1997. Hong Kong will keep its own capitalist system, judiciary and police, but the head of Hong Kong will be a Hong Kong Chinese.

1984 The British Ambassador to China and the Chinese Vice Foreign Minister initial "A Draft Agreement on the Future of Hong Kong", ending two years of acrimony. The Hong Kong government starts to plan for the territory's administration in the years running up to 1997.

1985 Britain and China ratify the Sino-British Joint Declaration initialled the previous year. A Sino-British joint liaison group is created in regard to Hong Kong's

1991 Beijing and London announce an agreement regarding the new airport. Later, British Prime Minister John Major goes to Beijing, the first Western leader to do so since the Tiananmen massacre in 1989.

1992 Hong Kong's 28th and last British governor, Chris Patten, arrives in the territory and proposes political reform. The move draws attacks from Beijing.

1994 The Legislative Council passes Patten's proposed electoral reforms. Beijing and London continue to argue.

1997 China resumes sovereignty on 1 July, Tung Chee-hwa appointed Chief Executive, Legco is temporarily replaced by the Provisional Legislature and Hong Kong becomes a Special Administrative Region. The Stock Market dives in response to the Asian economic crisis.

COLONIAL GOVERNORS 1900–1997

Hong Kong's first British governor, Sir Henry Pottinger, took over administration in 1841.

1898–1903: Sir Henry A. Blake
1904–1907: Sir Matthew Nathan
1907–1912: Sir Frederick Lugard
1912–1919: Sir Francis H. May
1919–1925: Sir Reginald E. Stubbs
1925–1930: Sir Cecil Clementi
1930–1935: Sir William Peel
1935–1937: Sir Alexander Caldecott
1937–1940: Sir Geoffry Northcote
1941–1947: Sir Mark Young
1947–1957: Sir Alexander Grantham
1958–1964: Sir Robert Black
1964–1971: Sir David Trench
1971–1982: Sir Murray Maclehose
1982–1987: Sir Edward Youde
1987–1992: Sir David Wilson
1992–1997: Christopher Patten

future. The colony holds its first election for the Legislative Council, drawing criticism from China, which insists that any political changes not accepted by Beijing will not be respected after the handover.

1988 The proposed Basic Law, Hong Kong's operating constitution after handover, is published.

1989 One million people take to the streets to protest against the Tiananmen Square massacre. The government announces plans for a new airport; Beijing attacks the British government for not having been consulted. The forced repatriation of Vietnamese boat people begins.

LEFT: Viceroy of Guangdong province, 1870.
RIGHT: Sir Edward Youde arrives for duty as governor.

POST-HANDOVER

1998 Elections held for the Legislative Council (Legco). Chek Lap Kok airport opens.

1999 The rule of law is undermined as government asks Beijing to overturn Court of Final Appeal's ruling on the right of abode. Typhoon York, Hong Kong's first "direct hit" since 1983, kills two and injures over 500.

2003 The economy continues to flounder, particularly from March to May when the deadly SARS virus spreads to Hong Kong. Proposals for national security laws ("Article 23") spark mass protests on 1 July; over half a million people take to the streets. The government backs down and shelves the plans indefinitely.

2004 Up to half a million protestors again march on 1 July, calling for more democracy. ❑

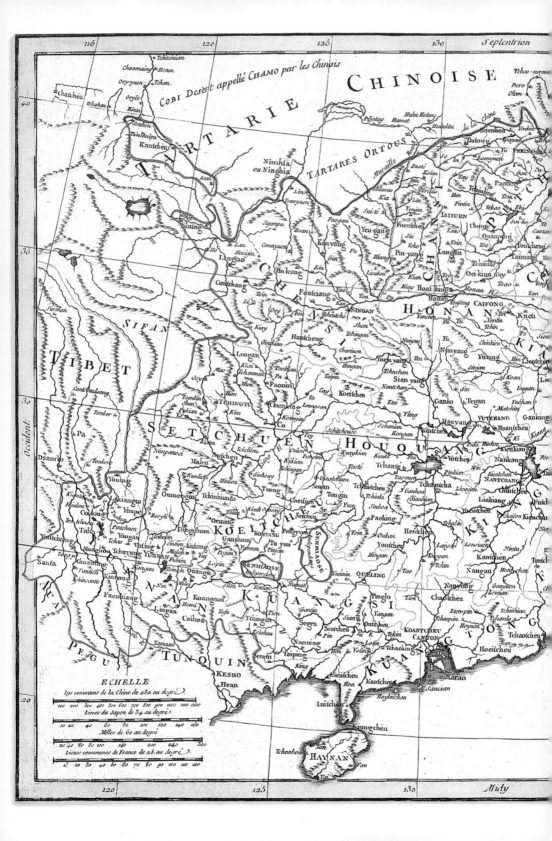

L'EMPIRE
DE LA CHINE
d'après l'Atlas Chinois,
AVEC LES ISLES DU JAPON?
Par M. Bonne
Hydrographe
au Bureau de la Marine.
A PARIS
Chez Lattré Graveur rue St. Jacques
à la Ville de Bordeaux
Avec Priv

Sealed by the Plenipotentiaries on board
Her Britannic Majesty's Ship
"Cornwallis" this twenty ninth day of August
1842, corresponding with the Chinese
date, twentyfourth day of the Seventh month
in the twenty Second year of Taoukwang.

大清欽差便宜行事大臣等

大英欽奉全權公使大臣各為

約者

君上定事蓋用關防印信各執一冊為據俾即日按照和約開載之條施行妥辦無礙矣要至和

道光二十二年七月二十四日即英國記年之

大英君主汗華帥大臣關防

一千八百四十二年八月二十九日由江寧省會行

A BARREN ISLAND

At first considered an ill-chosen gain from China, Hong Kong became an important
British colony almost through circumstance and even serendipity

To most people, Hong Kong's history starts from the Opium Wars in the 1840s. However, archaeological studies have uncovered evidence of ancient human life in Hong Kong more than 6,000 years ago at many sites along the winding shoreline. A growing number of scholars believe that during the earliest prehistoric periods, from the close of the fourth millennium BC, the region was within the framework of a changing environment in which sea levels rose from as much as 100 metres below the present level. Most of the excavated stone tools, pottery and other artifacts have been found preserved in coastal areas, suggesting a strong dependence on the sea.

Recent excavations have revealed two main neolithic cultures lying in stratified sequence. Coarse, cord-marked pottery has been found at the older level, together with a fine, soft, fragile pottery decorated with linear carvings, perforations and sometimes paintings. Chipped and polished stone tools have also been found. Current indications suggest a fourth millennium BC date for this initial phase.

At the later level appears a new ceramic form, decorated with a wide range of impressed geometric patterns. In this phase, beginning in the mid-third millennium BC, polished stone tools show better workmanship and a variety of shapes, suggesting improvements in techniques. Ornaments such as rings, some slotted, were also made from quartz and other suitable stones. These adornments came in a range of sizes, sometimes displaying exquisite craftsmanship.

Bronze appeared in the middle of the second millennium BC. Weapons, knives, arrowheads and halberds, and tools such as socketed axes and fish hooks, have been excavated from Hong Kong sites. There is evidence, too, in the form of stone moulds from the islands of Chek Lap Kok, Lantau and Lamma, that the metal was

worked locally. The pottery of the Bronze Age was fired at a much higher temperature and decorated with designs, many of which are reminiscent of the geometric patterns of the late neolithic period. But some patterns, such as the "Kui-dragon" or "double F" patterns, were characteristic of the region in the Bronze Age.

Ancient Chinese writings have been found with descriptions of the lives of maritime people that resemble those in China's southeastern coastal areas, suggesting they might come from similar origins. Rock carvings, most of which are geometric in style, have also been discovered around Hong Kong island and on some of the smaller, mostly uninhabited islands.

An increasing number of people from the mainland came to settle in the region during the Qin (221–206 BC) and Han (206 BC–AD 220) dynasties, and these migrants influenced the indigenous populations. Coins of the Han period have been found in Hong Kong, and a brick tomb was uncovered at Kowloon's Lei

PRECEDING PAGES: 17th-century French map of Asia; signatories page of the Treaty of Nanjing, 1842.
LEFT: "A Family Group in Macau", by George Chinnery.
RIGHT: Chinese junk on the high seas.

Cheng Uk in 1955 with a collection of typical Han tomb furniture. Other findings included pottery and iron implements. Findings of engraved writings, coins and celadon pottery from the Song dynasty suggest strong links between that Chinese dynasty and Hong Kong during the 13th century AD.

The many Ming-style blue-and-white porcelain works discovered on Lantau suggest increasing contact between the mainland and Hong Kong during the Ming (1368–1644) and

SEAGOING EUNUCH

In the 1500s, Zheng He's fleets had ships that were four times the size of European ships. Powered by a dozen sails on four or six masts, each ship carried 500 men on four decks.

The Western world began to show an interest in China and Asia during the 15th and 16th centuries due to the increased trade in Chinese products such as silk and tea through the Silk Road, which stretched from northwestern China to eastern Europe. In the 16th century, Chinese admiral Zheng He of the Ming dynasty led a fleet of ships to West Asia, Southeast Asia and even as far as East Africa in search of tribute, diplomacy and trading partners.

Gradually, more and more

Qing (1644–1911) dynasties. The same kind of fine porcelain was used in the courts of Southeast Asia and further west, and dates from the first few decades of the 16th century.

The excavation of a Qing-period fort on the island of Tung Lun has revealed fascinating details of the internal structure of the fortification and the nature of everyday utensils of a remote garrison during the final stages of imperial China. Recent investigations at the site of the former Kowloon Walled City have uncovered remnants of the old garrison wall and two stone plaques above the original South Gate, which bore the Chinese characters "South Gate" and "Kowloon Garrison City".

Europeans wanted to come to the region, and Hong Kong, with its sheltered harbour located on the trade routes of the Far East, became a hub of burgeoning entrepot trade between Western businessmen and China in the 16th century. The Portuguese who settled in Macau in 1555 were the first group of Westerners to arrive en masse in China. However, the British dominated foreign trade in China's southern region of Guangzhou (Canton) during the early stages of Western involvement in China.

In 1685, Emperor Kangxi, under whose reign the Qing dynasty experienced the peak of its power, opened trade in Guangzhou on a limited basis. Ships began arriving from the British East

India Company stations on the Indian coast. Fifteen years later, already the world's largest commercial organisation, the company received permission to build a storage warehouse outside of Guangzhou.

At first, trade with Western countries was in China's favour. Western traders paid huge amounts of silver for fine Chinese tea and silk products. Isolated from the outside world, the Chinese were proud of their ancient civilisation and regarded themselves as a highly civilised race and treated foreigners as barbarians.

There were tough terms for foreign traders who wanted to do business in China. Foreign eign traders. But despite these restrictions, the southern coastal region prospered with foreign trade, and even impoverished Macau had a minor renaissance as a destination for merchants seeking sumptuous off-season retreats.

The ancient Confucian classics, published in Latin in Paris in 1687, sparked a China craze in Europe. For some intellectuals in strife-torn and bigoted Europe, the Chinese empire seemed a model of order and reason with its just laws, a learned bureaucracy and, above all, a benevolent philosopher-king.

Chinese porcelain and furnishings, mock-Chinese landscape paintings and Chinese archi-

traders could only live in restricted areas in Guangzhou, and were only allowed to stay until the trading season ended. They could not bring in arms, warships, or women, and they had to pay for everything in hard cash, normally silver. Afraid of their potential bad influences, the Chinese rulers banned foreigners from learning the Chinese language. Foreign traders also had to put up with the Chinese system of royalties, bribes and fees. Local merchants were appointed by the emperor to keep an eye on for-

FAR LEFT: Emperor Kangxi opened trade in Guangzhou on a limited basis. **LEFT:** traders using the scales. **ABOVE:** Causeway Bay, in the mid 1800s.

tecture became fashionable among European aristocrats. In 1763, a 10-storey pagoda was built in London's Kew Gardens.

The British East India Company tried to balance its huge purchases from China by increasing its sale of opium to the Chinese, and by the beginning of the 19th century, the volume reached 2,000 chests a year. Alarmed at the outflow of silver, the Chinese emperor banned the drug trade completely in 1799. But neither foreign traders nor Guangdong merchants were willing to give up the profitable business, and they resorted to smuggling. By 1816, annual opium imports amounted to at least 5,000 chests. After the British East India Company lost its monopoly on the opium trade in 1834, traders from other countries hoped to get rich quickly by joining the lucrative but illegal opium business.

To eliminate the drug trade, in 1839 the emperor appointed Lin Zexu as a special commissioner to Guangzhou. Lin surrounded foreign factories with troops, stopped food supplies and refused to let anyone leave until all stocks of opium had been surrendered. Large amounts of opium were burned in the port city of Humen, at the mouth of the Zhu Jiang (Pearl River), and dealers and ship owners were forced to sign a pledge promising to stop importing opium or else face execution.

After a six-week siege of the British compound, the British government's representative, Capt. Charles Elliot of the Royal Navy, finally agreed to surrender more than 20,000 chests of opium to the local government.

Queen Victoria's Foreign Secretary, Lord Palmerston, instructed Lord Napier of the Royal Navy, who was Chief Superintendent of Trade, to deliver a letter to Lin Zexu. But Napier had no right under Chinese law to enter Guangzhou because only merchants were so privileged, and his rank only permitted him to pass a petition, not a letter, to Lin, who had by now been promoted to viceroy.

Deadlocked, Napier returned to Macau and Lin ordered the halt of all trade with the British. Napier sent two frigates up the Zhu Jiang to force passage past Guangzhou's forts, but the ships were cut off and hopelessly stranded. (Napier died three weeks later of natural causes.) The British community, mainly traders and their families, retreated to Macau, but were warned by the Portuguese governor that he could not be responsible for their safety. During the summer of 1839, the British took refuge on board ships in Hong Kong harbour.

Still reluctant to give up the lucrative opium business, British forces began to arrive in Guangzhou to force Lin to open up the province to opium trade. He refused, and in a diplomatic gesture to demonstrate his authority over British traders who had retreated to Macau, he made an official visit to the Portuguese colony.

At this point, the British decided to resort to more resolute measures to protect their interests in China. Claiming that the British in Guangzhou were in danger because of the Chinese government's anti-opium movement, Foreign

Secretary Palmerston proposed a settlement for Britain's trade relations with China. He suggested either a commercial treaty that was in favour of British traders, or British occupation of a small island where the British could live under their own flag, free from control of the Chinese government.

When negotiations broke down between Lin's representative and Capt. Charles Elliot in 1840, the British fleet attacked Guangzhou and occupied the city's forts, thus sparking the First Opium War (1839-1842). Intimidated by the British military threat, the Qing commissioner, Qi Shan, who had replaced Lin, agreed in Janu-

ary 1841 to the Convention of Chuen Pi, which gave away Hong Kong island to Britain.

On 26 January 1841, the British flag was raised at Possession Point on Hong Kong island, and the island was officially occupied by the British. Five months later, British officials began selling plots of land and the colonisation of Hong Kong began.

Despite the solution agreed upon, neither China nor Britain was happy with the terms of the Chuen Pi agreement. The Chinese government and its people saw the loss of a part of its territory as an unbearable shame, and Qi Shan was ordered to Beijing in chains.

The British government, particularly Palmerston, was unhappy with Hong Kong, which he contemptuously described as "a barren island with hardly a house upon it" and refused to accept it as the island station that his representative, Charles Elliot, had demanded as an alternative to a commercial treaty.

Blaming Elliot for failing to use full use of the troops sent to China for the purpose of getting a better deal, Palmerston replaced him with Sir Henry Pottinger, Hong Kong's first governor, in August 1841. This

ANTI-OPIUM HERO

Although his course to eliminate opium failed because of the weak Qing court, Lin Zexu is still remembered by the Chinese. Pictures and statues of Lin can be found in parts of China.

once and for all, he ordered his troops north up to the Chang Jiang (Yangzi River) and threatened to attack Nanjing (Nanking).

The Chinese capitulated in August 1842. The two governments signed the Treaty of Nanjing, which officially gave Hong Kong island to the British "in perpetuity". The Chuen Pi Convention agreed upon earlier by the the British and Chinese representatives had not been signed and so was never accepted as an official agreement, especially by

decision virtually ended Elliot's professional career. In modern-day Hong Kong, Elliot's name is hardly remembered, while the names of his successors adorn buildings, streets, parks and bars throughout Hong Kong.

Pottinger soon realised Hong Kong's potential future, despite the fact that Britain had treated Hong Kong as just another pawn in ongoing negotiations with the Chinese over trade terms. He encouraged long-term building projects and awarded land grants.

To settle hostilities between Britain and China

the British. Under the Treaty of Nanjing, which Communist China naturally regarded as "unequal" more than a century later, five Chinese ports, including Guangzhou, were opened for foreign trade. The treaty included the supplementary treaty of the Bogue (Humen) in October 1843, under which the Chinese were permitted to go to Hong Kong island freely for trading purposes, although it was officially a British territory.

With the eventual silting of Macau's harbour and the weakening of Portuguese power in Asia, Hong Kong thus began its growth under British rule into one of the greatest port cities the world has ever seen. ❏

ABOVE: panorama of Victoria Harbour, with Hong Kong island and Victoria Peak as seen from Kowloon, 1860.

THE COLONIAL DECADES

For nearly a century, Britain believed it had outmanoeuvred other European powers and China. In the end, the Chinese would have the upper hand

The 1842 Treaty of Nanjing (Nanking) ended the Opium War and formally put Hong Kong under British control. In its early days, the new British colony grew slowly. In 1856, a dispute over the interpretation of the two earlier treaties – the Chuen Pi Convention and the Treaty of Nanjing – and the British gov-

to send diplomatic representatives to China and travel freely throughout China.

However, hostilities between the Chinese and the British were renewed in 1859 when Chinese soldiers fired on the first British envoy to China as he made his way to the court in Beijing to present his credentials. Fighting continued until

ernment's anger over the boarding of a British ship by Chinese authorities in search of suspected pirates, led to the outbreak of the Second Anglo-Chinese War – or the Second Opium War, as mainland Chinese historians refer to it.

During the two-year war, many companies in Guangzhou (Canton) transferred their offices to Hong Kong, enabling the British colony to take its first step towards becoming a full-fledged Asian entrepot. China, weak with a corrupt government, lost the conflict again. By the summer of 1858, the allied forces of Britain and France had moved far north, forcing the Chinese government to sign the Treaties of Tianjin (Tientsin). The terms gave foreigners the right

1860. In that same year, the allied British and French armies sacked the emperor's Summer Palace and Yuan Ming Palace just outside of Beijing and took most of the royal family's treasures. The Yuan Ming Palace ("Garden of Perfection"), one of the most magnificent in the world, was torched by the foreigners as they retreated. During this period, Britain used the Kowloon peninsula to billet soldiers serving in the Second Opium War; later, the British government wanted to make it a military base. The British consul in Guangzhou secured the perpetual lease of the peninsula all the way north to what is now Boundary Street, including Stonecutters Island.

By this time, other countries – Russia, France, Germany and Japan – realised the importance of having easy access to trade with China. Not to be outdone by the British, these countries began to make similar incursions to secure treaty ports all along the Chinese coastline. In 1862, a Sino-Portuguese treaty gave Macau a colonial status similar to that of Hong Kong. A second treaty in 1887 confirmed Macau as a Portuguese colony in perpetuity and defined the land area to include the old town

BRITISH BLUNDER?

Signing a limited lease on the New Territories proved to be a strategic blunder that weakened Britain's possession, in perpetuity, of Hong Kong island and Kowloon.

as well as over 230 islands off the mainland coast. The British later regretting having signed this treaty, which only leased, not gave, the land to them, while Hong Kong island and the Kowloon peninsula had been given to Britain in perpetuity. (It would later be geographically impractical for Britain to keep Hong Kong island and Kowloon when the New Territories lease ran out in 1997.) At first, Chinese warships were allowed to use the wharf at Kowloon City, and Chinese officials were per-

and two off-shore islands, Taipa and Coloane. In 1895, China lost a war with Japan, and with an increasing number of countries making inroads into China, the British realised the need to control the land around Hong Kong's harbour to ensure efficient defence.

Thus, in 1898 another treaty was signed in Beijing between China and Britain, leasing the New Territories to Britain for 99 years. The New Territories consisted of a 900-square-kilometre (350 sq mi) stretch of land north of Kowloon extending up to the Shenzhen River,

LEFT: early English impressions of Chinese aristocrats.
ABOVE: the British negotiate to open China's ports.

mitted to remain in office. However, a year later, the British unilaterally took over the city completely. The New Territories was declared a part of the overall territory of Hong Kong, although it kept a separate administrative body from the urban area. Under a liberal British rule, Hong Kong people, both Chinese and British, were left alone to concentrate on their businesses. The colony soon became a magnet for Chinese immigrants and a centre of trade with Chinese communities abroad. Shipping through Hong Kong increased from under 3,000 ships annually in 1860 to over 23,000 by World War II.

Hong Kong's administration followed the usual pattern for a British colony, with London appointing a governor as well as members of the administrative Executive Council (Exco) and the law-making Legislative Council (Legco).

At first there was a system of two parallel administrations, in which the British had its own within its community, while the Chinese were governed through Chinese magistrates from the mainland. But the system proved to be inefficient, and the dual system was dropped in 1865.

Hong Kong was governed as a free market operating under the principle of equality of all

reclamation project was completed in Wan Chai. In fact, today more than five percent of Hong Kong is reclaimed land.

In the second half of the 19th century, both public and private schools were encouraged. The College of Medicine for the Chinese was founded in 1887, with Dr Sun Yatsen, the revolutionary leader, as one of its first two students. The college later developed into the University of Hong Kong, considered the most prestigious university in today's Hong Kong.

NO RESPECT

"You cannot be two minutes in a Hong Kong street without seeing Europeans striking coolies with their canes or umbrellas", wrote Isabella Bird in 1879.

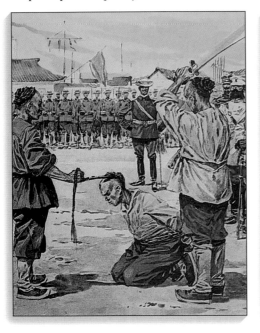

races before the law. The governor could not issue ordinances subjecting non-Europeans to restrictions that didn't apply to Europeans.

During the late 19th and early 20th centuries, the colony began a period of rapid development, and several public service companies were established, including the Hong Kong and China Gas Company in 1861, the Peak Tram in 1885 and the 137-kilometre (85 mi) Kowloon-Canton Railway in 1910. The colony also began massive land reclamation projects in 1851. In 1904, the first stage of land reclamation was completed in Central District, creating new land area for what is now the area of Chater, Connaught and Des Voeux roads. In 1929, another

From the beginning of the 20th century, China experienced a series of political upheavals. In 1900, a peasant uprising known as the Boxer Rebellion seriously challenged the authority of the Qing government. Nationalistic peasants in northern China revolted against what they saw as an invasion of their country by foreigners. These sometimes superstitious peasants believed that with help from the gods, they could resist modern weapons and bullets with their skills in the martial arts. The rebellion was soon quashed by the Qing rulers, but the Qing dynasty began its terminal decline.

A few years later, Sun Yatsen led an anti-Qing movement, which in 1912 overthrew the feudalist empire and established the Republic of China. Although Sun travelled to Hong Kong many times to enlist support for his cause, his revolution did not have a huge impact on the British colony, apart from the fact that many mainlanders came to Hong Kong to escape the unrest on the mainland.

China's history between 1920 and 1940 was dominated by the Japanese invasion and the civil war raging between Mao Zedong's Communist Party, founded in 1921, and the Nationalists (Guomintang), led by Chiang Kaishek.

On 8 December 1941 (7 December in Hawaii), the Japanese bombed the U.S. naval

Japan and Portugal, Macau became the only "neutral pocket" in China; many Europeans found refuge in Macau during the war.

During the Japanese occupation, Hong Kong's trade virtually stopped, the currency lost its value, food supplies were disrupted, and government operations were seriously impaired. But most of the local residents remained loyal to the Allied cause. Chinese guerrillas fought against the Japanese invaders in the New Territories, while peasants helped foreign residents from Allied countries to escape.

In August 1945, the United States dropped an atomic bomb on Hiroshima, Japan. Eight days

base at Pearl Harbour in Hawaii, forcing the Americans into World War II. At nearly the same time, Japanese troops attacked Hong Kong from across the mainland border, and the British army was forced to withdraw from the New Territories and Kowloon to Hong Kong island. After a week of resistance on the island, Hong Kong surrendered on Christmas Day. The Japanese occupation lasted for three years and eight months. Under an agreement between

FAR LEFT: a Boxer is executed by foreign troops.
LEFT: Dr Sun Yatsen. **ABOVE LEFT:** Japanese pilots prepare to attack in World War II. **ABOVE RIGHT:** Mao Zedong during the civil war against the Nationalists.

later, the Japanese agreed to an unconditional surrender, thereby ending World War II in Asia. That same month, the British fleet arrived in Hong Kong to re-establish English presence in the war-ravaged colony, and a provisional government was established.

After the war, Hong Kong Chinese who had moved to the mainland areas not completely controlled by the Japanese returned in large numbers. China's civil war, which broke out in 1946 soon after the Japanese surrender, drove more people – many of whom were affluent Shanghai entrepreneurs and property owners – into the British territory. By 1949, Hong Kong's population had reached two million.

In China's civil war, the Communist army pitted their old-fashioned rifles against the Nationalists' tanks, fighter planes and machine guns provided by the United States. But despite their military disadvantage, the Communists had the support of the masses, who had become fed up with the corrupt Nationalist government. The Communist army eventually got the upper hand in the war against Chiang Kaishek, and by 1949, the Communists controlled all of China, with the exception of Taiwan and Tibet. In October of that year, Mao Zedong declared the establishment of the People's Republic of China, and the defeated Nationalists fled to Taiwan.

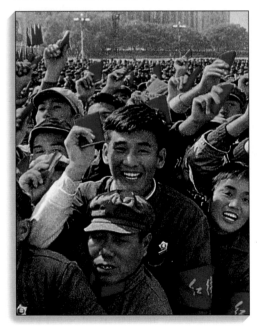

The Western world refused to accept Communist China, which they saw as a threat to world peace and order. During the 1950–53 Korean War, the United Nations faced off against the newly established government in China, with U.N. forces fighting on the side of the anti-Communist South Koreans and China fighting alongside Communist North Korea. At the same time, the United Nations imposed an embargo against trade with China, with the intention of killing the new Beijing government in its cradle. Hong Kong's economy suffered from the embargo, and since revenue from the port was not enough to support the rapidly increasing population, the colony was forced into industrialisation. Entrepreneurs from Shanghai who had earlier come to Hong Kong with their capital and business skills established themselves in the colony by setting up textile factories. By the 1960s, the textile and garment industries accounted for more than half of the colony's exports.

Famine swept China in the early1960s due to impracticable socialist policies. According to unofficial figures, up to 30 million died of hunger during this period. The famine started another wave of immigrants to Hong Kong. This time, the colonial forces tried desperately to keep them out because the numbers were becoming alarming.

During the Vietnam War in the late1960s and early1970s, U.S. Navy vessels, en route to or leaving Vietnam, were a familiar sight in Victoria Harbour. Hong Kong became a favourite destination for American soldiers on leave, and troops spent their dollars liberally in the bars and nightclubs of the Wan Chai red-light district and across the harbour in Tsim Sha Tsui bars and restaurants.

Meanwhile, in China, the disastrous Cultural Revolution was underway. Knowledge was condemned as anti-socialist, intellectuals were persecuted, and young people were sent to the countryside to be "re-educated" by the peasants, who were considered to be the poorest group in society and therefore the best revolutionaries. According to Mao Zedong, only hard labour could teach young people to remain proletariats. Schools were closed and students were forced to work in the fields. In hindsight, historians believe that Mao started the Cultural Revolution to get rid of his political rivals. The turmoil on the mainland drifted into Hong Kong, where tensions developed into a series of disturbances in the mid 1960s.

The chaos in China also spilled over into Macau. Rebellious Red Guards waged a propaganda war with posters and slogans, calling on the Chinese residents in the Portuguese colony to rebel against their government and start a revolution. In Hong Kong, Chief Superintendent John Tsang, of the police department's intelligence arm, was unmasked as a Communist spy. He disappeared across the border, only to reappear as the chief of security for Guangdong province. Later, he became a legendary figure and was featured in several works of fiction written about the colony.

The chaos caused by the Cultural Revolution in China almost paralysed Hong Kong's economy during the late 1960s. Stories circulated that criminal gangs, called "triads", were keeping Wan Chai free of Communist cadres so that police could concentrate on protecting other districts. By the end of 1967, the disturbances provoked in Hong Kong by the instability in China were quelled, and Hong Kong and Macau remained colonies.

China's position in the world began to change during the

China, where he met Mao Zedong and Chinese Premier Zhou Enlai. Diplomatic relations between the two countries were established.

During the 1970s and 1980s, Hong Kong's economy developed at an amazing pace, and the colony continued to expand its role as an entrepot with its neighbours and as China's trading partner. It was during this period that Hong Kong saw the first generation of wealthy Chinese business tycoons, such as the Macau-based casino magnate Stanley Ho, shipping

PROLETARIAT PIQUE

China's Cultural Revolution spilled into the colony. In 1966, a riot began over a simple price rise for the first-class – ironically – Star Ferry fares.

1970s, as the international community came to realise the country's growing power. In 1971, China won its first significant international political victory when Beijing gathered enough support from third-world countries to have Taiwan removed from the United Nations. Despite strong opposition from the United States, the People's Republic was finally recognised as the "real" China, replacing Taiwan in the General Assembly. The next year, the world was stunned by U.S. President Richard Nixon's visit to

FAR LEFT: Red Guards and Mao's little red book.
ABOVE: an example of Social Realism art – Mao huddled with the masses.

tycoon Y. K. Pao, and the property giant Li Ka-shing, whose group makes up a large percentage of the stock exchange's Hang Seng Index.

To keep pace with economic development, infrastructure throughout the colony was improved, and the territory was transformed into a modern, efficient and cosmopolitan city. Growing wealth pushed up the standard of living and made it possible for the government to increase investment in education, housing and other social welfare projects. The development of public housing in the late 1950s enabled many people to own their own homes.

An efficient civil service system introduced by the British government played a major role in the economic boom. To keep the local government clean and efficient, an independent commission against corruption was set up in 1974 with a mandate to stamp out corruption.

In 1973, Sir Murray MacLehose became the first Hong Kong governor to be appointed from the British diplomatic circle. London's choice of MacLehose, a diplomat who was familiar with China and spoke the Chinese language, demonstrated Britain's concern about Hong Kong and its future. Since then, all Hong Kong governors have been professional diplomats and China experts, with the exception of the last governor, Chris Patten, a career politician.

After the Cultural Revolution ended in 1976, China began to take measures to modernise its economy and open its tightly shut doors to the outside world. Hong Kong, as China's window to the world and the world's gateway to China, began to play a more important role. An increasing number of Hong Kong businessmen began moving their manufacturing operations north to the mainland, where labour and raw materials were cheaper.

With the city becoming increasingly populated, Hong Kong ended an immigration policy in 1980 that allowed Chinese refugees to remain in the colony if they managed to reach an urban area. Now, all illegal immigrants are sent back.

By the 1980s, the Hong Kong government had near complete autonomy from London and even had the power to conclude certain negotiations with foreign powers. The colony, for example, regularly negotiated its own economic agreements with other countries and was admitted into several international financial institutions such as the Asian Development Bank. On rare instances when the territory could not be included in an international forum directly, it joined a British delegation.

However, amid the growing prosperity and affluence was concern over Hong Kong's future after the 99-year lease on the New Territories expired in 1997. The New Territories made up 90 percent of the total territory of Hong Kong and without it, the vibrant economic entity that Hong Kong had become would not exist.

Most Hong Kong people would have preferred to stay under British rule rather than embrace the Communist regime. Although they were unhappy with the fact that British companies and expatriates had been enjoying privileges in business and in government positions, most locals appreciated the fundamental policies by the British government that enabled people to compete in a free market. Having escaped earlier from the authoritarian system in socialist China – or in some cases, having suffered political persecution on the mainland – they feared going back to the Communist system. But their destiny was not in their own hands.

China had always expressed its stance that it would take back Hong Kong when it was "ripe". In the 1970s, China had refused the Portuguese government's offer to hand back Macau earlier, for fear of causing instability in Hong Kong. But circumstances had changed by the early 1980s, and Chinese leaders began thinking about getting Hong Kong back.

It was under such circumstances that British Prime Minister Margaret Thatcher paid a visit to Beijing and Hong Kong in 1982. During the trip, she brought up with Chinese leaders the issue of Hong Kong's future. Confident with her recent victory in the Falkland Islands, Thatcher believed she could win another battle and get the Chinese to allow Britain to extend the 99-year lease on the New Territories. ❑

LEFT: Margaret Thatcher takes tea in a resettlement estate during her 1982 visit. **RIGHT:** a young Prince Charles with a group of Hong Kong admirers.

THE RETURN TO CHINA

Generations of Hong Kong people grew up living under British rule. Then, in a single day, they were living according to the dictates of the Chinese Communist Party

Since the early 1980s, life in Hong Kong has been dominated by the issue of its return to China. Even now, although the former British colony is a part of the People's Republic of China, its relationship with the mainland still remains a priority above all other issues.

Hong Kong people have not been unfamiliar with the mainland Chinese, as immigrants from mainland China have long played a key role in the development of Hong Kong. Those who arrived in the years following the Communist victory in 1949 brought their money and entrepreneurial skills, laying the foundation for a sustained economic boom in the British-run territory. Mao Zedong's disastrous Cultural Revolution, during which knowledge was condemned as bourgeois and intellectuals were persecuted, led to another influx of immigrants from the mainland in the late 1960s. When Hong Kong's economy began to take off in the late 1970s, and immigrant numbers again increased, the authorities ended a policy that granted citizenship to illegal immigrants who managed to enter the urban areas.

In the years just before Hong Kong's return to China in 1997, mainlanders again flowed into the territory. In 1996, the governments of Hong Kong and Beijing agreed to limit immigration to the colony to 150 people per day. But this new wave was different from previous flows of immigrants. Most notably, it included some of the mainland's top business executives and professionals, lured by Hong Kong's opportunities.

Several opinion polls taken shortly before the handover showed most Hong Kong people would prefer to remain under British rule if they could control their own destiny, although they agreed it was politically correct to say they loved the Chinese homeland. And although many were sceptical that the Beijing government leaders would keep their promise to let Hong Kong's present political system continue

PREVIOUS PAGES: happy on handover day, 1997.
LEFT: lowering the Union Jack, Victoria Harbour.
RIGHT: illegal immigrants from mainland China.

for another 50 years, most people had decided to accept the reality and adapt.

Negotiating the return

The issue of Hong Kong's return to China came up in 1982, when British Prime Minister Margaret Thatcher paid a visit to Beijing and

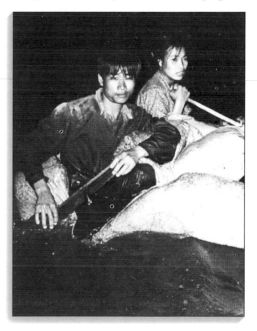

Hong Kong. This visit began the discussion on what would happen to Hong Kong after the 99-year lease on the New Territories, nine-tenths of the colony, expired in 1997. The reaction to the news that the territory's future was being negotiated was typical of Hong Kong – a nose dive in the local stock market.

The following year, the Chinese government revealed its plan: Hong Kong would become a Special Administrative Region (SAR) and would keep its own capitalist system, judiciary and police, but the future head of the special region would be a Chinese resident of Hong Kong.

During the 1982 Sino-British negotiations, Thatcher tried to persuade China to extend the lease for the New Territories another 50 years after it expired in 1997. But Chinese leader Deng Xiaoping dismissed the idea, curtly pointing out that he could legally send his People's Liberation Army troops across the border the day after the lease's expiration.

In September 1984, Britain and China came to an agreement, ending two years of often acrimonious negotiations between the two countries on Hong Kong's fate. Whereas Britain had initially gone into

Declaration and registered it as an international treaty at the United Nations. The declaration provided that Hong Kong's way of life would remain unchanged for 50 years after 1997.

The territory would enjoy a "high degree of autonomy", except in foreign affairs and defence, and China's socialist system and policies would not be imposed on post-handover Hong Kong. As former Chinese leader Deng Xiaoping put it, "Horses will keep racing, and nightclub dancing will continue".

the negotiations expecting to extend the lease on the New Territories, China intended to regain all of Hong Kong. Britain left the negotiations, it must be said, rather humbled, if not humiliated.

At the same time, plans were drawn up for Hong Kong's administration in the years running up to 1997. Key points included elections to the Legislative Council (Legco), the District Boards and new Regional Councils. The Hong Kong government expressed its intention to train local policymakers during the years preceding 1997 to prepare the territory for its role as a Special Administrative Region. In 1985, Britain and China signed the Sino-British Joint

Beijing soon appointed a committee of 59 members, only 23 of whom were from Hong Kong, to draft the mini-constitution – known as the Basic Law – for the Special Administrative Region and which would rule Hong Kong for 50 years starting in 1997. Britain announced it would phase out its garrison by 1997, while China said the People's Liberation Army would be stationed in Hong Kong after the handover.

During Hong Kong's first Legislative Council elections in 1985, initiated by the British, 24 of the 56 members took their places through indirect elections. Out of a total population of 5.5 million at the time, only 70,000 people were eligible to vote under Hong Kong's restricted system of indirect elections. Of that number, only 47,000 registered to vote and only 25,000 actually went to the polls. Nevertheless, this election was enough to touch off a debate about whether the Hong Kong government would allow open elections for the 1988 elections, as promised in 1984.

Strained relations

China began to worry about the territory's fledgling attempts at democracy – something with which the socialist country was not familiar – and the ensuing debate about the future of Hong Kong. Beijing's top man in the territory, the director of the New China News Agency, insisted that Britain was deviating from the joint declaration and arousing fear and anxiety amongst Hong Kong's people. Amid the political tension, however, Hong Kong's economy continued to thrive.

In 1987, Sir David Wilson, who had served as political advisor to the Hong Kong government, was sworn in as governor of the territory. Wilson stepped into the middle of the debate on representative government, which had been the focus in the 1985 Legislative Council elections. The British government wanted direct elections to be held before 1997, and China became more and more riled. Eventually, China insisted that political changes not following the Basic Law would be overturned – nullified – in 1997. Deng Xiaoping added that universal suffrage might not be beneficial for Hong Kong. According to a BBC documentary and various newspaper accounts, Britain reached a secret agreement with China during the 1980s, promising not to encourage democracy in Hong Kong.

The anxiety amongst the people of Hong Kong about what would happen in 1997 led to the "brain drain" – large-scale emigration of the territory's professionals to better political climes, encouraged by favourable changes in immigration laws in popular destinations such as Australia, Canada and the United States.

In December 1987, China and Portugal signed an agreement to return the Portuguese colony of Macau to China on 20 December 1999. The agreement was similar to that stipulating Hong Kong's handover, but it allowed Macau citizens to hold dual nationality. The

Sino-British Joint Declaration did not give dual nationality to Hong Kong citizens.

In 1988, a report on representative government was published jointly by Beijing and London, postponing direct elections to the Legislative Council, the territory's law-making body, scheduled for that year to an unspecified later date. Under Hong Kong's system of indirect elections, still fewer than 100,000 people out of 5.5 million were eligible to vote.

In June 1989, the Chinese government crushed a pro-democracy demonstration centred in Beijing's Tiananmen Square. Although no official figures have been released, interna-

tional human rights organisations estimate thousands of civilians were killed. Horrified by Beijing's brutality, one million people took to the streets in Hong Kong. They marched to a mass rally at the Happy Valley racecourse, in sight of the New China News Agency, Beijing's quasi-diplomatic mission in the territory. The massacre raised a new political awareness among the people of Hong Kong and alerted them to the possibility that they could lose their freedoms after Beijing took over the territory.

The Tiananmen Square massacre exacerbated the Hong Kong brain drain, with more than 50,000 Hong Kong Chinese leaving the territory annually after the incident. Britain tried to

FAR LEFT: unhappy with Thatcher. **LEFT:** Gurkha troops at the ready. **RIGHT:** Tiananmen Square protest, 1989.

internationalise its Hong Kong problem by bringing the subject up at international forums, but gained little more than verbal sympathy. At the end of the year, Britain said it would grant British citizenship to just 225,000 Hong Kong Chinese before Hong Kong reverted to China.

The British government tried to find a balance in keeping earlier promises of democratic reform made to the people of Hong Kong without provoking China's displeasure at free elections for the Legislative Council. Pushed by budding political awareness among its citizens, the Hong Kong government agreed to speed up the process, saying it would put 18 Legco seats up

Special Administrative Region government might be saddled with debt. The Hong Kong government found itself in the position of being at loggerheads with its future master.

After numerous consultations, the Hong Kong and Beijing governments agreed in early 1990 that members elected to the Legislative Council in 1995 would serve until their term ended in 1999, even after the handover, and that they would be among the 400 people who would select Hong Kong's first post-1997 handover Chief Executive.

In April 1990, the Basic Law, Hong Kong's post-1997 constitution, was promulgated, giv-

for direct elections in 1991 (China later reneged on the agreement after Governor Chris Patten carried out electoral reforms against Beijing's wishes; China replaced the elected Legco with a Beijing-appointed provisional legislature).

Funding the new airport

To boost the economy and confidence battered by the Tiananmen Square massacre, the Hong Kong government announced a scheme in October 1989 to use HK$78 billion to build a new airport on Lantau Island, then scheduled to be completed in early 1997. But the scheme was attacked and stalled by China, which insisted that it should be consulted because its future

ing China's law-making congress the final say over Hong Kong's affairs.

The Hong Kong government announced it would self-finance the HK$7.8 billion Lantau fixed crossing (a series of bridges to the new airport) because it could not get international financing. As expected, China took the announcement as a direct challenge.

The argument between China and Britain over the airport project began to move beyond the question of finance to the broader issue of Hong Kong's autonomy. If Hong Kong did not have the autonomy to build a new airport, then its autonomy over other matters would be in doubt. Hong Kong and British government representatives paid many visits to Beijing to win approval for the airport project, all the time trying not to appear they were grovelling. Beijing was unrelenting.

Finally, Beijing and London announced that an understanding about the airport had been reached. But like the 1984 Sino-British agreement, its conclusion was without Hong Kong's participation. The document gave China's support for the airport project in exchange for fiscal guarantees and membership on the board of the airport authority. A few days after the announcement, Hong Kong's stock market indicator, the Hang Seng Index, hit an all-time record high – a sigh of relief from Hong Kong's business community that the two governments had worked out their differences.

But the optimism did not last long. Soon, another issue came up to ruin the good mood. In June 1991, Hong Kong's new Bill of Rights backing the "rights and freedoms" guaranteed in the 1984 Sino-British Agreement became law, despite China's insistence that the move was against the principles stated in the Basic Law, Hong Kong's post-handover constitution.

The political instability pushed more Hong Kong residents to emigrate. In 1990, about 60,000 of Hong Kong's most accomplished professionals and businessmen moved overseas, mainly to Canada and Australia. Britain called on its allies to accept Hong Kong immigrants; the United States amended its immigration laws to increase Hong Kong's quota to 10,000 annually until 1994 and 20,000 thereafter. The Hongkong and Shanghai Bank, the territory's largest bank, moved its headquarters to Britain, generally seen as reflecting the company's lack of confidence in Hong Kong's future.

The first direct elections in the 150-year history of the Legislative Council took place in September 1991. For the first time in Hong Kong's history, the incumbent government faced opposition and the potential of legislative defeats from the opposition under barrister Martin Lee. China, in a not-too-subtle move, advised Hong Kong voters to take candidates' "attitudes toward the mainland" into account when casting their votes. The comment was widely interpreted as a call to vote for the pro-Beijing candidates and not those of the pro-

democracy and freedom camp represented by Martin Lee's United Democrats. But people were not cowed. They demonstrated political independence by giving 15 of the 18 seats up for direct election to pro-democracy candidates.

The last governor

In April 1992, Britain's Conservative Party chairman Chris Patten was named Hong Kong's last governor. It was the first time Britain appointed a politician instead of a diplomat to govern Hong Kong. Patten's arrival heralded the most tense period in relations between Britain and China.

Unlike his predecessors who arrived in the territory decked out in full ceremonial dress, plumed helmet and all, Patten arrived in a dark business suit – and changed the image of the office of governor in Hong Kong. Despite, or perhaps because of some of his unorthodox ways, Patten soon proved to be a popular leader. Instead of sitting in his office, he went out into the streets to meet ordinary people, listened to their opinions, and frequently held question-and-answer sessions in public during which he addressed politically sensitive issues with a candid, sometimes controversial attitude.

Patten announced proposals for increased spending on welfare, health, housing and the

LEFT: street demonstrations in Hong Kong following the Tiananmen Square massacre. **RIGHT:** border watch.

The Handover

The handover of Hong Kong back to China on 30 June 1997 was the media event of 1997, with more than 8,000 journalists descending upon the tiny territory. Hong Kong saw more parties, spontaneous street celebrations and fireworks in one night than at any other time in the territory's history.

On The Peak and Mid-Levels, where most of Hong Kong's wealthier expats live, guests at glitzy handover parties were glued to the windows facing the harbour to see the night lit up with fireworks. Most Hong Kongers, Chinese and Western residents

alike, forgot the political implications of the handover for the night and celebrated the historic occasion with a festive spirit and a sense of humour. Some of the British revellers were calling the all-night celebrations, in understated fashion, "The Last Night of the Poms".

At midnight, all the major figures who either had, or were to have, a hand in Hong Kong's future gathered in the new, glass-encased extension to the Hong Kong Convention and Exhibition Centre: Chinese President Jiang Zemin and Prime Minister Li Peng, Hong Kong's new Chief Executive Tung Chee-hwa, out-going Hong Kong Governor Chris Patten, British Prime Minister Tony Blair, Prince Charles, and the woman who went head-to-head with the Chinese and lost the Crown's most prosperous colony

to Beijing, former British Prime Minister Margaret Thatcher. The man who had won the territory back for the Chinese was conspicuously missing – Deng Xiaopeng had died more than four months before.

Just before the clock struck midnight, the Union Jack made its slow descent down the flagpole as the British military band played "God Save the Queen". Then, the red-and-yellow Chinese flag was raised as a Chinese military band played their country's national anthem. After 156 years of colonial rule, Hong Kong was back in the hands of the Chinese, thus ending what Beijing called the most shameful episode of China's history.

A man of the people to the very end, Chris Patten shook hands with the crowds of people near the picr in Ccntral before stepping on board the royal yacht *Britannia* just after midnight. With the Royal Navy band playing "Land of Hope and Glory" in the background, Patten and Prince Charles waved to the crowd as the *Britannia* sailed away. Also at midnight, a brief ceremony was held at East Tamar, the British naval base, as a British honour guard was replaced by a Chinese army contingent.

Inside the Convention Centre, after bidding their old British rulers goodbye a few hours earlier, Hong Kong civil servants swore allegiance to the People's Republic of China in Mandarin, the mainland's official language. The Chinese delegation was led by President Jiang Zemin, the first Chinese head of state to have visited Hong Kong since the founding of the PRC in 1949.

The elected law-making Legislative Council, which China refused to recognise, was scrapped immediately after the handover. But in a reassuring sign that the handover did not mean the end of democracy in Hong Kong, Martin Lee and members of the opposition Democratic Party climbed up onto the balcony of the Legislative Council Building in Central just after midnight to hold the first democracy rally under the new rulers. Several thousand Hong Kongers braved the rains to listen to Lee speak against Beijing's replacement of the elected legislative body with its own.

In the early morning of 1 July, People's Liberation Army troops crossed the border into the New Territories with their armoured personnel carriers along rain-slicked roads, welcomed by hundreds of villagers lining the roads.

That evening, the Chinese out-performed the festive display put on by the British the night before with a HK$1 million spectacular in Victoria Harbour, with fireworks that transformed the night sky and harbour into a blaze of coloured light. ❑

environment. The most controversial move, however, was his proposal to reform the political system. China wanted no such shift towards greater democracy and openly attacked Patten's political reforms. The Beijing-funded daily *Wen Wei Po* accused Patten of wasting time in dressing himself up as a "God of Democracy" and of gambling with Hong Kong's future. On his first official visit to Beijing, Patten was snubbed by Premier Li Peng. The highest official he met, China's Foreign Minister Qian Qichen, told him the Hong Kong government was jeopardising relations between Britain and China.

In response to China's attacks on Hong Kong's new governor, the Hang Seng Index dropped about five percent in October 1992. Brokers warned that unless Patten made a U-turn on his push for greater democracy, the stock market could suffer further falls.

Beijing's Communist mouthpiece, the *People's Daily*, accused Patten of conspiring with Western allies against China. Beijing declared that all contracts, leases and agreements signed or ratified by the British Hong Kong administration without the approval of China would not be honoured after 30 June 1997, the last day of Britain's rule. Beijing also pointed its accusing finger at the private sector, including the British company Jardines, which it accused of supporting Patten's political agenda and damaging the international community's confidence in Hong Kong's future.

In 1994, the Legislative Council passed Governor Patten's proposed electoral reforms by a narrow margin, inviting strong condemnation from China. The reforms were a halfway point between full direct elections for all members of the legislature and a more muted electoral plan. Legco remained far from being a directly-elected legislature, but the change was still enough to draw attacks from China.

The electoral reform was Patten's last major act in office. As China began to play an increasingly important role in Hong Kong society – although the territory had not yet returned to China – and the business sectors competed with each other to get on Beijing's good side, Patten was more and more sidelined. Beijing simply refused to talk to him, making it difficult for him to take any further action.

Left: Prince Charles via television at handover dinner, Mandarin Hotel. **Right:** Hong Kong Chinese bagpipers.

Sunset over the Empire

A chief executive of the Hong Kong Special Administrative Region government was selected by a Beijing-appointed committee at the beginning of 1997 from among three candidates. Tung Chee-hwa, a shipping tycoon who had received financial help from China in his earlier business days, was chosen as the first leader of post-handover Hong Kong. Ironically, before the handover, Tung had been a member of the colonial government appointed by Patten.

Despite the many humiliating insults the Chinese leaders threw his way during his five years in office, Patten's political reforms and personal

charisma won him the respect of Hong Kong's residents. At the British farewell ceremony on the night of 30 June 1997, Patten's moving and forceful farewell speech received long applause from the crowd, and people shouted, "We will miss you" as he boarded the royal yacht *Britannia* for England.

The handover meant the dismantling of the elected Legislative Council, because China refused to recognise its legitimacy, reneging on an earlier promise with the excuse that Patten had changed the electoral process. After taking office on 1 July 1997, Tung formulated a voting system for Hong Kong's first legislative election set for May 1998, when the Beijing-appointed provisional legislature was replaced. It gave the biggest say to business groups, a move believed to have been designed to sideline the most popular party, the Democrats.

Future anxieties

Although China's recent economic development and the successes of the younger generation of mainlanders have helped change Hong Kong people's opinions of their northern compatriots, the mutual prejudices will take years to overcome. The 1989 student massacre in Beijing's Tiananmen Square horrified the world and shattered the hopes of most Hong Kong people for the region's future. But, while they distrust the socialist regime, Hong Kong is their home where they have prospered, and where most of them must remain.

Although the Beijing government kept its promise not to interfere in Hong Kong's internal affairs during the early posthandover period, some aspects of society have been changing. More locals are learning Mandarin, the language of mainland China; more mainland artists are putting on shows and exhibitions in Hong Kong; and local businessmen are competing feverishly to get a share of the huge market in the north.

Hong Kong's school curriculum has also changed. The Basic Law (Hong Kong's miniconstitution) and Mandarin have become new subjects; classes on the British political system have been replaced by courses on the structure of the Special Administrative Region. These measures are aimed at strengthening young Hong Kong students' sense of belonging to China. Cantonese has replaced English as the language of instruction in most schools, and many observers have commented that local English-speaking ability has suffered as a result.

Hong Kong's first post-handover Chief Secretary, Anson Chan, said before the handover that in a hundred years, Hong Kong and China would merge into one system, the Hong Kong system. She might be right. Few certainly believe that China can change Hong Kong much. But to most Hong Kong people, impatient and expecting immediate results, and who are used to the efficiency that created an economic wonder in just a few decades, a hundred

SUICIDAL PRETENSES?

"Hong Kong," wrote Richard Hughes in 1975, "persists on borrowed soil and borrowed time... because it affects no suicidal pretenses of 'democracy' or 'independence'". Will Hong Kong prove him wrong?

years is far too long to wait and see. Before the handover, a popular view was that Hong Kong under Communist China would undergo political changes, while remaining stable and prosperous economically. What happened in the months after the handover was just the opposite. There were few political confrontations, apart from some dissent concerning the makeup of the SAR's first legislative body. The People's Liberation Army kept a low profile in Hong Kong and its headquarters, the Prince of Wales Barracks, retained its colonial name, despite later attempts to disguise the name engraved on the side of the building.

However, in 1997 Hong Kong experienced a major economic crisis, as did many Asian countries. The Hang Seng Index dropped 6,000 points – about 40 percent – late in the year, from its historical height right after the handover. One leading international investment company openly expressed its negative view on the city's economic future, forecasting that Hong Kong would suffer from a long period of economic recession and financial turbulence, if not political uncertainty. By 2003, the economy had still not recovered, unemployment had soared and, in an ironic reversal of history, many locals began seeking work on the mainland. From March to May 2003 the SARS virus epidemic killed hundreds of people in Hong Kong and China. The Hong Kong public wore surgical masks and plastic gloves outdoors, and tourist numbers dried to a trickle.

The dictum of "one country, two systems" has been called into question a number of times since the handover, notably when the government asked Beijing to overturn the Court of Final Appeal's ruling on the right of abode, and then on July 1st 2003, when more than 500,000 demonstrators marched peacefully to protest against plans to introduce controversial antisubversion laws. People feared they would limit freedoms and that Beijing would use the legislation to ban groups it considers a threat to the Party. After the protest, the government backed down and postponed the new laws, saying the time was not right. ❑

RIGHT: celebrating the handover of Hong Kong.

GEOGRAPHY

Lacking in exploitable natural resources, Hong Kong relies instead on its exploitable and strategic location, and on its fine, deep-water harbour

Hong Kong is made up of a peninsula protruding from southeastern China and hundreds of islands scattered off the coast. The peninsula consists of Kowloon and the New Territories, and due south off the mainland is Hong Kong island (from which the entire territory takes its name) and hundreds of outlying islands.

The only valuable natural gift the territory enjoys is its deep, wide harbour protected by mountains in the north and south. Its favourable geographical location between the Taiwan Straits, the South China Sea and the Pacific Ocean makes it a strategic channel for sea traffic in Asia and the world.

Hong Kong lies just south of the Tropic of Cancer on a similar latitude to Calcutta, Havana and Hawaii. It shares the same longitude as Wuhan in central China, Bali and Perth. To its north is China's Guangdong Province, while its southern side is surrounded by the South China Sea.

Hong Kong covered 1,095 square kilometres (423 sq mi) in 1997, but that land area is constantly expanding due to land reclamation projects. From 1851 to 1997, in fact, the total area of land reclaimed from the sea amounted to 60 square kilometres (23 sq mi). In area, the island of Hong Kong is 80 square kilometres (31 sq mi); Kowloon peninsula, 47 square kilometres (18 sq mi); the New Territories, 794 square kilometres (306 sq mi); and the outlying islands total 174 square kilometres (67 sq mi).

People and land

The former British colony, which was returned to the People's Republic of China in July 1997, is one of the most densely-populated cities in the world. Hong Kong's 6.7 million people live in a cramped urban environment, and only 300 square kilometres (116 sq mi), about 30 percent of the total land area, is inhabitable. The remain-

der is mostly undeveloped. In 1997, the overall population density was 5,780 people per square kilometre, while the crowded Kwun Tong District in eastern Kowloon had 53,610 people per square kilometre.

Although the urban areas are densely packed, the countryside is fairly deserted. Twenty-one

parks and 14 natural preserves cover about 40 percent of the total land area – a striking proportion considering the high population density.

Hong Kong's foundation is volcanic, and its landscape is dominated by hills and mountains. A series of ridges running from northeast to southwest form the backbone of Hong Kong. Flat land is mostly concentrated on the Kowloon peninsula and northwestern New Territories. There are large alluvial plains in the New Territories, which served as farmland for the city in the past. Now, only about three percent of the total land area is cultivated. Hong Kong's waters are dotted with over 250 islands, mostly small and uninhabited. There are three

PRECEDING PAGES: classic view of Victoria Harbour from Victoria Peak; Repulse Bay. **LEFT:** people have lived on the water for centuries. **RIGHT:** the final destination of over half of cargo reaching Victoria Harbour is China.

larger islands – Lantau, Hong Kong island and Lamma, all of which are mountainous.

On Hong Kong island, there is only a narrow piece of flat land (most of it landfill) between the mountains and the sea along the north shore. Most people live on this narrow belt, while the south shore has luxury residential buildings and several sandy beaches, such as Stanley and Repulse Bay. A tunnel through the mountains links the north and south shores.

Hong Kong's highest point is Tai Mo Shan, located in central

MAKING LAND

Land reclamation in the 1990s added an area the size of 700 soccer fields to Kowloon's western edge.

Climate

Although Hong Kong's latitude places it within the tropics, the seasonal differences in temperature are greater than in most places at similar latitudes. Because of the relatively wide temperature range and cool winter, climatologists classify the climate as subtropical. The continental high pressure of Siberia and China ushers cold and dry air southward in winter to cool down the region. Hong Kong's climate is dominated by monsoons – the seasonal alternation of winds. In

New Territories at 957 metres (3,140 ft) above sea level. A dramatic backdrop to the skyscrapers of Hong Kong island's Central district, Victoria Peak ("The Peak") is 552 metres (1,811 ft) high and provides a bird's-eye view of much of the island, Victoria Harbour and Kowloon and – on a clear day – over to the Chinese mainland.

Hong Kong is in an area of minor but significant seismic activity, resulting in frequent minor tremors, although no major earthquakes have occurred in the region in recent history. The latest major earthquake recorded was in 1874, with a magnitude of 5.75 on the Richter scale, and it caused only minor property damage.

summer, low pressure to the north brings in warmer, moister air from over the Pacific.

The best weather is during autumn and early winter – roughly October to January – when the weather is mostly sunny and temperatures are comfortable. The rest of the year is usually damp and, from May to September, very hot. Summers are so humid that many Hong Kong residents have dehumidifiers in their homes to prevent furniture from warping and clothes from getting mouldy.

February is usually the coldest month, with an average daily high of about 17°C (63°F). July is the hottest, with average highs of around 31°C (88°F). The average daily temperature range (the difference between day and night) is only around 5°C – on summer nights the temperature almost always remains above 25°C (77°F).

The transitional period from winter to summer, between February and May, is considered miserable by some, with fog, frequent cloud and rain. But the weather is at its most variable in these months, and in some years March and April can be glorious.

June to September is the time of the southwest monsoon, with sky-high heat and humidity and torrential downpours (but also a fair amount of sunshine). July to September sees typhoon season in the South China Sea, but direct hits on

of 60kmh are expected – at which point shops and offices close and everyone heads home.

Visitors to Hong Kong during the summer should keep an umbrella handy at all times. It is also a good idea to bring along a jacket or sweater, since most offices, restaurants and shops have very powerful air-conditioning, making it difficult for newcomers to cope with the temperature differences.

Natural resources

Despite its economic success, Hong Kong is not blessed with natural resources. Its soil is generally acidic, low in organic matter,

Hong Kong are quite rare. Usually, typhoons pass within several hundred kilometres of the territory, hitting China's Guangdong Province. But heavy rains often cause landslides and flooding. On average, about 30 tropical cyclones form over the western North Pacific and the South China Sea each year, and about half of them reach typhoon strength, with maximum winds of 120 kilometres per hour or more. If a typhoon approaches, the standby signal no.1 will be upgraded to a warning "3" signal and then an "8" signal if winds in excess

nutrient-poor, and with low levels of nitrogen, phosphorous and calcium. Almost everything Hong Kong needs to sustain itself – food, industrial materials, energy, machinery, and even water – must be imported. Each day, Hong Kong's people consume about 900 tonnes of rice, 1,400 tonnes of vegetables, 7,000 tonnes of pork and nearly 2,000 tonnes of fruit. About 45 percent of the territory's food is imported from mainland China. Hong Kong is also dependent on China for fresh water. Surrounded by ocean, Hong Kong used to have a rich supply of seafood. But pollution and over-fishing mean that fishermen have to travel increasing distances for a sizeable catch. ❑

LEFT: a Peak Tram climbs Victoria Peak. **ABOVE:** the Port Authority's control tower for Victoria Harbour.

HONG KONG'S PEOPLE

Outsiders may see Hong Kong's people as materialistic and brusque, if not rude.
But there are reasons for this, including an obsession with success

The people of Hong Kong have a reputation for being the most business-minded, materialistic, competitive and restless population on the planet. No other city in the world has such a complex, unsettled society of people. It is a place where everyone moves at lightning speed because time is money, and every minute costs. Love it or hate it, life in Hong Kong is addictive, and even those who have escaped to more peaceful places – vowing never to return – have been drawn back like iron filings to a magnet. Even the most jaded visitor usually finds something seductive about it.

Hong Kong's 6.8 million people are packed into just 1,100 square kilometres, and certain areas have some of the world's highest population densities. During rush hour, overwhelming crowds of commuters squeeze themselves into trains and buses. Lunch hour in the Central District is a crazed feeding frenzy as thousands of office workers dash for restaurants, jostling and barging their way into tiny noodle shops and delicatessens. Elbowing strangers, stepping on toes, jumping queues and honking horns in traffic jams are unavoidable features of daily life here.

As a major trading port situated on the fertile Zhu Jiang (Pearl River) Delta, Hong Kong has long been a magnet for immigrants in search of a better life. New arrivals continue to flood in from China and overseas, all sharing one dream: to make money quickly and to enjoy spending it. This continual injection of new blood into the region is what gives Hong Kong its excitement and intensity.

For those seeking a settled, peaceful existence, Hong Kong will be a hard slap in the face. This place resounds with rags-to-riches tales of entrepreneurs who built up their business empires from scratch, and this promise of success is in the minds of almost every immigrant who heads here.

LEFT: dawn in Hong Kong brings out large groups starting the day with taijiquan practice.
RIGHT: rural woman with traditional hat.

Ethnic backgrounds

Hong Kong is, and always has been, Chinese. In spite of more than 150 years of colonial rule, the Chinese, who now make up 98 percent of the population, never had a sense of allegiance to the British Crown. Those of the older generation, who originated from elsewhere, often

have identified with their home provinces or towns in China rather than Hong Kong. However, after a century and a half of separation from their homeland, local Chinese are naturally more inclined to view themselves as Hong Kong citizens rather than Han Chinese.

The vast majority of Hong Kong Chinese are Cantonese, and their dialect, cuisine and customs make up the fabric of society here. The Cantonese language often sounds harsh and argumentative to unaccustomed ears, but its humour, slang and interspersed English words make for lively, often hilarious conversation. Cantonese is also centuries older than Mandarin, the official language of China, which evolved later in the courts of Mongol emperors during the Yuan dynasty (1271–1368). Therefore, the original rhythms and sounds of classical Tang and Song dynasty poetry are probably closer to modern-day Cantonese.

The Cantonese have traditionally been regarded as rebellious, ungovernable people who will take spontaneous action if angered, and they have always been feared and mistrusted by successive emperors and regimes. The Nationalist revolution, which toppled the Qing dynasty in 1912, was insti-

SQUEEZED

Eighty percent of Hong Kong's population lives on less than 10 percent of the territory's land.

land, which is passed down through sons only, so that the family can retain ownership of its land. The Tanka and Hoklo "boat people" once spent their lives on junks bobbing in the waters off Aberdeen, Yau Ma Tei and other typhoon shelters, but most of them have now come ashore to earn a living. The Tanka are allegedly the descendants of General Lu Tsun, who revolted against the emperor; after his death, his people were persecuted and deemed unworthy to live on land.

The Hoklo originate from Fuzhou (Fujian province) and

gated by a Cantonese – Dr Sun Yatsen. In 1966, public discontent in Hong Kong erupted into serious rioting, ostensibly against an increase in Star Ferry fares. At the height of the Cultural Revolution in 1967, hundreds of Communist supporters besieged Government House; rioting and strikes broke out, and a bomb exploded on Hong Kong Island, injuring nine people. Since then, the Hong Kong government has been rather sensitive to public opinion.

Hong Kong's oldest landowners, the Hakka ("guest people"), immigrated from central and southern China centuries ago, fortifying villages around Hong Kong against marauding pirates. Hakka women are forbidden from inheriting

were mainly fishermen and manual labourers. The sea goddess Tin Hau's birthday on the 23rd day of the third moon is celebrated by the descendants of these boat people, who sail in elaborately decorated fishing boats to her temples to pray for protection at sea.

From the 1930s onwards, thousands of immigrants began arriving from other parts of China, especially Shanghai and Fuzhou. Shanghai and Chiu Chow (Shantou) people, renowned for their cunning business acumen, clung together in powerful clan networks and established successful family businesses. As a result, many of Hong Kong's top professionals hail from these regions. The Chinese government had a formidable Shanghai clique under former President Jiang Zemin, who was once mayor of Shanghai, and it's likely that the appointments of Hong Kong Chief Executive Tung Chee-hwa and Chief Secretary Anson Chan were partly due to their roots in Shanghai.

Between 1978 and 1980, some 500,000 illegal immigrants from mainland China swam the shark-infested tidal waters, or climbed hills along the Sino-British border under the cover of darkness, to come to Hong Kong. Pitted against them were battalions of the People's Liberation Army (PLA) and Chinese coastal gunboats, which cooperated with British and Gurkha troops, police and the Royal Navy and Air Force to stop the flow of illegal immigrants into the territory.

Nowadays, mainlanders can enter Hong Kong legally on an entry permit. Once derided as *ah tsan* (country bumpkins) by the Hong Kong Chinese, many of them are now assimilated into the local culture. However, China-trained professionals such as doctors, nurses and engineers often have to accept menial jobs here because their credentials are not recognised by Hong Kong authorities. A medical board examination was set up in the 1990s to qualify Chinese doctors to practice in Hong Kong, but some mainland medical graduates feel that the test discriminates against them. The English section of the test alone eliminates many candidates.

Previously, it was difficult for mainland wives and children of Hong Kong men to register as local citizens. In 1997, 66,000 of these illegal immigrant children known as *siu yunseh* (little snakes) were deported, causing fierce debate over residency rights. Since then, priority has been given to these women and children in the quota of new arrivals allowed, but they still sometimes need to bribe mainland officials.

Foreign devils and ghost people

Hong Kong's cultural diversity is largely a result of the many different foreign nationals who have made their home here, either temporarily or permanently. Indeed, the two percent of the population that is not Chinese have made valuable contributions to cuisine, arts, culture and religion in Hong Kong, while assimilating Chinese customs and traditions.

LEFT: Fire Dragon Festival, Kowloon. **RIGHT:** the British celebrated the 1997 handover with a bit of style.

American, Australian, Canadian, British and other European expatriates – *gweilo* ("ghost person" or "foreign devil") as they are known in Chinese – make up the majority of the foreign business community in Hong Kong. During British rule, expatriates were often given preferential treatment in the workplace, commanding much higher salaries than the Chinese. Today, these inequalities are less apparent.

One of the more established foreign communities in Hong Kong comprises the descendants of early merchant traders and soldiers who followed the Union Jack from the Indian subcontinent to Hong Kong: Indians, Sri Lankans,

Pakistanis, Bangladeshis, Sikhs and Parsees. Their descendants, many of whom speak fluent Cantonese and hold Hong Kong passports, are not recognised as Chinese nationals, even though they were born in the territory. However, most of them have now been granted British citizenship. The survival of this community is largely due to a family-oriented approach to running cost-effective, profitable companies.

A few thousand ex-Gurkha troops, who once served in the British army, are now working as security guards in Hong Kong; eventually, they will probably retire to their homes in Nepal.

Hong Kong is home to a large number of Filipinas working as *amahs* (domestic helpers).

There are also many Filipinos working as singers and musicians. On Sundays and holidays, thousands of *amahs* gather in Chater Garden, Statue Square and surrounding streets in Central on their day off from work.

Several thousand Vietnamese boat people, who first started arriving in 1975 after the Communist North Vietnamese took over their country, have stayed on in Hong Kong. In the 1970s and 1980s, asylum was granted to over 100,000 refugees, many of whom had no hope of resettlement abroad. But after international discussions to resolve the issue of the Vietnamese boat people, it was concluded that all Vietnamese believed that a person should always carefully examine motives before acting, since all individuals are directly responsible for their fate. Therefore, the Chinese believe that anything can be achieved through sheer will and hard work. Their attitude is, "If you don't have any money, then go out and earn some!" rather than relying on government support or charity to provide financial assistance for one's family.

With this work ethic in mind, many parents work at least nine or 10 hours a day, six days a week to provide for their children who will, one day, look after them in old age. Most of the family budget goes towards children's clothing,

were to be removed from local refugee camps by the end of 1995. Those deemed "economic migrants" were repatriated to Vietnam, by force when necessary, while political refugees, who comprised about 10 percent, were resettled elsewhere overseas.

Values

Traditional Chinese values such as humility, perseverance, reverence for ancestors and respect for elders have been adapted to Hong Kong's modern, capitalist society. In fact, its community is based upon a paternalistic, family-oriented system that was perpetuated by China's most venerable sage, Confucius. He healthcare and education, so that they may enjoy what their parents never had in their youth. Children are expected to support their elderly parents and to honour the memory of deceased parents by regularly visiting their graves and making offerings.

The Chinese tend to be rather reserved about displays of affection; love is expressed through acts of kindness, rather than through words or embraces common in Western cultures. Family values are very strong, and parents dote on their children by spending time and money on them. On Sundays and holidays, parents take the whole family, with grandparents in tow, for Western-style buffets, *yum cha* ("drinking tea"), or *dim sum*. After lunch, families wander around the streets and shopping malls and buy new toys and clothes for the children.

Money madness

Successive famines, wars and political upheaval in China have taught the Hong Kong Chinese not to be complacent about financial security. They are eagle-eyed at spotting opportunities for making money, and for Hong Kong people, money does buy happiness, since material

A FLAT FOR A CASTLE?

A premium flat of around 130 square metres in Hong Kong will cost about three times as much as a castle in the Scottish highlands with 16 bedrooms.

At the end of a meal, diners will fight to pay the bill, since generosity also gains face. Face and *guanxi* – lifelong obligations of mutual assistance – are crucial to relationships. That's why the Chinese prefer to give business to family and friends rather than dealing with strangers, who might prove to be unreliable. In friends there is certainty.

Hong Kong people are often blamed for lacking a spirit of civic duty, but they are anything but miserly. Millions of dollars are donated annually to the

security is vital to one's sense of well-being. There is no other place in the world where people, rich or poor, are as business-minded and clued-in about property, stocks and horse-racing. It's no coincidence that *kung hei fat choi* – literally "Congratulations on your wealth" – is a common greeting at Lunar New Year.

The quest for wealth is also motivated by "face" or self-respect. Driving expensive cars, wearing designer labels and living in a beautiful apartment are ways of winning face.

LEFT: an expecting couple without a seat on the Kowloon Canton Railway. **ABOVE:** Hong Kong's two race courses draw seriously focused punters.

Community Chest, a charitable organisation in Hong Kong.

Security overseas

Since the 1984 Sino-British agreement to return Hong Kong to China in 1997, emigration has been a constant feature of life in Hong Kong. During the 1980s and 1990s, around 60,000 people left each year to secure foreign passports, mainly from Canada, Australia and the United States. The price of such security has meant sacrificing businesses, family and friends, and starting out from scratch in an alien country. Many emigrants have returned to Hong Kong after establishing permanent residence overseas, shuttling back and forth annually to retain their status in both places. In theory, China insists that all ethnic Chinese Hong Kong residents are Chinese nationals; therefore, they are not entitled to foreign consular protection. However, Hong Kong residents are free to travel on foreign passports, since attempts to change their status could lead to economic disaster.

Pragmatism versus passion

For financial reasons, Hong Kong Chinese marry at an older age than mainland Chinese. Women generally marry at the age of 25 and

men, at 28. Because of high property prices, most people, even married couples, have no choice but to live with their parents until they have saved enough money. Cramped living conditions, however, make life difficult for would-be lovers. Moments alone are rare, and the prying eyes of relatives are not conducive to romance. Among the few romantic retreats are public parks, and at night, the benches are often taken by courting couples. Another option is the love motel rented by the hour in Kowloon Tong, a popular escape for couples looking for a few hours of undisturbed passion.

Hong Kong is a capitalist society where Darwin's theory of the "survival of the fittest" predominates. Local tax laws give residents incentive to be among those that not only survive, but thrive. Hong Kong residents get to keep most of what they earn – income tax does not take away more than 15 percent of a worker's salary, and only around two percent of the working population pays the highest rate, with over half paying no income tax at all.

However, Hong Kong has a high cost of living due to rising inflation, limited land, the expense of bringing raw materials and food from China, and high import duties imposed upon petrol and cars. In spite of this, luxury cars score high points in the "face" game, and people will gladly blow all their cash on a Mercedes-Benz or BMW even though they can't afford much else. The cost of a parking space in certain residential blocks is the price of an apartment in other countries, and like property or stocks, speculators buy and sell parking spaces at enormous profits.

The government has generated enormous revenue from auctioning land to private developers who are willing to pay astronomical prices, and from taxes imposed on the sale and purchase of property. Before the Asian economic crisis, the property market remained the fastest and most consistently reliable way of earning a buck.

The expected arrival of an additional two million immigrants from mainland China by the year 2000 prompted Hong Kong's Chief Executive Tung Chee-hwa in 1997 to promise 85,000 new flats by 2002. The most costly method of releasing land to create more housing has been through urban renewal projects – purchasing run-down buildings in old areas, such as in parts of Kowloon, and often resettling the tenants elsewhere.

Old factory areas such as Cheung Sha Wan and Tsuen Wan and rural land in Sheung Shui and Fan Ling, have been developed into residential areas at minimal cost. However, the main problem of developing high-density residential areas in the New Territories is that of infrastructure – efficient transportation and employment opportunities are essential to draw people to move into this new housing. The earliest New Towns, as these developed areas are called, lacked these facilities, causing unemployment and social problems to soar.

A more cost-effective solution to the shortage of space for building new public housing has been land reclamation, as there is no need to compensate tenants or buy property.

Families living in public housing have the benefit of low rents, as well as shared income from family members, so they are relatively well-off compared to low-income families in other parts of the world. However, lower-middle-class families are often caught: they do not qualify for public housing, and most property prices are way out of their budget. Since the 1990s, the Hong Kong government has allocated "sandwich-class" housing for these families in the form of affordable rental or private property.

Social welfare and health

Primary medical care is largely dominated by market forces in Hong Kong, while the government subsidises secondary health care in hospitals. The problem of overcrowded public wards and long waiting lists has drawn a great deal of criticism. But despite these problems, affordable government medical care is assured for the entire population through public funds and private donations. There are no government-aided schemes for comprehensive health care, except in extreme cases when people cannot afford private health care and insurance and

LEFT: shopping for gold is always auspicious.
RIGHT: mahjong action, Lantau.

their employers do not provide medical insurance. This has led to substantial growth in private medical and life insurance funded by both companies and individuals.

Crime

Hong Kong's over-the-top action movies often give the impression of a crime-ridden city and a perpetual hunting ground for chopper-wielding tattooed triads and armed robbers. In reality Hong Kong is fairly safe, although mainland crime syndicates have become an increasing problem in recent years, especially in Macau.

Crime syndicates called triads (so-called

because their emblem symbolises harmony between Heaven, Earth and Man) rely on a hierarchical structure, with ranks denoted by numbers that begin with four, representing the four elements, compass points and seas. The most high profile gangs are "14K" and "San Yee On", whose illegal activities include loan-sharking, gambling, narcotics, prostitution, smuggling and extortion.

Hong Kong has an estimated 40,000 drug users, 96 percent of them heroin addicts, so the government takes a particularly tough stance on narcotics. Possession of marijuana carries the same penalties as hard drugs: a criminal record and possible imprisonment. Codeine-laced cough medicine has become the drug of choice amongst teenagers, and police carry out sporadic raids on pharmacies to bust shop owners who sell codeine to teenagers.

Education

Hong Kong's educational system is every bit as competitive as its business community. Children suffer tremendous pressure to gain entrance into prestigious schools. The most sought-after are English or bilingual schools, because English is widely used in business, medicine and law. A number of students commit suicide each year because they fail an

important exam. Parental pressure often proves too much for children, who spend most of their time doing homework, cramming for exams and studying foreign languages for overseas study. Tutors are hired to prepare even toddlers for kindergarten entrance exams, an ordeal that sometimes requires two hours of testing to determine a child's Chinese, English and arithmetic skills.

The government recently conducted a programme to ascertain the standard of English spoken by teachers, to ensure that students get every opportunity to become confidently bilingual. The core competency remains Chinese, English and maths. Language proficiency surveys conducted in the late 1990s have shown that the majority of school dropouts are competent in neither Chinese nor English, and that over 60 percent of students are more receptive to lessons taught in Chinese.

Many schools claim to use English, but teachers and students often resort to "Chinglish" – Cantonese peppered with English phrases – when studying English-language textbooks. Outside the classroom, English is seldom used. It's hardly surprising that the most popular, over-subscribed university courses are in science, business and engineering – more easily rote-learned and leading to more financially rewarding careers than the arts and humanities.

The future

During the 1989 pro-democracy movement in China, over 500,000 demonstrators took to the streets in Hong Kong in a show of solidarity. Hong Kong residents donated millions of dollars to the cause and sent tents to Beijing for student protesters camped out in Tiananmen Square. After the 4 June massacre, more than one million people in Hong Kong marched to the New China News Agency, the unofficial headquarters of the Chinese Communist Party in Hong Kong. Preconceptions of a socially compliant population evaporated.

Hong Kong's economic success can be credited above all to one thing: its industrious people. Any heavy-handed attempts to restrict freedoms (such as the proposed anti-subversion laws that hit the headlines in late 2002) could result in an unprecedented exodus of a talented, highly educated workforce with disastrous consequences for China, negating the benefits brought about by the reforms, modernisation and acceptance into world markets that have been so encouraging for the region as a whole.

However, stories of the economic success possible in Hong Kong have reached even the remotest parts of China, and the tide of migrants heading south is gaining momentum. It is here in Hong Kong that China's economic reforms must coincide with the advance of democracy rather than its suppression, if Hong Kong is to thrive. ❑

LEFT: children at play on statue.
RIGHT: a woman is a dog's best friend.

RELIGION AND PHILOSOPHY

Daoism, Confucianism and Buddhism define the way that Chinese approach life.
Adding to the complexity of the Chinese world-view is ancestor worship

The Chinese have three primary religions or philosophies – Buddhism, Confucianism and Daoism – each with elements of animism and superstition that have made their way into these belief systems throughout their long histories. Some elements of these also overlap, with values and deities shared amongst them. Added to the mix is the Chinese tradition of ancestor worship. And because Hong Kong's population originates from so many different cultures, Muslims, Christians, Jews and Hindus also mingle with followers of these Chinese beliefs.

Daoism

There are two concepts central to Daoism: *dao* (also *tao*), the way or path, and *wuwei*, or passivity. Daoists believe in dao as the guiding principle of all reality and truth, and that such a path must be pursued with humility and a life of simplicity. They believe events in the world are determined by the forces *yang* and *yin*. Yang represents masculinity, brightness, activity and heaven, while yin elements are feminine, weak, dark and passive.

The Daoist philosophy is said to have begun in the sixth century with a man named Laozi, who was an archivist for the Chinese government. Numerous legends have been told about Laozi, and some historians question whether such a man actually existed. Laozi's philosophy is said to be contained in a book entitled the *Daodejing* (The Way and Its Power). The book was, at first, credited to Laozi, but it now seems certain, according to many scholars, that this work was not written by a single author.

The earliest, and also most significant, followers of Laozi were Liezi and Zhuangzi. Liezi (fifth century BC) was particularly concerned with the relativity of experiences, and he strived to comprehend the dao through meditation. Zhuangzi (fourth century BC) is famous for his poetic allegories.

PRECEDING PAGES: coils and coils of temple incense.
LEFT: brass deer and incense smoke, Man Mo Temple, in Western District. **RIGHT:** old print of Laozi.

Ordinary people were not particularly attracted by the abstract concepts and metaphysical reflections of Daoism. Even at the beginning of the Han period (206 BC–AD 220), there were signs of both a popular and religious Daoism. As Buddhism also became more and more popular, it borrowed ideas from Daoism, and vice versa, to the point where the two overlapped in many ways.

Both the Daoists and Buddhists believed that the great paradise was in the far west of China, hence the name, Western Paradise. It was believed to be governed by the Queen Mother of the West (Xiwangmu) and her husband, the Royal Count of the East (Dongwanggong). The Daoists also borrowed the idea of hell directly from Buddhism.

Daoism as a religion developed in various directions. The ascetics retreated to the mountains or to monasteries and devoted all their time to meditation. Daoist priests played the role of medicine men and interpreters of oracles. They carried out exorcism and funeral rites, and prayed for the dead or conducted sacrificial offerings for them.

Historical and legendary figures were added to the Daoist pantheon. At the top of the hierarchy were the Three Commendables. The highest of the three deities, the heavenly god, is identical to the Jade Emperor and is worshiped by the common people. There is hardly a Daoist temple without Shouxinggong (the God of Longevity), a friendly-looking old man with a long white beard and an elongated, bald head. There are also gods for every aspect of daily life: the God of Wealth (Caishen), the God of

Fire (Huoshen), the Kitchen God (Zaoshen), the God of Literature (Wendi) and the God of Medicine (Huatou), among others.

Confucianism

While Laozi's philosophy took off in the southern part of China, another system of beliefs was popularised by Confucius in the northern regions of the country. For more than 2,000 years, the ideas of Confucius (551–479 BC) have influenced Chinese culture, which in turn sculpted the world-view of neighbouring lands such as Korea, Japan and Southeast Asia. It is debatable whether Confucianism is a religion in the strictest sense, or simply a philosophy of liv-

ing. But Confucius was sometimes worshiped as a deity, although only officially made equal to a heavenly god by imperial edict in 1906.

Confucius lived during a time of poverty, corruption and turmoil. Mencius, a Confucian scholar, describes the political and social atmosphere during Confucius's time: "There are no wise rulers, the lords of the states are driven by their desires. In their farms are fat animals, in their royal stables fat horses, but the people look hungry and on their fields there are people who are dying of starvation."

Confucius himself came from an impoverished family of the nobility in the state of Lu,

CONFUCIAN WISDOM

A man of humanity, wishing to establish himself, also establishes others, and wishing to enlarge himself, also enlarges others.

It is a pleasure to have friends come to visit you from afar.

It is these things that cause me concern: failure to cultivate virtue, failure to go deeply into what I have learned, inability to move up to what I have heard to be right, and inability to reform myself when I have defects.

He is the sort of man who forgets to eat when he engages himself in vigorous pursuit of learning, who is so full of joy that he forgets his worries, and who does not notice that old age is coming on. (Describing himself)

west of Shandong province. For years, Confucius – or Kong Fuzi (Master Kong) in Mandarin – tried to gain office with some of the feudal lords but was dismissed again and again. So he travelled around with his disciples and instructed them in his philosophy. He is said to have had 3,000 disciples, 72 of them highly-gifted scholars who are still revered today.

Confucius taught literature, rites and music, and is thus regarded as the founder of scholarly life in China. The Chinese word *ru*, which is usually translated as "Confucian", actually means "someone of a gentle nature" – a trait that was attributed to a cultured person. Confucius did not publish his philosophical thoughts in a book. His teachings were written down by his loyal students in a collection entitled the *Lunyu* (Conversations). Some of the classic works on Confucianism are: *Shijing*, the Book of Songs; *Shujing*, the Book of Charters; *Liji*, the Book of Rites; *Chunqiu*, the Spring and Autumn Annals; and *Yijing*, the Book of Changes.

Confucianism is, in a sense, a philosophy of law and order. Just as the universe is dictated by the world order, and the sun, moon and stars move according to the laws of nature, so a person, too, should live within the framework of world order. This idea, in turn, is based upon the assumption that man can be educated about eth-

their husbands; a younger brother must obey his older brother; and subjects must obey and be loyal to their ruler.

In the 12th century, Zhu Xi succeeded in combining the metaphysical tendencies of Buddhism and Daoism with the pragmatism of Confucianism. His work included teachings about the creation of the microcosm and macrocosm, as well as the metaphysical basis of Chinese ethics. This system, known as neo-Confucianism, reached canonical status in China; it was the basis of all state civil-service examinations, a determining factor for Chinese officialdom until the 20th century.

ical principles. Confucius was a very conservative reformer, yet he significantly reinterpreted the idea of the *junzi*, a nobleman, to that of a noble man whose life is morally sound and who is, therefore, legitimately entitled to reign.

Confucius believed an ideal social order could be achieved if each member of society fulfiled his role. Confucius defined social roles very clearly, beginning with family relationships and extending to the relationship between a king and his subjects: the son must obey the father without reservation; women must obey

FAR LEFT: portrait of Confucius.
ABOVE : Pai Tak Temple, Cheung Chau.

Buddhism

Although Buddhism is often associated with China, the religion actually originated in India. Buddhism was introduced to China at the beginning of the first century by merchants and monks who came from India over the Silk Road. The Buddhism that is prevalent in China today is the Mahayana (Great Wheel), which – as opposed to Hinayana (Small Wheel) – promises all creatures redemption through the so-called *bodhisattva*, or redemption deities.

Buddhism offers two things that are particularly attractive to the Chinese: an explanation for individual misfortune and the promise of existence after death. Nevertheless, at first there was considerable opposition to Buddhism, which contrasted sharply with Confucian ethics and the tradition of ancestor worship.

During the Three Kingdoms period (AD 220–280), Confucianism spread in each of the three states. The trading towns along the Silk Road as far as Luoyang became centres of the new religion. During the rule of Emperor Wudi (502–549), hostility towards Buddhism spread among Confucians. And from 574 to 577, during the relatively short-lived northern Zhou dynasty, Buddhism was banned.

CROSSOVER

The Buddhist Goddess of Mercy, Quanyin, is worshipped in Daoist temples, too.

influential: Chan (school of meditation or Zen Buddhism) and Amitabha Buddhism (Pure Land). The masters of Chan considered meditation to be the only path to knowledge.

In Mahayana Buddhism, worship focused on the bodhisattva Avalokiteshvara. Since the seventh century, this ascetic bodhisattva has been a popular female figure in China. She is called Quanyin (Kuanyin), a motherly goddess of mercy and compassion who represents a central deity for the ordinary people. Quanyin means "the one who listens to complaints".

Buddhism was most influential in Chinese history during the Tang dynasty (618–907). Several emperors officially supported the religion. The Tang empress Wu Zetian, in particular, surrounded herself with Buddhist advisors. During the years 842 to 845, however, Chinese Buddhists also experienced the most severe persecution in their entire history: a total of 40,000 temples and monasteries were destroyed, and Buddhism was blamed for the economic decline and moral decay of the dynasty.

In time, ten Chinese schools of Buddhism emerged, eight of which were essentially philosophical ones that did not influence popular religion. Only two of the schools have remained

In Chinese Buddhism, the centre of religious attention is the Sakyamuni Buddha, the founder of Buddhism who was forced into the background in the sixth century by the Maitreya Buddha (called Milefo in China, or redeemer of the world). In Chinese monasteries, Sakyamuni greets the faithful as a laughing Buddha in the entrance hall. Since the 14th century, the Amitabha school has dominated the life and culture of the Chinese people.

The most influential Buddhist school was the so-called School of Meditation (Chan in China, Zen in Japan), which developed under the Tang dynasty. It preached redemption through buddhahood, which anyone is able to reach. It despises knowledge gained from books or dogmas, as well as rites. Liberating shocks or guided meditation are used in order to lead disciples toward enlightenment. Other techniques used to achieve final insights are long hikes and physical labour. The most important method is a dialogue with the master, who asks subtle and paradoxical questions, to which he expects equally paradoxical answers.

When the People's Republic of China was founded by the Communist Party in 1949, there were approximately 500,000 Buddhist monks and nuns, and 50,000 temples and monasteries in China. By the beginning of the Cultural Revolution in 1966, Buddhism faced complete eradication by the Communist Party, which approved of no belief system other than Communism. Autonomous Tibet was hard-hit by these excesses. Only a few monasteries and cultural objects survived the large-scale destruction of temples and religious monuments during the 10-year Cultural Revolution.

In the seventh century AD, another type of Buddhism, called Tantric Buddhism or Lamaism, was introduced into Tibet from India. With the influence of the monk Padmasambhava, it replaced the indigenous Bon religion, while at the same time taking over some of the elements of this naturalist religion. The monasteries in Tibet developed into centres of intellectual and worldly power, yet there were recurring arguments amongst followers. A sect of virtue (Gelugpa) was established, which declared absolute celibacy to be a condition and reintroduced strict rules of order. Because followers wear yellow caps, this order came to be known as Yellow Hat Buddhism.

Two of the founder's disciples are said to be reborn as heads of the order: the Dalai Lama and Panchen Lama. The Dalai Lama represents the incarnation of the bodhisattva of mercy, worshiped as the patron god of Tibet. The Panchen Lama is higher in the hierarchy of the gods.

In Lamaism, a complex pantheon exists; apart from the Buddhist deities, there are figures from the Brahman and Hindu world of gods and the old Bon religion. Magic, repetitive prayers, movements, formulae, symbols and sacrificial rituals are all means for achieving redemption.

LEFT: images surrounding the Buddha statue, Po Lin Monastery, Lantau. **RIGHT:** cemeteries are only temporary; the bones must be dug up and cremated.

Ancestor worship

The Chinese tradition of worshipping ancestors is based upon the assumption that a person has two souls. One is created at the time of conception, and when the person dies, the soul stays in the grave with the corpse and lives on the sacrificial offerings. As the corpse decomposes, the strength of the soul dwindles, until it eventually leads a shadow existence in the underworld. However, it will return to earth as an ill-willed spirit if sacrifices are not offered.

The second soul only emerges at birth. During its heavenly voyage, it is threatened by evil forces and is also dependent upon the sacrifices

and prayers of the living descendants. If the sacrifices cease, then this soul, too, turns into an evil spirit. But if the descendants continue to make sacrificial offerings and look after the graves, the soul of the deceased ancestor may offer them help and protection.

At first, people believed that the soul of the ancestor would search for a human substitute – usually, the grandson – during sacrificial ceremonies. About 2,000 years ago, genealogical tables were introduced as homes for the soul during sacrificial rites.

Today, the Chinese visit their ancestors' graves to offer sacrifices of food and wine to the spirits of the dead. ❑

TRADITIONAL BELIEFS

Nearly as old as China's recorded history, beliefs such as fortune-telling, feng shui,

and the idea that numbers can be lucky continue to influence Hong Kong's destiny

Few modern-day city residents take their traditional beliefs more seriously than the Hong Kong Chinese. Fortune-telling and real estate dealing are two professions where making pots of money is guaranteed in this cosmopolitan international city. Following the fortune-tellers' advice to the letter can involve

radical behaviour, such as having your hair shorn off skinhead-style to appease the fortune god, or wearing a bright red belt, no matter what outfit.

It is easy for non-believers to sneer at what they may call "superstition", but most Hong Kong Chinese take it very seriously, pointing out that the beliefs go back a long way.

Like any cultural phenomenon, fortune-telling is historically related to the social environment. In primitive society, everyone was equally poor, so there was no need for fortune-telling. The idea of fate came with the introduction of slaves as a social class. It was believed that "the god" – the emperor – decided who would be slave or master, poor or rich, fortunate or unfortunate. Still, there was no fortune-telling then. Since a person's fate was decided by the emperor, why worry about it?

When the Yin dynasty was overthrown by rebellions in the 11th century BC, the myth that the emperor was infallible was broken and people began to think about the existence of fate and ways to influence, or at least know, their fate. At first, they worshiped horses and cows, animals essential to an agricultural society. People soon came to believe that the different physical features of animals, such as shape, frame, hair and skin colour, decided the animal's capabilities, temper and life span. They gradually applied this observation to people.

During the Tang (618–907) and Song (960–1279) dynasties, life became more complex, people were more concerned about their fate, and fortune-telling became a popular profession. Officials not only asked about their own fortune, but also that of their colleagues and superiors, so they could know the best time to request a promotion or a new posting. From then on, fortune-telling developed into a number of branches, including the reading of palms and facial features, and predictions based on mathematical calculations from birth dates.

Feng shui

Feng shui ("wind and water") is a form of geomancy, based on the belief that wind and water were created by the gods and therefore reflect the will of the gods concerning the earth and its people. After government departments complete a new development plan, a businessman buys a new office, or before a family moves into a new house, feng shui masters are hired to study the surroundings and determine which direction the building should face and where desks, beds, or even a vase should be placed to attract the best luck and prevent bad fortune.

The most important tool of feng shui masters is a compass-like device that has eight ancient trigrams representing nature and its elements: heaven, water, fire, thunder, wind, hills and earth. These elements, in turn, represent eight animals: horse, goat, pheasant, dragon, fowl, swine, dog and ox.

Feng shui is based mainly on the principle of *qi*, the spirit or breath that is believed to exist in nature and in all living creatures. The qi is divided into *yin* and *yang*, or female-passive and male-active elements. The concept of *wuxing* also plays a prominent role in Chinese philosophy, medicine, astrology and superstition. The term can be directly translated as "five elements", or the five types of energy that dominate the uni-

LUCKY CHARITY

As of 1997, more than 370 lucky license numbers had been sold, raising more than HK$547 million for the government's charity fund.

height, a Buddhist ceremony was carried out to calm the spirits of those who had died there.

One of the most famous cases of the psychological influence of feng shui involves tycoon Li Ka-shing. The street between his head office, China Building and the building opposite was dangerous for pedestrians because the traffic was very heavy during rush hours. But despite government requirements, Li was reluctant to build a pedestrian bridge, believing that a bridge would channel the evil spirits in from across the

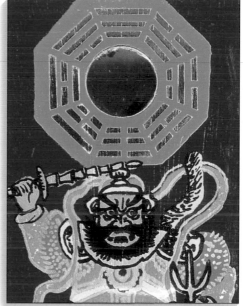

verse at different times. Water dominates in winter, wood in spring, fire in summer and metal in autumn; earth dominates in the transitions between the seasons.

Big business takes superstitious beliefs seriously. In Central District, at the site where Hutchison House, Bank of America Tower and a multi-storey carpark stand, a mass execution was conducted by Japanese army during World War II. When Hutchison House reached its full

street. To protect the good luck that made him one of the richest Chinese in the world, he finally placed two giant stone lions at the entrance of his building to deflect evil spirits.

Even government officials believe in the power of feng shui. When morale within the Hong Kong police force dropped substantially in 1973, a senior officer went to seek advice from a geomancer who concluded that the headquarters' entrance facing a fairground made it susceptible to evil spirits. At the geomancer's suggestion, two old cannons were placed on either side of the entrance to keep away the evil two-horned monster that was threatening the police force's morale.

LEFT: slow night for the fortune-teller. **ABOVE LEFT:** the Bank of China Tower's angles are said to cast bad feng shui on the nearby buildings of competing banks. **ABOVE RIGHT:** mirrors are used to deflect bad feng shui.

Most feng shui experts can also tell people's fortunes by reading faces and palms, or by doing complicated calculations based on a person's name or the time and date of birth. But if you want detailed information such as when you will get married and how many children you will have, it'll cost significantly more.

Lucky numbers

Hong Kong may be the only place in the world where someone would pay US$1.7 million for an automobile license plate. In 1994, Hong Kong tycoon Albert Yeung did just that. He thought the license plate bearing the single digit

nine was lucky because the Cantonese word for "nine" sounds like the word for "longevity".

The number two stands for "easy", three for "living or giving birth", six for "longevity", eight for "prosperity" and nine for "perpetuity" or "eternity", or even "longevity". But it is the combinations that are in most demand. For example, 163 means "live forever" or "give birth non-stop"; 168, "prosperity all the way"; and 162, "easy all the way".

Lucky license-plate numbers became so much in demand that, in 1973, the government's transport department began auctioning off these number plates to the highest bidders. The number eight has consistently drawn the highest bid.

But trading lucky numbers was a profitable business long before the auctions began. Prior to the auction scheme, sought-after numbers were freely traded on the open market without restrictions. In 1970, a foreign car owner drove his dilapidated 1959 Sunbeam Rapier convertible into a petrol station and the station owner offered him HK$2,500 in cash for the lucky number plate,1479, on the car, which (with the number) had been bought a few years before that encounter for HK$1,000. The car number plate was (and still is) considered an antique.

In late 1997, despite a plunge in the Hong Kong stock market and a financial crisis in the region, a license plate reading HH88 – meaning "good, good, prosper, prosper" – was purchased for HK$555,000 by an anonymous Chinese couple. However, a similar number, HH4444 – its pronunciation means "good, good, death, death, death, death" – fetched only HK$60,000 as it was not lucky enough, although it could be lucky with a bit of mathematical fudging.

Before the big car boom in the 1960s and 1970s, car license-plate numbers had no letter prefixes, so these surviving plates have become expensive collector's items. Licenses of three digits, double digits, or even a single digit are now worth many thousand times the amount offered by the astute pump attendant.

Today, all license plate numbers considered lucky in Cantonese and prestige numbers in single, double, triple and quadruple digits without prefixes are reserved and available only through auctions. The government has designated a batch of lucky numbers and carefully restricts their sale to about a dozen numbers at a time and at regularly spaced auctions.

The superstition over numbers also applies to street, apartment and telephone numbers. For example, the price for an apartment on the 14th floor can be 20 percent cheaper than that for the same flat on the 18th floor, because 14 in Cantonese means "definitely dies", while 18 means "definitely prospers".

If you want to get hold of the boss of a Hong Kong company without having to go through the receptionists and secretaries, try extensions 13, 18, 19 and other lucky number combinations. Most likely, the boss has the luckiest telephone number in the company. ❑

LEFT: a lucky "6" for longevity. **RIGHT:** lucky "red papers" at a Hong Kong temple.

HONG KONG'S FESTIVALS: OF SPIRITS AND DEITIES

For the visitor, it's all a matter of timing. But if the timing is good, one may see some of the world's most elaborate festivals occurring in Hong Kong.

Although firecrackers are officially banned for private use in Hong Kong, hardly a month goes by without the crackle of explosions to scare off evil spirits.

Lunar New Year can fall as early as January or as late as February, depending upon the lunar calendar. Children and the unmarried receive *lai see*, lucky red packets containing newly minted money. Employees get a bonus. Shops are decorated in fine style. The standard good wish is *Kung Hei Fat Choy*, roughly interpreted as "May You Be Lucky and Get Rich."

Even more high profile is the Cheung Chau Bun Festival in early May. Intended to placate the spirits of former residents of the island who were either slain by pirates or, depending on the legend, died in a plague, it's a riot of colour and invention. And the buns? In days gone by the young men of the island used to compete to get as many buns as possible from a bamboo tower, but the event got out of hand and nowadays people simply eat them.

Perhaps the most glorious sight is the Tin Hau Festival, dedicated to the goddess of the sea. As someone who can calm the waves, protect seafarers, and ensure fishermen of a bountiful catch, the offerings made to her many temples and the decoration of junks and craft paying her tribute are all on a grand scale.

PERFORMANCE FACE ▷
The performing arts are prominent during the many festivals of Hong Kong.

△ **LOOMING DEITY**
Incense is burned for a temple god on Hong Kong's outlying Cheung Chau island.

▽ **OFFERINGS**
During Hong Kong's festivals, offerings are made at the appropriate temples.

△ BUN FESTIVAL

In May, on the tiny island of Cheung Chau, there is a bun festival. Towers of buns rise from the ground at Pak Tai temple. Its origins are vague.

◁ LION DANCE

The lion dance, like the dragon dance, usually takes place whenever there's a festive occasion.

▽ FESTIVAL BOATS

Junks are decorated for the Tin Hau Festival, with variable dates in April or May.

DRAGON BOATS ON THE LOOSE

Hong Kong's most international celebration, the Dragon Boat Festival, owes its existence to an odd event around 200 BC. Chu Yuan, a poet who had fallen out of political favour with the king, jumped into a river in protest and drowned. The frantic paddlers of today recreate the desperate actions of Yuan's friends as they tried to save him.

Although the main event of today's festival is in Sha Tin, in the New Territories, all over Hong Kong one can find teams enduring a back-breaking test. The test is of endurance as they propel their heavy wooden craft through the water, cheered on by crowds who've come to watch the fun. Many boats are sponsored by corporations and crewed by their employees.

Thanks to some clever marketing and the growing numbers of Hong Kong Chinese who've emigrated to various places around the world, dragon boating is international with teams from all over the globe. In 1971 the first women's event was held in Hong Kong.

Tuen Ng – Hong Kong's Dragon Boat Festival – is held in June and is a public holiday. If you can't make it up to Sha Tin, there are usually races in other areas, including Stanley. Contact the hotel concierge or look in the newspaper for locations.

TRADITIONAL MEDICINE

Long considered by Westerners to be primitive and of little use, traditional Chinese medicine's 4,000 years of background have made inroads into Western scepticism

Whenever traditional Chinese medicine is mentioned nowadays, most Westerners immediately think of acupuncture. In some countries, orthodox Western medicine is still somewhat reluctant to accept acupuncture as part of an alternative approach to medicine. However, it is increasingly accepted by many Western physicians, and there is hardly a "pain centre" anywhere in the Western world that does not offer acupuncture as a therapy. In 1997, medical authorities in the United States approved it as a legitimate – and insurable – treatment for pain.

Yet medicine in China is not just so-called traditional medicine. In fact, Western-style medicine is the primary form of medical treatment in China. The large public hospitals in all cities use the Western approach (*xiyi*) to treatment almost exclusively. The hospitals for Chinese medicine (*zhonggi*) are smaller, less well-equipped and harder to find. Nowadays, the Chinese will usually visit a doctor trained in Western medicine if they feel that they are seriously ill and wish to be diagnosed. If no organic failure is found, the patient will go and see a traditional doctor who is far more likely to be able to restore the lost harmony in the body.

Traditional Chinese medicine entails more than just acupuncture. The knowledge of remedies (*zhongyao*) is an important factor. Patients are treated with different kinds of massage and chiropractics (*tuina*), as well as breathing and movement therapies, such as *taijiquan* (shadow boxing) and *qigong* (breathing therapy).

The practice of traditional cures does not only take place within the walls of a hospital or pharmacy. When travelling through China, travelers have many opportunities to observe – in public parks and open markets – the efforts of the Chinese to keep healthy.

Wandering through the streets of a Chinese town, again and again one will see farmers in the street selling herbs and produce. Often it is not obvious that these are remedies; one would

LEFT: early morning breathing exercises, Stanley.
RIGHT: herbalist in his store.

naturally think of them as food. For example, *giou qize*, a small and oval-shaped fruit, carmine red and tasting rather bitter, is used to relieve "congestion" of the liver and for getting rid of "anger". Farmers who raise it tend to claim that it is also somewhat beneficial in fighting high blood pressure.

The pharmacy

In the pharmacy there is a unique smell, or rather a mixture of 1,001 scents. You will also recognise the acupuncture needles and the cupping glasses made of glass or bamboo. You will find all sorts of animals, insects and vegetables: birds' eggs, snakes wound up in spiral shapes, dried monkeys, toads, tortoises, centipedes, grasshoppers, dried fish, octopi, stag antlers, rhinoceros horns, and testicles and penises of various unfortunate – and often endangered – animals. And then there are the thousand kinds of herbs, blossoms, roots, berries, mushrooms and fruits – dried and preserved. In fact, there is hardly a plant, mineral, or animal substance in the world that is not used as a remedy or pre-ventative. All traditional Chinese pharmacies are well-stocked with ginseng roots, dried or immersed in alcohol and often shaped like a human figure. In fact, the Chinese character for ginseng contains the sign *ren*, which means person.

The *Encyclopaedia of the Traditional Chinese Pharma-copoeia*, published in 1977, has 2,700 pages listing 5,767 sub-stances with medicinal or pre-ventative properties.

BENEVOLENT VITAMINS

Herbalist Sun Ssu-mo established the tradition of "benevolent art, benevolent heart" that has guided Chinese doctors since. He also diagnosed vitamin-deficiency 1,000 years before Europeans did so in 1642.

medicine. The two most important schools of thought at the time were those of Confucianism and Daoism. Both shared the wish for harmony, but their views on how this was to be achieved differed.

Harmony was interpreted as the interaction of opposite forces, for example, the adjust-ment of human behaviour to ecological and social conditions. If this harmony was interfered with, then the disturbance would result in social or physical ill-ness. The theory of the opposite

Historical roots

The foundations of traditional Chinese medi-cine were laid over 2,000 years ago, in the era of the Warring Empires, a time in which China was split up into many quarrelling fiefdoms and kingdoms. This stage in Chinese history, marked by fighting and misery, lasted a few centuries. So it is hardly surprising that people began to search for a solution to the endless strife. Innumerable thinkers, philosophers and social reformers with as many diverse ideas emerged – a collection of thought often referred to as the "hundred schools". It was the time when ideas were born that were to influence life in China for the next 2,000 years, including

forces of *yin* and *yang*, the theory of the "five phases of change" and the idea of *qi* – the life force – were the most influential in the theoret-ical background of traditional medicine. They formed the framework of medical thinking.

At a time when there existed very little knowledge of human anatomy and physiology, these theories provided points of reference. They enabled people to observe not only the relationship of the human microcosm to the macrocosm of the environment, but also the effect that physical and emotional changes have on each other.

Thus, the feeling of fury was related to the wind that can come up very suddenly and with elemental force; fury was also brought into connection with a sour type of taste, and with muscles and sinews that can become cramped due to aggression.

The *Inner Classic of the Yellow Emperor*, which is around 2,000 years old, mentions that people with gall-bladder problems must have fallen ill due to unsatisfied ambition and pent-up anger. Thus, over the centuries, a special form of medicine and treatment evolved in China that concentrated particularly on the functional body. And as Chinese influence grew in Asia, these treatments and techniques spread to Korea, Japan and elsewhere.

A new form of painless acupuncture is that of ear acupuncture, which does not use needles. Small, round seed kernels are stuck onto certain points of the ear and massaged by the patient from time to time. This method is not only very successful in the treatment of pain, but it is also said to relieve some allergies such as hay fever.

When entering an acupuncture clinic, you will notice the similar 1,001 scents of the Chinese pharmacy. This is the typical smell of the *moxa* herb, which is the same thing as Artemisia, or mugwort. It is considered especially helpful in the treatment of illnesses that, in Chinese medical terminology, are classified

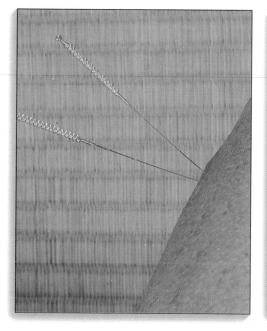

Acupuncture

Certainly not a cure for everything, acupuncture seldom performs the miracles that were often attributed to it in the past. In one aspect, however, its effect is undisputed and valued by a billion Chinese: the relief of pain. While Westerners rely on drugs to moderate physical pain, the Chinese go to the acupuncturist. Many cases of acute back pain, for example, can be cured by sticking just one needle in the *ren-zhong* point between the top lip and nose.

LEFT: Song dynasty illustration of a village doctor using acupuncture.
ABOVE: acupuncture needles, and taijiquan, Kowloon.

as "cold" – for example, stomach and digestive complaints without fever, certain rheumatic illnesses, chronic pains in the back and cramped shoulders and neck.

The mugwort is placed onto the acupuncture point or on the end of the acupuncture needle, or, it is molded into the shape of a cigar and rolled back and forth over the skin.

Exercise

At some stage while travelling in China, visit a public park at dawn to witness the Chinese exercise arts of taijiquan and qigong.

The most common type of exercise is taijiquan, the so-called shadow boxing. You will probably not be familiar with the qigong exercise, which is often translated in the West as breathing therapy.

Both exercises are based on the belief that the human body is endowed with the life energy, qi. If this life energy can be harnessed and controlled, a person can influence the course of certain ailments that afflict the body. Body and breathing exercises are thus preventative forms of "medicine".

During the Cultural Revolution in China, qigong was banned because it was said to be too close to superstition. But in 1980, new qigong groups sprang up throughout the country. It was

a lay movement that soon gained a large following. Some forms of qigong involve hardly any movement: breathing and "sinking into oneself" are of prime importance. Other forms, like the "wild goose qigong", entail a great deal of movement and are aesthetically appealing.

In both taijiquan and qigong, the changes of the mental and emotional state follow a certain pattern of movement.

The most extreme of these forms is the "crane qigong", which involves violent, sometimes cathartic emotional outbursts. Practitioners may scream, cry or laugh and dance or jump around. They experience what the Chinese call *fagong*, abandoning oneself to spontaneous movements.

It's in the diet

For much of China's history, herbalists have attributed medicinal value to various foods. At times, the distinction between food and treatment can blur.

While the Chinese have little doubt of the efficacy of different foods for treating ailments and healing certain parts of the body, Western science, always empirical, has been somewhat sceptical. Tentative research in Europe and North America, however, has substantiated many claims of the Chinese herbalist.

Consider three traditional delicacies: shark's fin, abalone and bird's nest. These are exquisite parts of an extensive cuisine, eaten in part for their sensory delights.

Yet each is claimed to have medicinal value. Shark's fin, for example, is said to benefit internal organs, including the heart and kidneys. Abalone also calms those internal organs. Moreover, it regulates the liver and reduces dizziness and high blood pressure. Bird's nest, usually taken as a soup, cleanses the blood and assures a clear skin complexion.

Verifying such claims is difficult. The scientific method, which involves controlled experiments using known values and quantities, doesn't lend itself well to the analysis of claims that a food item can help cure physical illnesses. Moreover, to be valid, a result must be independently verifiable. Consideration must also be given to the placebo effect, where a valid result occurs because one believes in something's efficacy. Many say the success of Chinese cures are simply a question of mind over matter. However, recent research on the health effects of soy beans and green tea, for example, suggests that components in these two items have substantive medicinal value, perhaps against some forms of cancer.

Herbal remedies have gained respect in the West. Why not culinary ones? Besides, Western science has proved certain foods provide necessary vitamins and minerals that are good for the body – carrots for good eyesight, calcium for strong bones. Traditional Chinese medicinal foods simply take these scientific remedies one level further. ❑

LEFT: shark's fin comes in several quality grades, and prices vary accordingly. **RIGHT:** tigers are killed for their eyeballs (epilepsy), whiskers (toothache) and especially bones (rheumatism).

Threatened Wildlife

The use of animal parts for medicine is not new. The Chinese have been using them for well over 1,000 years. The practice spread from China to other countries such as Korea and Japan, as well as throughout the world wherever there are significant East Asian populations.

Increased respect for and patronage of traditional Chinese medicine has helped countless people around the globe treat their ailments. In some cases, traditional medicine is even reputed to be more effective than Western medicine, or at least less harsh on the body.

Yet this renewed interest in alternative medicine has a darker side. Wildlife, already suffering from the intensive industrial and economic growth of many Asian countries since the 1970s, is now being pushed to the brink of extinction by the increased demand for their body parts. Unfortunately, the demand in Asia also threatens species in the Americas and Africa.

The demand for tiger parts, for example, is forcing three of the world's five remaining subspecies of tiger ever closer to extinction, threatening the long-term survival of the species as a whole. Various tiger parts are used for traditional medicine: eyeballs are used to treat epilepsy; the tail for various skin diseases; the bile for convulsions in children; whiskers for toothaches; and the brain for laziness and pimples. Yet of all tiger parts, it is the bones that are most valued. Tiger bone is often used to treat rheumatism, but can also be used for treating weakness, stiffness or paralysis.

Studies carried out in 1997 estimate that there are only 30 to 80 South China tigers, 150 to 200 Siberian tigers and 600 to 650 Sumatran tigers left in the wild. In addition, tigers have vanished from much of their former range worldwide and may now number as few as 5,000. Without radical intervention, tigers may disappear from natural habitats within a decade. And tigers are not the only species suffering from the Asian medicine trade.

Rhinoceros, bear and even shark populations are also rapidly shrinking. Rhinoceros horn has a reputation for being an aphrodisiac, and the number of rhinoceros in the wild is quickly dropping: only 12,500 rhinos remain in the wild and another 1,000 in captivity. About half of these are white rhinos and the remaining half consisting of about four species. Without assistance, these four species of rhino could be extinct within a decade or two. Also

greatly threatened by Chinese demand, bears from as far away as North America are valued for their paws, which are believed to have medicinal value. Shark's fin, though not used exclusively for medicine, is a fancy delicacy. Served most commonly as shark's fin soup, this broth is believed to benefit the internal organs. Sharks are caught and their top fin sliced off. They are then tossed back into the ocean, alive, to drown. In some areas, the shark population – essential to the ecosystem, as the shark is the top predator – is declining.

In recent years, human populations and expendable incomes have increased dramatically in East Asia, along with a resurgence of interest in tradi-

tional cures. Use of traditional medicines is seen as a status symbol and also as a way to hold onto traditional customs amidst the rapid social and economic changes.

While the effectiveness of these endangered animal products in medicine is still disputed, researchers today are confirming the effectiveness of the active ingredients present in a considerable number of Chinese prescriptions.

But as endangered animal populations are rapidly dropping off, the use of their parts to feed an ever-growing demand is no longer sustainable. What is clear, however, is that one way or another, the trade in endangered animal parts for medicine must stop. This means finding an alternative to alternative medicine. ❑

CUISINE OF HONG KONG

Cantonese cuisine has been exported around the world for decades. Much of what is unique about it, however, is rarely found outside of southern China

It has been said that when confronted with something they have never seen before or do not understand, the first impulse of a Chinese is to try eating it. This canon of Chinese folk philosophy has helped inspire the greatest cooking the world has known.

Ancient Chinese cooking bears little resemblance to what you'll savour in Hong Kong today, but certain basic principles remain. Steaming, roasting, smoking and fermentation of meats were practiced at least as early as 1000 BC, as was the now-forgotten practice of "scorched" roasting of a whole pig with all its innards intact.

Archaeologists have unearthed heavy, ornate, bronze cooking cauldrons and tripods from the Zhou dynasty (1122–256 BC) – items that were used together as a double-boiler. Recipes of that time were also elaborate. A suckling pig, for example, was stuffed with dates, wrapped with hemp and mint and baked in a shell of clay. After the clay was removed, the pig was deep-fried until crisp, then steamed for three days, thereby producing a layer of fragrant oil.

Rice was steamed in an earthenware vessel that had several holes at the bottom and was lined with bamboo matting. Fish was steamed in a bamboo tube. Meat was preserved by salt curing, grilling with spices and by fermenting with a yeast-and-wine mixture.

New culinary refinements came gradually as China's developing agriculture provided steady supplies of new ingredients. Each region naturally evolved a distinctive cooking style that reflected its topography, climate, flora and fauna, the temperament of its people and their contact with outsiders.

Foods of northern and western China, for example, developed apart from the mainstream of China's southern coastal rice bowl. This northern region, centred on Beijing, was heavily influenced by Mongols who swept into Han

China during the late 13th century. When the flat arid plain of northern China fell to these "outer barbarians" from the western netherlands, the splendour of Chinese agrarian cuisine began a new taste odyssey.

This newly evolved western Asia cooking – rooted in the hearty flavours of the wintry, wind-

swept steppes – was fine fare, but it was further refined by China's indigenous Han chefs. The Mongols, who founded the Yuan dynasty in AD 1279, were a nomadic tribe. They lived in tents and dressed in furs, and their tastes – based on what was available, primarily milk, butter and lamb – were quite different from the Han Chinese of Beijing.

These "uncivilised" wanderers preferred a rough and simple cuisine: whole animals were roasted in stone pits or steamed with rock salt. They made fruit preserves and used pine nuts, rosewater, almond oil and sugar for seasonings. Lamb dumplings were made with bean paste and dried tangerine peel, and lamb cakes

---

PRECEDING PAGES: the elegant simplicity of dim sum.
LEFT: preparations at Stanley's Oriental.
RIGHT: attempt at self-promotion.

included innards, ginger, gourds and eggs. More than three centuries later, China was engulfed by yet another horde – this time by Manchurian warriors from the north who founded the Qing dynasty (1644–1912). Like the Mongols, the Manchus further influenced the local Mongol-Han cuisine to suit their unusual tastes.

Indeed, even today, four centuries after the Manchus and Mongols have added new alien recipes to the vast Chinese menu, there are still great battles fought over food preference in

FAST, BUT BUSY

The McDonald's outlet in Kowloon's Star House is the second-busiest McDonald's in the world.

fan mei – an expression which literally means "Have you eaten?". Every Chinese dialect is rich in food symbolism. "You are breaking my rice bowl", wails the Chinese man whose livelihood is threatened.

And even to learn simply how to say rice in Chinese, one needs an annotated dictionary. Consider the Cantonese linguistic variables for the common Chinese staple of rice: plain rice is *mai*; cooked rice is *faan*; rice porridge (commonly called congee) is *juk*; and harvested but unhusked rice is *guk*.

China's kitchens. Southern Chinese (mainly the Cantonese, but also sub-groups such as the local Hunan, Chiu Chow and Hakka people) like to complain that Beijing-based food lacks smoothness and subtlety. Beijing folks, meanwhile, argue that southerners grind, chop and dilute the flavour out of their food.

Whatever their regional biases, Chinese everywhere talk about their food the way Westerners talk about art. This is probably because Chinese cuisine is indeed an art form.

But even if they aren't conscious of their food as a major cultural accomplishment, no Chinese can ever avoid talking about it. The most common Cantonese greeting, for example, is *sik tzo*

Eating for the Chinese is not just a matter of necessary sustenance for the body. Granted, there has been an exponential increase in Western or Western-style fast-food outlets in Hong Kong, but when eating here, one is still expected to enjoy a measure of entertainment and, most important, a tasty titillation of the palate.

The Chinese concept of a meal is very much a communal affair and one that provides a strong sensory impact. Dishes are chosen with both taste and texture in mind – a stomach-pleasing succession of sweet-sour, sharp-bland, hot-cool and crunchy-smooth.

In a land that has experienced recurrent famine and natural disasters, no wastage of food is acceptable. Even today, children are warned by their parents that if they leave any rice in their bowls, they will marry a pock-marked spouse – and the more grains left in the bowl, the more pock-marked the partner will be.

In spite of traditional poverty and privation, or maybe because of it, the Chinese nearly always insist on fresh food. It is only recently that refrigeration and freezing methods have been adopted by Chinese households. Most Chinese still shop three times a day for fresh meats and vegetables. A Chinese cook does not start with a particular dish in mind, but rather goes to the market to buy what's fresh and in season, then creates the meal with what's available.

To most Westerners, some Chinese foods seem bizarre, if not downright repulsive. In fact, many dishes considered rare delicacies by Chinese make the Westerner ill. Among them are monkey's brain (eaten directly from the skull of a freshly killed monkey), bear's paw, snake, dog, pigeon, frogs, sparrows, live baby mice (good for ulcers) and lizards. Unfortunately for the average Hong Kong Chinese who savours such gourmet fare, many of these delicacies are either banned by law or virtually impossible to obtain. Hence, many are rare and expensive.

Tools and techniques

Many Westerners have a hard time eating with chopsticks. Small and loose rice grains are a particular menace to the *gweilo*, or foreigner. Thankfully, it's perfectly acceptable to raise the rice bowl to your lips and shovel the elusive little grains into your mouth with the chopsticks. Scraping and slurping are not considered a *faux pas* among the Chinese.

Chopsticks are thought to have been adopted for eating because of a Confucian distaste for knives – potentially dangerous weapons – on the dining table. In Hunan, China's agricultural rice bowl, extra long chopsticks are supplied in restaurants. Stories are told of people who feed each other across the table because the chopsticks are so long they can't manoeuvre the ends into their own mouths.

If chopsticks prove impossible to manoeuvre, it is perfectly acceptable to use the porcelain spoon provided for soups as a scoop for other courses. And no one minds if you make a mess

– it is even permissible to wipe your hands on the edge of the tablecloth. The object is to get the food into your mouth efficiently.

A typical Chinese meal starts with a cold dish, which is followed by several main courses. Soup – usually clear, light broth – may be eaten after the heavier entrees to aid digestion. However, a thick and full-bodied soup may be served as a main dish, and a sweet soup often serves as a dessert at meal's end. There are no rules when it comes to ordering your meal. The main thing is to enjoy the food.

One mistake Westerners make, however, is the unseemly swamping of their rice with soya

sauce, a crude act that robs it of its character and function. A meal should include enough spicy and savoury dishes to make the neutral and relative blandness of steamed rice an essential balancing agent.

Cantonese cuisine

Given the diversity of Chinese cuisine, eating and enjoying Chinese food is largely a matter of personal taste. However, since you are in Hong Kong, largely influenced by Cantonese cooking, consider the oft-repeated Chinese proverb: Live in Suzhou (a city noted for its refined manner and beautiful women), die in Luzhou (where teakwood coffins are made), but

LEFT: food court in Kowloon's Tsim Sha Tsui.
RIGHT: fresh fish in Mong Kok market.

eat in Guangzhou (Canton). Indeed, if Chinese cooking is the world's finest, then judging by popular worldwide demand, Cantonese cuisine just may be the premier regional food of China.

The Cantonese live to eat and, at its most refined level, Cantonese gastronomy achieves a finicky discrimination that borders on cultism. Of these decadent eaters, it was once written about Confucius: "For him the rice could never be white enough and minced meat could never be chopped finely enough. When it was not cooked right, he would not eat. When the food was not in season he would not eat. When the meat was not cut correctly, he would not eat.

When the food was not served with its proper sauce, he would not eat".

The search for rare delicacies is common to all Chinese, but the Cantonese have pushed it to the extreme with dishes made of bear's paw, shark's fin, bird's nests, duck webs, deer tails, chicken testicles and live monkey's brain.

Visitors to Hong Kong who are familiar with Chinese food in Western countries soon learn the authentic cuisine has little to do with what they have been served in Chinese restaurants abroad. Take, for example, two supposed Cantonese dishes popular abroad: sweet-and-sour pork is said to have been invented by ever resourceful inhabitants of Guangzhou solely for sweet-toothed foreigners. And chop suey is said to have been invented in San Francisco when a customer entered a restaurant at closing time, and the cooks threw their leftovers into a pot, served it up and in quiet jest called this Oriental goulash "chop suey". Also, despite Hong Kong people's preoccupation with luck and superstitions, fortune cookies do not exist here. They are another romantic *gweilo* invention.

In the Cantonese method of preparation, food is cooked quickly and lightly, usually stir-fried in shallow water or an oil base in a wok. The flavour of the foods is thus preserved, not cooked away, in preparation. Many dishes, particularly vegetables or fish, are steamed. This discourages overcooking and preserves a food's delicate and natural flavours. Sauces are used to enhance flavours, not destroy them. The sauce usually contains contrasting ingredients such as vinegar and sugar, or ginger and onion.

A Cantonese restaurant is the place to eat fish, steamed whole with fresh ginger and spring onions and sprinkled with a little soy sauce and sesame oil. Cantonese, unlike finicky Western eaters, consider fish eyes and lips to be delicacies. However, in keeping with a traditional superstition among fishing families, seldom will a Chinese diner turn over a fish to reach the meat underneath. One doesn't want a capsized boat and drowned men on the conscience.

Prawns and crabs cooked in various styles – steamed or in a black-bean sauce – are also popular Cantonese seafood dishes. If you hear the term "jumping prawns", this signifies that they are alive (and obviously fresh), but it doesn't mean you are expected to eat them that way. Shark's fin soup – golden threads of gelatinous-like shark's fin in a broth – is the centrepiece of Cantonese banquets.

Chicken is the most widely-eaten fowl and, in keeping with the Chinese sense of economy and variety, a single chicken is often used to prepare several dishes. Chicken blood, for example, is cooked and solidified for soup, and the liver is used in a marvellous specialty called Gold Coin Chicken. The livers are skewered between pieces of pork fat and red-roasted until the fat becomes crisp, and the liver, soft and succulent. The delicacy is then eaten with wafers of orange-flavoured bread.

Cantonese chicken dishes can be awkwardly bony for chopstick beginners, but lemon chicken is prepared boneless with the skin coated in a crisp batter and served in a lemon sauce flavoured with onions, ginger and sugar.

For starters, choose something from the display of barbecued meats in the restaurant's display window. Cantonese barbecuing methods are unrivalled. Try goose, duck or, best of all, tender slices of pork with a golden and honeyed skin served on a bed of anise-flavoured preserved beans.

Also experience the taste sensation of double-boiled soups with duck, mushroom and tangerine peel, and a winter spe-

DUCK'S COOKED GOOSE

Over 7,000 ducks are eaten daily in Hong Kong. Only five percent of those come from Hong Kong; the rest are imported from China.

and Chinese smoked pork sausage. These sausages are sold in pairs and usually are served steamed on a bed of rice. In autumn, restaurants serve rice birds – yes, those cute and tiny winged creatures that frequent paddy fields at harvest time. These are quite often eaten together with succulent Shanghai hairy crabs. Frogs are also found in the rice paddies, and these "field chickens" are often served at banquets in southern China. In Hong Kong markets they are sold live in plastic bags, and restaurants prepare them in

cialty called Monk Jumping Over the Wall. This is a blend of abalone, chicken, ham, mushrooms and herbs so irresistible that monks are said to break their vows of vegetarianism if its fragrance is within smelling distance.

Snake is a traditional winter dish, but it is unfortunately a succulent food "misunderstood" by Westerners. Dog meat is also a winter dish but is illegal in Hong Kong, so special winter eating tours into China, specifically to eat dog meat, are available. Yet another Cantonese dish to sample in the winter is a casserole of chicken

many delicious ways. The best frog course is deep-fried frog's legs cooked in a crunchy batter mixed with crushed almonds and served with sweet-and-sour sauce.

And the others

Over the centuries, culinary elements from all over eastern Asia have been liberally adapted and absorbed into Chinese cuisine, and it's difficult to trace the origins of some dishes. Peking Duck was originally Mongolian, but it's now much more popular in Beijing than in Ulan Bator. Mongolian hotpot, called "steamboat" in Singapore and Malaysia, is of central Chinese Moslem origins. It is probably the second best-

LEFT: the scene is set at a typical Chinese restaurant.
ABOVE: wok cooking on high heat.

known of the northern dishes. Mongolian hot-pot is a winter food, served between November and March in northern-style restaurants.

The key utensil for hotpot is a chafing dish with a small charcoal stove burning underneath and a chimney rising through its centre. A trough around this centre contains soup stock to which vegetables and herbs are added.

When the soup stock begins to boil, the entire stove is set into a hole cut in the centre of the table. (Mongolian hotpot traditionally was a practical way to eat and keep warm at the same time.) Wafer-thin slices of various meats or fishes are served raw, and you cook the meal yourself in small wire baskets dipped in this hot-pot's bubbling broth. A spicy sauce, prepared to taste by the waiter, adds to the taste treat. The final course is the remaining soup broth. Another version of this dish is Mongolian bar-becue, for which a hot griddle is placed in the same hole in the table. In this variation of the hotpot theme, meats and fish are barbecued.

A surprise for Westerners at their first north-ern region Chinese meal is that rice is not served unless specially requested. Wheat is the com-mon grain staple in the north, so northerners tra-ditionally eat steamed bread (*pao*) or tasty onion cakes instead of rice.

PEKING DUCK

Peking Duck is the most popular northern Chinese dish served in Hong Kong. This dish is prepared by roasting the duck over an open charcoal fire and slowly basting it with syrup until the skin is a deep, crispy brown.

Part of the enjoyment of the meal is the "show" put on by the chef at your table as he deftly carves the duck with a large, razor-sharp butcher's cleaver. The chef slices the skin off for the first of three duck courses with a quick succession of exact strokes, starting at the neck. After the crispy skin is served, the waiter quickly follows with the meat. The skin and meat are eaten with a mild, sweet soya-bean sauce and spring onions and cucumber. The duck and sauce are placed on a wafer-thin wheat pancake, a thin layer of shredded onion and cucumber is laid on top, and the whole thing then rolled up and eaten with the fingers.

The third course from the duck is the soup. Dur-ing the first two courses, the duck's carcass is boiled with cabbage, mushrooms and herbs. When ordering Peking Duck, be sure to tell the waiter you want this soup. Some restaurants have been known to take advantage of visitors who do not realise there are three duck courses in a traditional Peking Duck meal.

One of the spectacular treats at a northern Chinese meal is hand-made noodles called *lie mien*, often made fresh at the table in a series of deft movements by the chef, who magically turns dough into strands of noodles within seconds. Noodles are a symbol of longevity, and so are served at weddings and birthday festivities to ensure long life. Related Western egg noodles are descendants of Chinese noodles and were first introduced to Europe in the 14th century by the explorer Marco Polo.

Chiu Chow cuisine is also known as Swatow food because this type of cooking originated around the city of Swatow in Guangdong Province. The people of this southeast coastal region have an original method of harvesting oysters. They simply push bamboo sticks into oyster beds and wait for the sticks to become encrusted with the mollusks. Harvesting of the oysters is merely a matter of pulling up the sticks, and the cooking is just as simple: they hold the sticks over a fire and grill the oysters right in their shells.

In Chiu Chow restaurants the preparation is more sophisticated but equally tasty. Seafood addicts like oysters fried in egg batter and clams served in a spicy sauce of black beans and chillies. Grey mullet is a favourite cold dish, and pomfret fish smoked over tea leaves and freshwater eel stewed in brown sauce are other highly recommended seafood wonders.

A Chiu Chow restaurant is also an appropriate place to try banquet-style food such as shark's fin soup and bird's nest soup. The dried saliva lining the edible swiftlet's nest provides the magic base for the famous bird's nest soup. The owner of one restaurant in Hong Kong reputedly rents a mountain in Thailand that is said to harbour the finest collection of swiftlet nests in Southeast Asia. The nest itself is virtually tasteless, but its nourishing saliva linings are believed to rejuvenate the old. This delicacy is also eaten as a dessert flavoured with coconut milk or almonds.

Baked rice birds are a seasonal fowl dish stuffed with chicken liver and served by the dozen. Minced pigeon, meanwhile, is cooked with water chestnuts and eaten wrapped in crisp lettuce leaves spiked with a healthy dollop of plum sauce. A Chiu Chow meal begins and ends with a thimbleful of Iron Maiden, an excellent bitter tea drunk to aid digestion. Desserts – made from taro, water chestnuts and sugar syrup – are for the sweet-toothed only.

The Hakka, who migrated south from the northern regions, settled in what is now Hong Kong's New Territories and contributed their own traditional cooking to the regional cuisine.

The Hakka main dishes are salt-baked chicken and stuffed duck. To prepare stuffed duck, the bird is first ingeniously deboned through a hole in the neck and then stuffed with

a rich assortment of glutinous rice, chopped meats and lotus seeds. Perhaps because they are peasants, and were thus always on the run from war or famine, the Hakka have created unusual flavours from obvious but generally unused food sources such as braised chicken's blood or pig's brains stewed in Chinese wine. Though these two dishes might be a bit too much for the average Westerner's palate, try the bone marrow if nothing else. It has a very delicate taste and is believed to be good for one's health.

There are numerous other regional cuisines that have made their way to Hong Kong from mainland China, including those from Sichuan, Shanghai, Hunan and Yunnan. ❏

FAR LEFT: Peking Duck is typically served in elegant and expensive surroundings. LEFT: snakes are served anywhere, on the street or on linen tablecloths. RIGHT: hanging poultry at the market.

DIM SUM: TOUCHING THE HEART ON A TROLLEY

Cantonese cuisine would be considerably less joyous without the delights of dim sum – exquisitely prepared, mouth-sized delights of infinite variety.

Dim sum is one of the great unheralded Chinese inventions, ranking alongside gunpowder and paper. It is a Cantonese invention, and to say it is popular today with Hong Kong's Chinese population would be an understatement. It is, in fact, indispensable, and not having one's daily dim sum would make life indigestible for many a Hongkonger.

Dim sum means "little heart" or "touching the heart". It refers to food that comes in small portions on equally small plates. The British called things like these "savouries", but that label does little justice to the complex universe of the dim sum.

In a dim sum restaurant, an infinite variety of offerings arrive at the table relentlessly. Servings are kept warm inside bamboo canisters stacked high on trolleys, which are wheeled from table to table by waiting staff. In the more traditional dim sum house, these women will sing traditional verses of praise about the food. Don't be shy. It is proper etiquette to take the tops off these canisters and marvel at the contents.

Don't ask the waiters to clear the table as the dishes and canisters pile up. While in an ordinary Chinese meal the dishes are cleared after each course, in a dim sum lunch the dishes are usually left on the table until it's time to tally the bill. The waiter counts the number of dishes served; each variably sized dish is of a certain price. If planning a dim sum lunch, make reservations by mid-morning at the latest. Otherwise, you'll find a table difficult to locate. Likewise, arrive around noon, or the remaining selection on offer may be thin.

△ **SIZZLING FRESHNESS**
One of the real treats of dim sum is its freshness. Minutes before it is wheeled out into the restaurant on trolleys, ingredients for dim sum are being cooked and put together in the sweltering hurly-burly, but orderly chaos of the restaurant's kitchen.

▽ **INSIDE AND OUTSIDE**
Depending upon the restaurant, presentation of dim sum can be as basic as that found with fast-food cuisine, or delightfully aesthetic. During *yumcha*, the tea break, the restaurant's ambience may be highlighted by customers' pet birds, brought along for a daily airing and some avian gossip.

MAKING SOME SENSE OF DIM SUM

Before you venture out to a dim sum restaurant, pick up a copy of a Hong Kong Tourist Association leaflet that features colour photos and descriptions of dim sum dishes. Of course, not all of these may be available in your chosen restaurant, so don't be surprised if the servers cry "Moaah" ("No") in response to your eager pointing. On second thought, forget the brochure and just point and eat away.

A pot of tea is delivered as standard. Despite their small size, dim sum soon mount up, and the Chinese believe that the tea's properties help with digestion. If you run out, stand the lid on top of the pot as a sign that you'd like it refilled.

Finally, for the sweet-toothed, there are desserts like hot custard tarts (*dun tat*) or *dun sun* — a crisp, sticky sweet cake topped with almonds. The savvy servers will figure out when you've had enough savoury and swing by with the sweets to round off a very Hong Kong meal.

◁ SHEER DELIGHT
Shrouded in a near-transparent envelope, some dim sum are delicate to the touch, like a fine skin.

▽ VOYEURS FOR DIM SUM
Some restaurant kitchens are on view to customers, and it's quite a sight to observe the dexterity of the chefs putting their culinary dim sum masterpieces together.

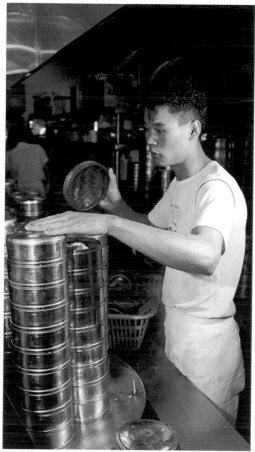

△ STEAMED FAST-FOOD
Dim sum as take-away food is kept warm in metal canisters, unlike the bamboo canisters found in a proper restaurant.

▽ SIDESHOW
One may find a variety of tempting side snacks in some dim sum restaurants.

PERFORMING ARTS

Spend any time in Hong Kong and one will encounter a diverse catalogue of performing arts, including traditional opera, lion dances, and Cantopop

Although Chinese opera is losing its popularity amongst the younger generation in Hong Kong and China, it remains an integral part of Chinese entertainment and culture. Originating from China's earliest folk music and dances, modern-day Chinese opera – a story put to music and dance – emerged during the Song dynasty (960–1279). Although Chinese opera came to be associated with festivals and state occasions at the 18th-century imperial court in Beijing, it was also popular among the common Chinese people.

In Hong Kong, a performance of Chinese opera is almost obligatory during important festivals on the Chinese calendar. Performances of Chinese opera are usually held in informal bamboo-and-mat theatres temporarily erected in public areas. Chinese opera has many cultural and regional variations. Cantonese operas, for example, are quite different from Chiu Chow operas, due to the area's development under imperial patronage. Beijing operas are performed in the court's official dialect, Mandarin. In Hong Kong, the most popular is Cantonese opera, as might be expected.

Folklore, legends and historical incidents are the dramatic sources from which Chinese opera's vast repertoire is drawn.

The backbone of Chinese opera is the actor-singer. Like Western opera stars, Chinese operatic singers undergo many years of intensive training to achieve a proper high-pitched falsetto. Singing artists are often accompanied by a traditional Chinese orchestra. Musicians playing percussion instruments occupy one side of the stage, while others responsible for wind and string instruments sit on the opposite side, leaving the main area of the stage clear for the primary performers.

To Western ears, Chinese opera may seem horrific, with the deafening sound of gongs and drums echoing from the music pit. There were no actresses during Chinese opera's early devel-

opment, because women were not allowed to make public appearances, so female roles were portrayed by male actors. As in Western opera, however, that tradition has died.

Makeup, movements, props and specific costume colours identify an actor's age, sex and personality the moment he or she appears on

stage. Actors in Beijing operas wear extremely heavy makeup, a cosmetic style derived from the use of painted masks in older operatic forms. In Beijing opera, a white patch on the nose indicates a comic character of low rank; a completely white face suggests an evil and treacherous character; a red face identifies a courageous but dim-witted man; and a black-faced actor is an average person. There are 18 types of opera beards, each symbolising a different personality.

Head-dresses are also a vital part of the Chinese opera costume; the more important the character, the more elaborate the headdress. Costumes are exaggerated in style to achieve as

LEFT: the painted mask is critical in Chinese opera.
RIGHT: colours of the face identify the character.

great a theatrical effect as possible. The colour code for costumes is important. Each colour identifies the rank, status and personality of the different operatic roles: purple for barbarians, yellow for emperors. Props are usually minimal, the idea being to leave the best part – the enjoyment of a performance – to the audience's imagination.

Chinese operas also incorporate mime, dance, sword-play and acrobatics. For the principal artists, gesture, movement and attitude are all as important as their spoken lines.

BUSY AUDIENCES

The audience of Chinese opera will talk, eat, walk around, walk out and call out during the performance of Chinese opera.

to expiate the sins of the dead. On each occasion, performances last up to five days.

Chinese operas are experiencing a crisis in relevance as younger people tend to find the traditional art form to be old-fashioned, slow in pace and simplistic in plot. Many top artists have either emigrated overseas, or else switched to movies and television acting, where there is more money and fame.

To revive the popularity of Chinese operas, some artists have taken measures to reform both operatic form and content.

It is perfectly acceptable for audiences of Chinese opera to arrive late for a performance, leave early, walk around and chat, or even eat during a show, which may run anywhere from three hours to a whole day. When an actor sings a beautiful or challenging tune, the audience is expected to respond by shouting out praise and applauding.

Most of the traditional opera performances in Hong Kong are called *sumkung* opera (god's eulogy opera) by the local Cantonese, as they are performed to celebrate special festivals or the birthdays of different gods. Many of these performances are related to Daoism and Buddhism. For example, during the Ghost Festival, operas are staged together with other activities

The most active reformer in Hong Kong is veteran actor Leung Hon-wai. He formed his own Hon Fung Cantonese Opera Group and paid writers to produce new scripts, while a symphony orchestra was introduced to accompany the performances, giving it a more modern tempo. "I will not give up my reform on Cantonese opera", says Leung. "I cannot let Cantonese opera die in the hands of our generation".

Ironically, the first major reform of Chinese opera was started by the late Chinese leader Mao Zedong's wife, who during the Cultural Revolution was notorious for persecuting intellectuals whom she found threatening. Under her instructions, traditional opera troupes put on "revolutionary model plays". They sang the praises of the Communist Party and condemned the evils of capitalism. Delicate and sentimental young girls yearning for love were replaced by iron ladies sweating away in the fields. Symphony music was introduced to add a strong mood, while Western opera-singing techniques were applied to make revolutionary leaders stand out.

The rigid political propaganda elements aside, these revolutionary plays introduced modern elements to traditional Chinese operas and convinced veteran artists that new stories could work.

accompanied by firecrackers to scare away evil spirits. There may also be a dragon dance to accompany the lion. The difference between the lion and dragon dances is simple to spot: the dragon is held aloft by a group of performers, who move the giant puppet from outside of it. They walk in set patterns to make the dragon look like it's flying. But the lion dance has a crew of only two, who move the large cloth or paper puppet from inside of it. Also, in the lion dance, performers can move the head in various ways, as well as move the eyes, mouth and ears.

There are generally two types of Chinese lions: the northern lion and southern lion. The

Lion and dragon dances

A lion dance, in which two performers wear and manipulate a large lion costume, is also a must-have item on special festive occasions. This *qongfu*-related Chinese entertainment form is usually performed at festivals or on special occasions such corporate anniversaries and the opening of a new business.

Since the lion is considered a holy animal and seen as a spirit that has its own importance in Chinese mythology, lion dances are believed to bring good luck. Sometimes performances are

LEFT: resplendent costumes embellish the opera performance. **ABOVE:** dragon dance.

differences are in their appearance and the way they move. While the northern lion has a furry yellow coat and a less-movable mouth, the southern lion has a movable mouth and a more colourful body, but no long hair for fur.

Cantopop

Despite traditional artists' efforts to adapt to modern times, young people's interest in traditional arts has been replaced by pop music and movies. Mainland Chinese immigrants in the 1950s and 1960s brought to Hong Kong not only money and entrepreneurial skills, but also arts, culture and the Mandarin language. During the 1950s and 1960s, most of the well-known artists in Hong Kong were immigrants from Shanghai, a prosperous and cosmopolitan city in eastern China before the Communists took over power in 1949. In the 1970s, when contact between Hong Kong and Taiwan increased, Hong Kong's music scene was dominated by Taiwanese songs, mostly written by college students on the island ruled by the Guomintang (Nationalist) party, defeated by the Communists in 1949. The best-known singer was the late Taiwanese singer Teresa Tang, whose classics *The Tale of A Small Town* and *When Will You Return?* still remain popular choices in local karaoke bars. Many Chinese believe that Tang's songs were the only media that linked together Chinese people in China, Hong Kong, Taiwan and abroad with a sense of community, despite their ideological, social and economic differences.

> ## PICTURE POWER
>
> The popularity of Cantopop stars is measured by album sales, the value of gifts and flowers they receive from fans at performances and the number of photographs sold. In Kowloon's Sino Centre, there are many shops selling photos of Cantopop stars. A "Sino Index" monitors popularity by the sale of the Cantopop stars' photos.

In the mid 1970s, some Hong Kong-born singers with a clear local identity, led by movie star Sam Hui, started a movement to promote Cantonese pop songs. They wrote and sang songs in Cantonese, mostly about love, friendship and life in the then-British colony. In the early 1980s, the first generation of Cantonese pop stars – dubbed "Cantopop" stars by the local press – appeared.

Since the late 1980s, the local Cantopop scene has been dominated by teen idols – young male and female singers in their late teens or early twenties – whose popularity depends on their attractive looks more than their voices or talent. In the 1990s, the biggest local pop stars were described as "emperors" and "empresses", with the most famous performers called the "four heavenly emperors" – singers Leon Lai, Jackie Cheung, Andy Lau and Aaron Kwok.

To maintain their position in the highly competitive entertainment business, stars have to grab every possible chance they have to promote themselves. They are forced to play mindless games on television programmes, take part in charity activities and give interviews. Some desperate artists have even been known to resort to love affairs, not necessarily image-improving ones or rational encounters, to attract the media's attention.

Only major concerts by superstars are held in the prestigious Hong Kong Coliseum; most performances are staged in the Queen Elizabeth Stadium. Competition is not only between performers, but also amongst fans. If fans of Andy Lau brought bigger bouquets of flowers, those of Leon Lai would try to win back points by shouting more loudly during the concert.

By contrast, few people in showbiz pay much attention to improving the singers' performance or coming up with higher-quality songs. Most of the local hits are sometimes cover versions of British, American, or Japanese originals.

Ironically, life for more traditional professional artists is a bit tougher, since the local society is so commercially-oriented that people do not have much time for serious art. However, as the city gets more and more affluent, the government and its citizens are beginning to appreciate the high-quality arts.

There are eight professional performance companies in Hong Kong and hundreds of amateur groups. The most prominent ones include the Hong Kong Philharmonic Orchestra, Hong Kong Repertory Theatre, Hong Kong Chinese Orchestra and the Hong Kong Dance Company. Founded in 1985, the Academy for Performing Arts in Wan Chai is one of the top performing arts schools in Asia. Major cultural events include the Hong Kong Arts Festival and the Fringe Festival.

Hong Kong is the world's third-largest movie production centre, with its films gaining international attention and its talent becoming more influential in Hollywood. The achievements in Hollywood of director John Woo, actor Chow Yun-fat and action-star Jackie Chan have increased international attention to Hong Kong's film industry.

But most local box-office hits are either action or romance productions. Still, Hong Kong remains one of only a handful of places in the world where locally-made films consistently out-perform Hollywood productions, even with bad English subtitles. ❑

RIGHT: carving of jade, a classic Chinese craft.

Arts and Crafts

Chinese arts and crafts have a long history and form a significant part of China's total exports. In Hong Kong, the best places to buy Chinese crafts are the China Arts and Crafts shop in Wan Chai, and the several department stores specialising in Chinese products on Hong Kong island and Kowloon. Most of these products are imported from China, as their manufacture is very labour-intensive and Hong Kong's wages are too high to make producing them in Hong Kong profitable.

Traditional Chinese arts and crafts include porcelain, embroidery, brocade, carpets, jade products, carvings (wood, bamboo and ivory), and paper decorations called "scissors-cuts" – all with different styles and regional influences.

Despite their long history, most Chinese arts and crafts today are not as attractive to overseas buyers as before, because factories have been turning out the same styles using the same materials for decades. Like many sectors in socialist China, whose economy is under reform, the arts and crafts industry needs new ideas and updated styles to cope with the ever-changing international market.

The traditional Chinese crafts of embroidery and brocade have had a reputation for excellent quality since the days of trade on the the Silk Road. The Silk Road in western China began the Middle Kingdom's trade with other countries. China's embroidery and brocade make up the largest part of its arts and crafts industry. The best silk products come from eastern and southeastern regions where the climate is suitable for raising silkworms, while the western regions produce fine-quality cashmere.

Silk embroidery from Suzhou in eastern China is especially well-known for its fine workmanship and long history of more than 2,000 years. Drawnwork from Shantou near Hong Kong also enjoys a good reputation overseas. In 1972, Chinese Premier Zhou Enlai presented a piece of Shantou drawnwork to the Queen of Iran as a gift, after which the product became a fashion in Iran.

Scissors-cut is traditionally a product of rural China, and it is mostly made by women. Before Lunar New Year, women make various kinds of colourful scissors-cuts to decorate their windows.

The only materials needed to make scissors-cuts are a pair of scissors, knife, and paper. Traditional patterns include animals, fruits, flowers, and characters from ancient Chinese folktales or operas, often with themes of good harvests, prosperity, and happiness. Scissors-cuts from different parts of China vary in styles. Those from Yangzhou in eastern China are known for their delicacy, while those from Fuzhou emphasise details.

Carvings of jade, ivory, wood, bone, rock, and bamboo are another traditional Chinese craft. The best known are jade carvings from Beijing, an art form that dates back to the Ming dynasty (1368–1644); ivory balls featuring legendary Chinese figures from Guangzhou; stone carvings from Shoushan in Fujian Province; bamboo carvings from Huangyan in Zhejiang Province; and high-quality ink-slabs made in Duanxi and Zhaoqing in Guangdong.

The best porcelain ware is from Jingdezhen

County in Jiangxi Province of central China, which has earned the moniker the "capital of porcelain". The region's blue-and-white porcelain is fine and smooth like those made during the Yuan dynasty, and the colourful styles have inherited the rich artistry of the Qing dynasty during its most powerful and prosperous period.

Artificial decorative flowers made in brocade, silk, paper, feather, plastic and synthetics are relatively new crafts coming out of China. Beijing is best known for its silk flowers, Liaoning in the northeast for its feather flowers, while Yangzhou in the east produces flowers made of grass.

Miniature paintings on shells, feathers, tree bark, deer horns, and even thin strands of wheat straw, are also popular souvenirs and gifts.

ARCHITECTURAL STYLE

Few of the world's cities confront the traveller with its architecture – good and bad – as does Hong Kong, whose skyline constantly shifts and realigns

If function is the guiding principle of architectural design, then Hong Kong is the epitome of this principle. The former British colony's architecture comprises a mix of Eastern and Western influences and styles. Buildings are planted on reclaimed land, then demolished as soon as they become unprofitable. A few trophy buildings are judged so exciting and innovative that they cause a sensation in the world of architecture. But for the most part, Hong Kong's architectural design is temporary, utterly pragmatic, ultimately profit-lead, utilitarian and, on very rare occasions, extravagantly glossy. The range of styles reflects the hodgepodge of cultures that have found their way to Hong Kong's shores.

Of all the myths about Hong Kong, none has been exaggerated more by the oxygen of publicity than the idea that there was nothing on the island or the Kowloon peninsula before the British arrived. True, you have to search hard to find examples nowadays, but they exist.

Tucked away in some of the remote villages in the New Territories are squat, stone houses that have been clustered together as much for protection from the elements as against the roving brigands who were once a very real danger. These stone houses are far more in harmony with their surroundings than the houses thrown up today. Thanks to the dictates of the *feng shui* (literally "wind and water") principle of geomancy, rooms were aligned with north, south, east and west, establishing a basic relationship with the environment. Many of these houses have been abandoned, their wooden front doors locked and bolted, and their highceilinged rooms sheltering only birds and rodents, but they are a reminder of a time when builders created structures that blended with the landscape, rather than subduing it.

Anyone spending a short time in Hong Kong who wants to understand the way the people think, live and breathe need only cast an eye

skywards – not for divine inspiration but to take in the ubiquitous static juggernauts of concrete and glass. And anyone spending a few months or more in the city soon runs up against one of its most startling phenomena, the Hong Kong Blink. Head down a side street in an area you haven't visited in a week or two in search of a familiar bank or shop and you are suddenly brought up short. It's vanished, either transformed into a completely new retail outlet or simply replaced by a pile of rubble, the victim of spiralling rents and Hong Kong's unremitting quest for a quick profit. Blink, and that old familiar landmark ceases to be.

Thus, little of Hong Kong's architecture sticks around long enough to be admired by posterity. Once-splendid examples of Edwardian design like the old Hong Kong Club building in Central would have been treasured anywhere else in the world with a bit more space. But located right in the middle of the most profitable piece of real estate in town, the

PRECEDING PAGES: building diversity, Central.
LEFT: Lippo Tower is nicknamed "The Koala Building".
RIGHT: classic architecture of The Peninsula.

building's restful proportions and elaborate cornices could only last so long and they were eventually offered up to the wrecker's ball. The best that can be said about its replacement is that it is bland and much more profitable.

One genre that fits in with no other but which is found all over Hong Kong is displayed in its temples and shrines. With green-tiled roofs and displaying the colourful porcelain figures of Chinese legends, temples are gaudy and ornate compared to their drab surroundings. But they are an important indication that while residents may put up with featureless blocks, they seek escape and comfort in their Daoist beliefs.

But not every old building has disappeared. The Peninsula Hotel, one of the grandest hotels in Asia, was given a new lease on life when its owners grafted a tower block onto its rear, preserving it from demolition. The lofty columns, stucco work and dome of the former Supreme Court Building (now the Legislative Council Building) off Statue Square are a pleasant reminder of a time when "maximising plot ratio" – making the building as big as possible to get the largest possible financial return – was not an architect's first and only priority.

The Repulse Bay Hotel, a gracious pre-war single-storey edifice with an ambience in tune

As far as aesthetics go, most of Hong Kong's modern constructions are not terribly inspiring. The Housing Authority, brought into being after a disastrous fire in 1953 left more than 50,000 squatters homeless, has produced rank upon rank of anonymous cruciform blocks that do their job of sheltering residents from the elements and not much more. And in much of the New Territories, where strict inheritance laws dictate that only sons (not daughters) may build new houses, and then only houses of limited size, the result is the "Spanish Style" villa, a three-storey cube that maximises the available space with a strip of tiles around the roof top doing duty as decoration.

with its slowly moving ceiling fans, was demolished, but it was rebuilt almost exactly as it had been. But unfortunately, a housing development has replaced Eucliffe, the folly which used to stand just up the road, built by an eccentric Malaysian tin millionaire who had been promised eternal life by a soothsayer as long as he continued to fund the construction of outlandish castles and other similar structures.

But the wonder of Hong Kong architecture is that, given the paucity of space and the city's dedication to Mammon, not only does a small quota of old structures survive, but a treasure trove of new ones also exists. Glancing across the harbour from Kowloon at night, it is easy to see why the Hong Kong skyline has been compared to Manhattan's. At one time the highest building in Hong Kong was St John's Cathedral. In the early 1960s, the Mandarin Oriental Hotel was the tallest. Now it is the banks and office blocks that dominate the skyline. With money to play with (the Hongkong Bank building is said to have cost US$1 billion, but the directors have refused to reveal the true price), designers working in Hong Kong have been able to produce structures

Naturally, Hong Kong's modern architecture has been shaped by the demands of feng shui. The front door of the Mandarin Oriental Hotel is askew to keep evil spirits – which must travel in straight lines – out, as are the escalators going up into the Hongkong Bank headquarters. The sharp, projecting corners on the Entertainment Building were chamfered off at a cost of several million dollars to prevent malignant forces being directed into a neighbouring office block.

that are not just bigger and better than their predecessors, but truly exciting as well. Young visiting architects have been known to go straight to Sir Norman Foster's Hongkong Bank building and stand underneath looking up at the cone of light that comes down the middle of the building. Nearby, the Bank of China building, designed by the Chinese-American architect I. M. Pei, is recognised as one of the finest examples of Post Modernism, while the Entertainment Building lives up to its name with quirky Gothic embellishments.

Left: Hong Kong island's classic skyline seen from Kowloon. **Above:** detail, Legislative Council Building.

But Hong Kong has not allowed itself to be overawed by the buildings that dominate its existence. With the Cantonese predilection for slang and penchant for a good joke, Central Plaza and its crowning spike – for a while the tallest building in Asia – became "The Hypodermic"; the Bank of China with its twin rooftop antennae, "The Chopsticks"; the gold-clad Far East Finance Centre, "The Amah's Tooth". The round-windowed Jardine building is called the "House of a Thousand Orifices", while the Lippo Tower, with extensions that seem to cling to its sides, is nicknamed "The Koala Building". When Britain opened the doors of its new consulate, it was only days before taxi drivers were calling it "The British Fort", as much at the expense of the designer as the beleaguered position of its occupants.

High rents paid for small spaces means that it's not just the major buildings that give vent to Hong Kong's humorous safety valve. Public housing tenants, often squashed in dirty, ageing blocks, refer to their homes as "Pigeon Lofts". And sometimes it's a developer's nomenclature that comes up trumps. Could any city but

BAMBOO TOWERS

Bamboo is the scaffolding of choice, even for skyscrapers. It goes up four times faster than steel and withstands typhoons better. There are around 250 experienced bamboo scaffolders in Hong Kong.

functional and in many ways poorly planned. Statue Square, once very much the centre of the city, lost its predominance as it was gradually overshadowed by outsize buildings. The waterfront on Hong Kong island, which should have granted a sweeping promenade on the harbour's edge, was swallowed by pedestrian constructions and freeways. Even the Cultural Centre in Tsim Sha Tsui, built on the site of the former railway station and nicknamed The Ski Slope for its

Hong Kong call a building the King Kong Commercial Plaza?

Finally, if you are not here long enough to experience the Hong Kong Blink, play another simple game. Try going for a short walk anywhere in town without seeing a construction crane or Hong Kong's characteristic bamboo scaffolding, hearing a jack hammer, without feeling the reverberations of a pile driver or getting a whiff of dust from a building site. As sensations go, Hong Kong's constantly changing architecture never stops.

As Hong Kong begins a new millennium, it is also approaching an architectural watershed. In the past, its buildings have been colonial,

sweeping roof, was constructed without a single window from which to enjoy the stunning panorama that lay across the harbour.

All too often the excuse given for a building design that could at most be described as workaday was the expense of construction and land, and the paucity of space. However, with the opening of Chek Lap Kok airport and reclamation of large areas of the harbour, Hong Kong will be granted new land on which to expand and breathe. True, the closure of Kai Tak has spelt the end of one of the world's best rollercoaster rides on the approach to landing, but the runway, apron and entire airport area will – together with land reclaimed from the surrounding area – provide an inner-city "green field" site the like of which Hong Kong has never experienced before. Some 285,000 people are expected to take up residence on Kai Tak, which will feature a park as its centrepiece and be bordered with a seaside promenade.

As a progenitor to Kai Tak's regeneration, the nearby Kowloon Walled City Park is a worthy example. Formerly, this was the site of the most notorious slum in the whole of Hong Kong, supposedly beyond the reach of authority and a place of refuge for criminals, drug addicts and illegal practitioners of every sort of craft. The edifice was a hotchpotch of oozing, evil-smelling tenements, festooned with wires and aerials and in every way vile in appearance and reputation. After lengthy and exorbitantly costly negotiations with the inhabitants, the block was finally demolished, and in its place a park, all waterfalls and lush paths and shady trees with a few quaint historical embellishments, has grown up into a truly genteel oasis.

The closure of Kai Tak spells good news for the rest of the Kowloon peninsula. Previously, building height was restricted so as not to interfere with aircraft taking off and landing. As a result, buildings were crammed together, subdivided and divided again to maximise on rental space, and then extended to the furthest permissible limits. Now this part of Hong Kong can grow vertically once again, rather than expanding on itself horizontally to near breaking point. Kowloon can finally provide a similar skyline to the Manhattan-like Hong Kong island. In years to come, as Kowloon sprouts like a crop of elongated mushrooms, the vista of Hong Kong island should be mirrored by a similar panorama on the other side of the harbour.

It is ironic that this urban regeneration should be poised to take place after so many years of haphazard development and half-hearted planning. The government-backed Land Development Corporation (LDC) was set up with the task of developing the more run-down areas of Hong Kong, clearing away older and poorly built areas and replacing them with new, well-planned housing and offices. But the organisation's powers were so weak and its operations so ponderous, that private companies moved in on areas it targeted, buying up property from poorer owners and then waiting for a fat profit. However the LDC has managed to complete 16 projects – including Western Market – and has another 30 or so on the stocks.

Hong Kong's architectural future cannot be examined without reference, again, to Chek Lap Kok, whose construction occasioned the closure of Kai Tak and thus the rebirth of building in Kowloon. The new airport terminal, designed by Sir Norman Foster, aims to steal the limelight from Singapore's Changi, whose superlative design has long been held up as an example of how Hong Kong's international airport should look and function. The energy-efficient

and environment-conscious Y-shaped passenger terminal features a unifying, wing-like roof, symbolic of flight and is functional if falling short of beautiful. But a concept of calm, clarity and convenience is maintained throughout the building, as interior designers have sought to create a serene atmosphere using subdued backgrounds and neutral colours. A feeling of open space makes the most of the airport's surroundings. It is profoundly apposite that the designer who came up with Hong Kong's first "world-class" building, the Hongkong Bank building, should also be giving new arrivals their first taste of Hong Kong architecture. ❑

LEFT: typical downtown buildings on Queen's Street West, Central District. **RIGHT:** cramped in Kowloon.

MONEY IS EVERYTHING. OF COURSE.

Nowhere else on the planet has the art of making money, and the style of spending it,

been as refined as in Hong Kong, where the tycoon and quick dollar are revered

Even with its limited resources and space, prosperity and affluence are among the first impressions a visitor gets after arriving in Hong Kong. But social grace doesn't always come with wealth. The man carrying a Gucci briefcase can be seen spitting on the floor, and a Chanel-wrapped *tai tai* (a rich man's wife) shouts coarsely at a shoe-shiner.

Hong Kong people are famous for their materialism, which turns off many newcomers. It is easy to sneer at this, but it does not take long to understand the reasons behind it. Consider what it takes to survive in this city. A new university graduate in Hong Kong makes about HK$11,000 a month, but the rent for a one-bedroom apartment can cost the same amount, if not more. An apartment – even one the size of a kitchen in many American or British homes – can't be bought for less than US$500,000. The belief among Hong Kong's people is that if you do not go into business, you will spend 30 years of your adult life earning a matchbox-size flat.

On top of this has been the mass psychology over the past decade feeding a desire to go abroad to escape China's clutches, particularly after the bloody 1989 crackdown of a students' democratic movement in Beijing's Tiananmen Square. After the massacre, many locals wanted to emigrate to the United States, Canada, Australia, Singapore – anywhere they could get away from the regime that would take over Hong Kong in 1997. But emigrating required money, and the deadline was tight.

The people of Hong Kong have the strongest business spirit in the world. As soon as they have saved enough money by working for other people, many of them venture into their own businesses. If they prosper, they move from Kennedy Town, a cheap area in the Western District, to the more privileged Mid-Levels. If they fail, they get a regular job and make a comeback once they have saved enough money. Hong Kong is rich with the stories of tycoons who have ascended to the summit, fallen into the financial abyss, then climbed to the top once more, attaining legendary status in Hong Kong.

Overview

The Hong Kong government's basic policy of minimum interference and maximum support for business has long been a key factor underlying Hong Kong's continued economic success. There are few places in the world where it is easier to set up and register a business. Con-

tributing to Hong Kong's economic wonder is a low tax environment, free and fair market competition, a sound legal and financial framework, a fully convertible and secure currency, a highly efficient network of transport and communication, a skilled workforce, the enterprising spirit of locals, a high degree of internationalisation and cultural openness.

Business decisions are left to the private sector, and the government has rarely sought to influence the structure of industry through regulations, tax policies, or subsidies. The tax system is simple, with the corporate tax rate at 17.5 percent, lower than international standards. The bureaucracy is small and efficient.

As a small city inhabited by almost seven million people, Hong Kong is one of the most densely populated urban economies in the world. Compensating for the lack of natural resources are Hong Kong's excellent deep-water harbour and a strategic location that bridges the time-zone gap between Asia and Europe. It has also benefited from economic ties with China and Southeast Asia.

Hong Kong currently operates the busiest container port in the world. Its airport is one of the world's busiest in the number of

ROLLS-ROYCE NIRVANA

One percent of all Rolls-Royces ever sold are in Hong Kong, which has the most Rolls-Royce cars per capita in the world.

To provide a stable currency, the government introduced a linked exchange-rate system in 1983 that pegged Hong Kong's currency to the U.S. dollar. The system was designed to keep interest rates close to interest rates in the United States with its reliable and stable economy. The currency exchange rate was fixed at approximately HK$7.8 to US$1. However, during the 1997 financial crisis that cascaded through Asia, many people questioned the wisdom of linking Hong Kong's currency to the U.S. dollar so rigidly.

passengers (visitor numbers have recovered after they dropped dramatically during the SARS outbreak in 2003), and the second busiest in the volume of cargo handled. Hong Kong is also the world's fourth-largest banking centre.

Hong Kong has established itself as a major international trade and financial centre with sound economic fundamentals. In January 2004, Hong Kong's foreign currency assets stood at HK$964 billion (US$ 123.6 billion), making it the world's fourth-largest holder of foreign currency reserves, only beaten by China, Japan and Taiwan.

LEFT: gold has an appeal in Hong Kong. **ABOVE:** safe deposit boxes, Hongkong and Shanghai Bank.

Manufacturing

While increasingly a finance and service-industry centre, Hong Kong's economy has its roots in manufacturing. In the 1950s, many entrepreneurs from China's commercial city of Shanghai fled to Hong Kong after the Communist Party took over power in 1949. Bringing along capital and business skills, these immigrants from the mainland re-established themselves in Hong Kong by setting up factories making textiles, toys and sundries.

Now, a large part of Hong Kong's industry is in electronics, textiles and garments, printing, publishing, machinery, fabricated-metal products, plastic products, watches and jewellery.

Since the late 1980s, however, most companies have moved their processing operations to China, where labour is cheaper.

Economic ties with China

Until the late 1970s, the Hong Kong business sector was dominated by British companies, called *hongs* by the Cantonese. The four leading British hongs were Jardine Matheson, Wheelock Marden, Hutchison Whampoa and the Swire Group. But since the 1970s, energetic and ambitious Hong Kong Chinese groups, with investments in shipping, property and the textile industry, have built new empires and taken

over some of the British-founded concerns. Considering mainland China to be the biggest potential market in the world, Hong Kong Chinese businessmen – with their blood and emotional ties to the mainland and their knowledge of the Chinese way of doing business – naturally became more competitive than British rivals.

Apart from the free-market spirit and the rule of law established by the former British administrators, Hong Kong owes its economic success, to a large extent, to the opening of the mainland Chinese economy in the late 1970s. Suddenly, Hong Kong's strategic position as the international community's gateway to China and China's trade window to the outside world

became even more important. Both China and Hong Kong have benefited from their fast-developing economic ties. China accounts for about 40 percent of Hong Kong's total trade in goods, making the mainland Hong Kong's largest trading partner. China's share in Hong Kong's re-export trade (export of goods made abroad) is even higher at around 90 percent, making China both the largest market for and the largest source of Hong Kong's goods for re-exports. In 2000, Hong Kong was China's third-largest trading partner (after Japan and the United States), accounting for 14 percent of China's total trade.

Financial links between Hong Kong and mainland China have also been increasing. The Bank of China, which has been in Hong Kong for decades, is now the second-largest banking group in Hong Kong after the Hongkong Bank. Hong Kong's favourable geographical position and the absence of restrictions on capital flows have helped it develop into an international financial centre. Hong Kong's financial markets have a high degree of liquidity and transparent regulations. About 80 of the world's top 100 banks are represented here.

Hong Kong is also a major service centre for China, especially southern China, providing financial and business support to mainland companies. For the international business and tourist interests that are not familiar with China and the mainland Chinese business culture, Hong Kong also serves as a bridge. In 2000, the Chinese immigration office recorded 34 million trips by Hong Kong Chinese to the mainland and an additional two million visits by foreigners who entered the mainland through Hong Kong.

The vast mainland market – with the world's largest population – has attracted an increasing amount of investment from Hong Kong, with a cumulative direct investment in China reaching US$100 billion, with 40 percent of that total in Guangdong province. Guangdong has an especially close economic relationship with Hong Kong because of its geographical location, cheap labour and because, unlike most of mainland China which speaks standard Chinese (Putonghua), Guangdong residents speak the same dialect as Hong Kong residents, Cantonese. ❏

LEFT: many manufacturers relocate to "mainland" China. **RIGHT:** if it's gold and shiny, it's worth something.

PLACES

*A detailed guide to Hong Kong, Macau, and Guangzhou, with
principal sites cross-referenced by number to the maps*

According to the opium merchants who took it as booty, all that
Hong Kong was ever good for was 45 square kilometres (17
sq mi) of the best deep-water harbour in the region – a harbour
that could shelter ships from any storm, be they torrential typhoons or
the emotional outpourings of an obstreperous Chinese emperor.

Today's Hong Kong can be divided into four parts: the island of
Hong Kong, Kowloon, the New Territories and the numerous outlying islands. Hong Kong Island is 75 square kilometres (29 sq mi) of
topsy-turvy real estate. The earliest British settlements were established here; it is now dominated by great banks and counting houses,
enormous futuristic buildings, opulent hotels, splendid residences
on Victoria Peak, fine beach resorts and the territory's oldest Chinese communities. Across Victoria Harbour – by the Mass Transit
Railway, Star Ferry or through three tunnels – is Kowloon, a resi-
dential-industrial complex packed into just a few square kilometres.
Kowloon was ceded to the British in 1860 so the insecure Brits could
better defend the harbour and Hong Kong Island. Most tourists see
only the tip of Kowloon – the Tsim Sha Tsui district – the site of many
hotels, bars and shops.

Boundary Street marks the demarcation line between the Hong
Kong granted to the British in perpetuity and the New Territories,
which were leased in 1898 for a 99-year period. The New Territories
used to be called unspoiled. A century ago, when it was known as the
"Emperor's Rice Bowl" for its fine arable land, it must have had a
verdant beauty. Today, though, its towns house countless factories
and apartment blocks; population pressures have caused the government to instigate "New Town" projects over the decades. However,
some quaint villages and rural areas can still be found.

Along with the New Territories, the British leased 234 islands.
Except for Lantau, Lamma, Cheung Chau and a couple of others,
few of these outlying islands are inhabited, which is part of their
allure, as they are reminiscent of what Hong Kong Island itself
looked like more than a century ago.

Always in the shadow of Hong Kong, except to those who gam-
ble, is Macau, once Portugal's base of commerce in Asia. What
brought the British and other Europeans to Macau and Hong Kong in
the first place was Guangzhou, known to colonials as Canton.
Guangzhou was China's port to the world, and from Guangzhou
came what the world knows of Chinese culture, including its famous
cuisine. Following the Cultural Revolution, Guangzhou was one of
the only cities open to foreigners, and it was where China first began
to experiment with capitalism, Communist-style. ❏

PRECEDING PAGES: New Territories scenery; Tin Hau Temple, Causeway Bay; Star
Ferry, Victoria Harbour; butcher shop, Hong Kong Island. **LEFT:** monastery on Lantau.

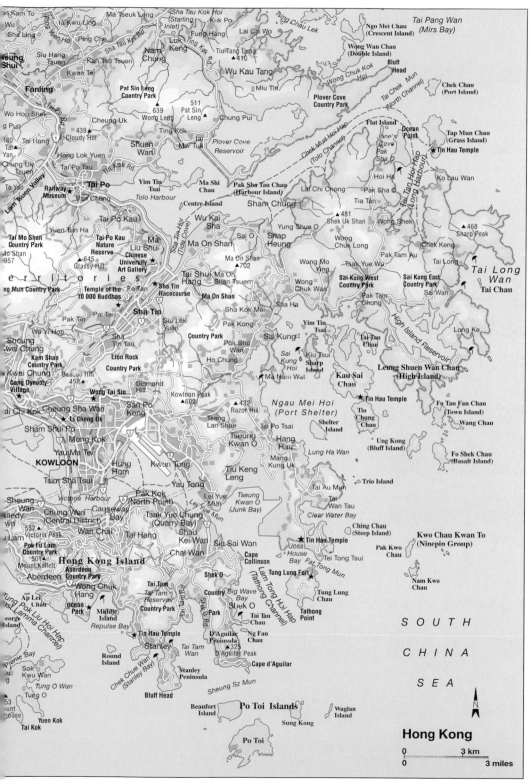

Sha Tau Kok Hoi (Starling Inlet)
Tsing Chau Lek
Tai Pang Wan (Mirs Bay)
Ma Tseuk Leng
Kuk Po
Ngo Mei Chau (Crescent Island)
Lai Chi Wo
Fung Hang
Wong Wan Chau (Double Island)
Wu Kau Tang
Bluff Head
Ting Kok
Tiu Tang Lung
Wong Chuk Kok Hoi
Chek Chau (Port Island)
Luk Keng
Tai Chek Mun (North Channel)
Nam Chung
▲416
Miu Tin
Plover Cove Country Park
Tap Mun Chau (Grass Island)
Chek Keng
Pat Sin Leng Country Park
511 Pat Sin Leng ▲
Chung Pui
Chek Mun Hoi Hap (Tolo Channel)
Flat Island
Ocean Point
Tin Hau Temple
639
Wong Leng
Ting Kok
Plover Cove Reservoir
Jane's Cove Pak Sha O
Ko Lau Wan
439
Cloudy Hill
Shuen Wan
Tai Mei Tuk
Hoi Ha
Pak Sha O
Hong Lok Yuen
Yim Tin Tsai
Ma Shi Chau
Pak Sha Tau Chau (Harbour Island)
Lai Chi Chong
Tia Tan
Wong Shek
Sharp Peak ▲468
Tai Po Tau
Tolo Harbour
Centre Island
Sham Chung
Shek Uk Shan ▲481
Tai Long Wan
Tai Po Kau
Wu Kai Sha
Sai O
Yung Shue O
Wong Chuk Long
Tai Chau
Tai Po Kau Nature Reserve
Ma Liu Shui
Ma On Shan
Shap Heung
Pak Tam Au
Chek Keng
Chinese University Art Gallery
Ma On Shan ▲702
Wong Mo Ying
Tsak Yue Wu
Sai Kung East Country Park
Temple of the 10 000 Buddhas
Tai Shui Hang
Ma On Shan Tsuen
Wong Chuk Wan
Sai Kung West Country Park
Sai Wan
Fo Tan
Sha Tin Racecourse
Ma On Shan
Pak Tam Chung
Sha Kok Mei
Sha Ha
Pai Tau
Sha Tin
Siu Lek Yuen
Pak Kong
Yim Tin Tsai
High Island Reservoir
Long Ke
Country Park
Pak Sha Wan
Sai Kung
Tai Tan Chau
Lion Rock
Country Park
Ho Chung
Sai Kung Hoi
Kiu Tsui Sharp Island
Kau Sai Chau
Leung Shuen Wan Chau (High Island)
Beacon Hill ▲452
Ma Nam Wat
Tin Hau Temple
Fu Tau Fan Chau (Town Island)
Diamond Hill
Kowloon Peak ▲602
▲432 Razor Hill
Ngau Mei Hoi (Port Shelter)
Tiu Chung Chau
Wang Chau
San Po Kong
Tseng Lan Shue
Tai Po Tsai
Shelter Island
Ung Kong (Bluff Island)
Fo Shek Chau (Basalt Island)
Kwun Tong
Tseung Kwan O
Hang Hau
Lung Ha Wan
Mang Kung Uk
Yau Tong
Tiu Keng Leng
Trio Island
Tai Au Mun
Tseung Kwan O (Junk Bay)
Tai Wan Tau
Clear Water Bay
Ching Chau (Steep Island)
Kwo Chau Kwan To (Ninepin Group)
Tin Hau Temple
Pak Kwo Chau
Tei Tong Tsui
Nam Kwo Chau
Joss House Bay
Fat Tong Mun
Tung Lung Fort
Tung Lung Chau
Shek O
Big Wave Bay
Tai Tau Chau
Tathong Point
Nam Kwo Chau

SOUTH CHINA SEA

D'Aguilar Peninsula
Ng Fan Chau
Cape d'Aguilar
D'Aguilar Peak ▲325
Po Toi Islands
Waglan Island
Beaufort Island
Sung Kong
Po Toi

Hong Kong

0   3 km
0   3 miles

HONG KONG ISLAND

Once considered completely worthless, the island of Hong Kong now is one of the priciest places on the planet

The fact that the Englishman who originally acquired Hong Kong Island for his queen from the Chinese has no street, hill, park, stadium, district, or footpath named after him seems odd today. Within months after he acquired the island, he was dismissed from his post. Queen Victoria even found humour in the acquisition.

In fact, the island of Hong Kong was without resources and with little flat land. Most of the flat area that lines Victoria Harbour today is landfill. The virgin island had little to recommend it, hence the British Empire's initial doubts about its merit as a colony. Its coastline was rugged, there wasn't a single river, it had little arable farmland, and it was completely lacking in mineral resources. The first place the British settled – today's Western District – turned out to be a malaria-infested hell. Yes, the island was of dubious value.

But the harbour wedged between its northern coast and the peninsula of Kowloon jutting out from the mainland was nearly perfect. The early opium merchants, as have all seamen since, found this 45 square kilometres (17 sq mi) of harbour to be the best deep-water port in the entire region. After a few colonial governors had come and gone, the value of Hong Kong Island gained clarity.

The "island" itself, as many call it, is 75 square kilometres (29 sq mi) of rolling real estate. Lining the entire northern shore today, from Western to Causeway Bay, is a wall of high-rise architecture housing some of the most powerful financial institutions in the world. Behind this wall is Victoria Peak, looming like a maternal protector. On the other side of Victoria Peak the vista is totally different. If the northern part of the island is the working side, this southern side is its playground. Aberdeen and Stanley offer superb restaurants along a rocky coast peppered with sandy beaches. There is an amusement park for those who are so inclined, and there are hilly hikes for the rest. ❑

LEFT: the spectacular Bank of China building, Central District.

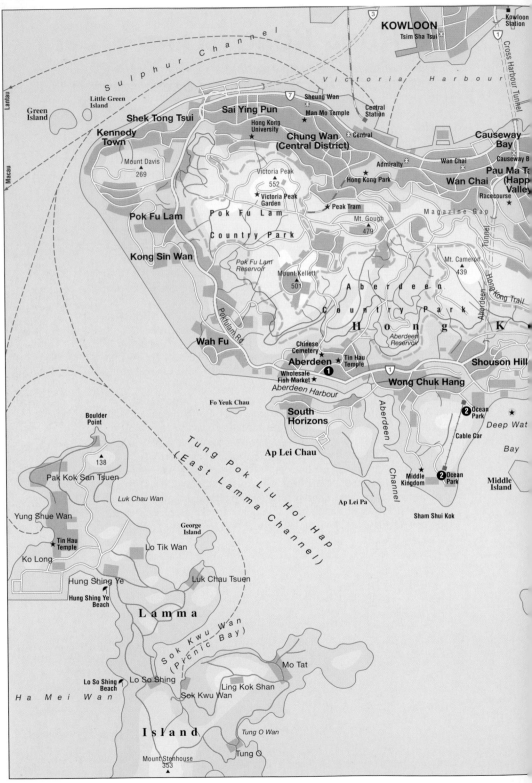

Sulphur Channel

Lantau

Macau

Green Island

Little Green Island

Shek Tong Tsui

Kennedy Town

Mount Davis
269

Pok Fu Lam

Kong Sin Wan

Sai Ying Pun

Hong Kong University
★

Pok Fu Lam

Country Park

Victoria Peak
552
▲

★ Victoria Peak Garden

Pok Fu Lam Reservoir

Mount Kellett
501
▲

Wah Fu

Pokfulam Rd

Sheung Wan

Man Mo Temple

Chung Wan (Central District)

Central

Peak Tram

Mt. Gough
479

Central Station

✠ Central

Admiralty

Hong Kong Park

Wan Chai

KOWLOON

Tsim Sha Tsui

Victoria   Harbour

Wan Chai

Kowloon Station

Cross Harbour Tunnel

3

7

1

Causeway Bay

Causeway B

Pau Ma Ta (Happ Valley

Racecourse

Magazine Gap

Mt. Cameron
439
▲

Hong Kong Trail

A b e r d e e n

C o u n t r y   P a r k

H o n g   K

Aberdeen Reservoir

Chinese Cemetery
★

Aberdeen
★ Tin Hau Temple

Wholesale Fish Market ★

❶

Aberdeen Harbour

Fo Yeuk Chau

South Horizons

Ap Lei Chau

Aberdeen Channel

Wong Chuk Hang

Shouson Hill

❷ Ocean Park

Cable Car

Deep Wat

★

Bay

Middle Kingdom
★

❷ Ocean Park

Sham Shui Kok

Ap Lei Pa

Middle Island

Boulder Point

138
▲

Pak Kok San Tsuen

Luk Chau Wan

Yung Shue Wan

★ Tin Hau Temple

Ko Long

Hung Shing Ye

Hung Shing Ye Beach

George Island

Lo Tik Wan

Luk Chau Tsuen

T u n g   P o k   L i u   H o i   H a p
(E a s t   L a m m a   C h a n n e l)

L a m m a

S o k   K w u   W a n
(P i c n i c   B a y)

Lo So Shing Beach

Lo So Shing

Sok Kwu Wan

Ling Kok Shan

Mo Tat

H a   M e i   W a n

I s l a n d

Tung O Wan

Mount Stenhouse
353
▲

Tung O

Hung Hom ▲ Ma Tau Ko — Kwun Tong **Chak Wo Ling**

Yau Tong

Eastern Harbour Tunnel

T s e u n g   K w a n   O
(Junk Bay)

**Pak Kok
(North Point)**

North
Point   Quarry Bay   **Tsak Yue Chung
(Quarry Bay)**

Fortress
Hill
Victoria   Tin Hau
Park
★   Tai Koo

Lei Yue Mun

**Junk
Island**

Sai Wan Ho

Tai Hang

Shau Kei Wan

Yiu Tung Est   **Shau Kei Wan**

Heng Fa Chuen

So Kon Po

Mt. Butler
▲ 435

Jardine's
Lookout

Mt. Parker
▲
531

Chai Wan   **Siu Sai Wan**

Chai Wan

Cape
Collinson

★ Parkview

n   g   *I   s*   *l   a   n   d*

Pottinger Peak
▲   312

Wong Nai
Chung Reservoir

T a i   T a m

Mount Collinson
▲
347

Shek O

Tai Tam
Reservoir

*L a m   T o n g   H o i   H a p
(T a t h o n g   C h a n n e l)*

f Course

Tai Tam
Intermediate
Reservoir

C o u n t r y   **P a r k**

C o u n t r y   *P a r k*

Wan Cham Shan
▲

Big Wave
Bay

Tai Tam Tuk
Reservoir

★ Golf Course

Repulse Bay Rd

3
*Repulse
Bay*

Repulse Bay

▲ 385

Middle Bay

*Tam Tai
Harbour*

Shek O Rd

Shek O

5

South Bay

Tai Tau
Chau

Chau
Tin Hau Temple
★

*Chung
Hom Wan*

T a i   T a m

**Tung Ah
Village**

D ' A g u i l a r

Ng Fan
Chau

ound
and

Chung Hom Kok

Stanley
Market
★

★ Stanley

W a n

P e n i n s u l a

4 Stanley

★ Stanley
Military
Cemetery

D'Aguilar Peak
▲ 325

Hok Tsui Shan

*Chek Chue Wan
(Stanley Bay)*

S t a n l e y

P e n i n s u l a

Cape d'Aguilar

S h e u n g   *M u n*

Hong Kong Island

N

Bluff Head

0 _____ 1 km
0 _____ 1 mile

CENTRAL AND THE PEAK

The Central District is Hong Kong's defining image because of its financial institutions, electric skyline, and the heights of Victoria Peak, or, simply, The Peak

Map, page 139

The centre of any great world metropolis is dominated by its government offices (usually of austere Roman-granite architecture), and perhaps a statue of a great ruler in an adjoining park. Hong Kong's Central District is no exception, if one concedes that the real governing power in Hong Kong is its banks and financial institutions. When you exit from the Star Ferry underpass and look ahead at the great concrete vista to the south, you will see the spires of two of Hong Kong's three main banks – the modernistic US$1 billion Hongkong Bank (reputedly the most expensive building in the world) and, to its right, the Standard Chartered Bank. Let your eyes wander past the old Bank of China Building (which now houses the trendy China Club, a private colonial-style, members-only club) to the left of the Hongkong Bank. Then look up to the gleaming 368-metre-high (1,209 ft) **Bank of China Tower ❶** designed by the Chinese-American architect I. M. Pei, with two antennae resembling a pair of chopsticks pointing upward from the roof. Behind it is Citibank Plaza, another gleaming office tower development leading to the high-rise apartments of the Mid-Levels area on the mountainside. The Bank of China's sharp angles point directly at the buildings of other financial institutions, which make for bad (or good, depending which side you're on) *feng shui*. The park in the foreground, Statue Square, was once graced with a statue of Queen Victoria, which has been replaced by a statue of Sir Thomas Jackson, an Englishman who managed the Hongkong and Shanghai Banking Corporation for 30 years at the end of the 19th century.

OPPOSITE: Star Ferry approaches Central.
BELOW: Bank of China Tower.

Ferries and rickshaws

The best place to begin a tour of Central is at the **Star Ferry Pier ❷**. The green-and-white ferries have been shunting passengers across the harbour between Hong Kong Island and the Kowloon Peninsula since 1898. The journey is one of Hong Kong's best bargains, costing just over a couple of Hong Kong dollars on the upper deck for an adult. If you really want to economise, travel second-class on the lower decks for even less.

In front of the busy Star Ferry Concourse are bright-red rickshaws pulled by the few old Chinese men who still earn a living in this old-fashioned way. These two-wheeled conveyances first appeared on the streets of Hong Kong in the late 1870s, but they actually originated in Japan. The first ones were designed and made by an American missionary living in Japan, and the name comes from the Japanese *jinrikisha*, which means "man-powered, wheeled vehicle". Today, they're only useful to provide photo opportunities for tourists or for a quick ride around the block – no further. Prepare to bargain hard.

To the right of the Star Ferry Pier is **Jardine House ❸**, whose distinctive 1,700-plus round windows

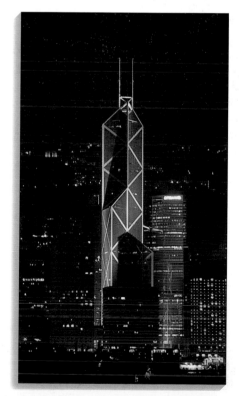

Jardine House was the model for the Struan family's headquarters in James Clavell's 1981 novel, Noble House. In the real world, when the new police emblem for post-handover Hong Kong replaced the Queen's crown with the skyline of Hong Kong, Jardine House was intentionally left out of the emblem's skyline, a reminder of Jardine's unpopular role in the Opium Wars.

BELOW: Central tram, and Jardine House.

have inspired the Chinese to nickname it the "House of a Thousand Orifices". Just behind this holey wonder is the General Post Office (GPO). Across the street to the west of the GPO and Jardine House are the shiny towers of **Exchange Square ❹**, home of the Hong Kong Stock Exchange, and the **International Finance Centre**, a combination of shopping malls and offices which sits atop the Airport Express terminus. Just in front, and still part of the IFC complex, is Hong Kong's tallest building, the prosaically-named **International Finance Centre Two**, which was finished in 2003. It stands at a staggering 420 metres (1,378 feet), and is capped by a mass of curving spires. To the north are the Outlying Islands ferry piers.

There is an underpass from the Star Ferry Concourse to Connaught Road Central, which is the first main avenue encountered when walking inland from the ferry dock. To the right, as you come out of the underpass, is the swanky **Mandarin Oriental Hotel**, one of the oldest and grandest hotels in Hong Kong and a favourite meeting place for the captains of industry. The hotel is connected by walkway over Chater Road to the Prince's Building office complex, which in turn has a walkway over Ice House Street to Alexandra House. From Alexandra House, a system of walkways leads to the Landmark mall and Swire House, which is interconnected to World Wide House and Jardine House, and beyond to the General Post Office, the Star Ferry and Exchange Square. *Don't panic.* These walkways sound more complicated than they are, and during the steamy summer months their air-conditioned passageways will be much appreciated.

Queen's Road Central was the area's original "Main Street", but a little footpath in front of the Queen's Road godowns (warehouses) and counting houses was turned into Des Voeux Road, which eventually upstaged it as the main thoroughfare.

Central Shopping

Toward the western end of Queen's Road is the first branch of Lane Crawford, one of the most expensive luxury department stores in Asia. Founded in the mid 1850s by a former butler, Edward Lane, and clerk Ninian Crawford, Lane Crawford is a typical Hong Kong rags-to-riches story — albeit with European rather than Asian beneficiaries. To the west along Queen's Road, there are dozens of ship chandleries on the site where, decades ago, ships docked and took on stock. Befitting its role as the site of "original" Hong Kong, Queen's Road beyond this point becomes less grandiose, whittling down from fancy department stores to small traditional crafts shops as you head toward Western District beyond Central Market.

Some of the side streets connecting Queen's Road and Des Voeux Road are well worth exploring. **Li Yuen Street** East and Li Yuen Street West (also known as The Lanes) are narrow alleyways lined with stalls and shops that sell clothing, fabrics and counterfeit designer fashion accessories. The atmosphere is a complete contrast to the glamorous high-rises on the larger avenues nearby. Bargaining is still expected here in these smaller streets, even though the neighbourhood is a bit more upscale than the outdoor markets, where haggling is *de rigueur*.

On Pedder Street, near the Central MTR station between Queen's Road and Des Voeux Road, is Shanghai Tang, one of Hong Kong's most successful home-grown fashion stores. British-Chinese entrepreneur David Tang, who first brought the territory the exclusive China Club, then Cuban cigars, turned his attention to making Chinese fashion chic. Neo-Mao suits and T-shirts are among the items on offer from this emporium, which also has branches in New York and Shanghai.

Map, page 139

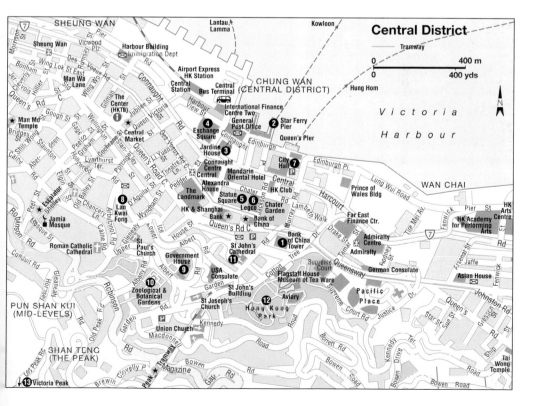

Across the road from Shanghai Tang is The Landmark, a shopping complex opened in 1980 on the site of the old Gloucester Hotel. The Gloucester was demolished for the New Gloucester Building, which in turn was destroyed to make way for The Landmark. Five floors surround a vast 6,000-square-metre (20,000 sq ft) atrium with 100 shops. The fountain in the middle is converted into a stage for performances on holidays and other special occasions.

In **Statue Square ❺** on Chater Road, Hong Kong's war veterans gather on Remembrance Day every November to commemorate both Chinese and expatriate victims of World War II. But the public square is most crowded on Sundays, when throngs of Filipina maids gather here on their day off in a festive, somewhat chaotic outdoor party. The 143,000 Philippine nationals, most of whom work here as maids, now form by far the single largest foreign community living in Hong Kong – over double the number of British, Canadian, Australian and American passport holders who together total around 70,000.

West of Statue Square is the Hong Kong Club, a prestigious institution for the SAR's upper crust. The Club's blue-and-white building was demolished in 1981 and has been replaced by a modern skyscraper. Fortunately, the colonial-style former **Supreme Court Building**, which is now the **Legislative Council (Legco) Building ❻**, escaped a similar fate. The building was once evacuated in mid-session because its foundations were undermined by the construction of the MTR (the underground railway) in the area. The building has been repaired and it now houses Hong Kong's legislature.

BELOW: The Landmark shopping mall, and the Legislative Council Building.

On the east side of this building is Chater Garden, a rare open space that on clear days is jammed with office workers eating their packed lunches. From here there is a walkway past the Bank of America Tower and the Ritz-Carlton hotel.

Under another walkway and to the left of the Star Ferry Pier is **City Hall ⑦**. The City Hall building not only houses administrative offices, but a concert hall and theatre as well. There are also billboards inside, which advertise cultural programmes for the month – a necessity for tourists searching for something beyond shopping, sightseeing and bar-hopping.

Mid-Levels

Behind Queen's Road Central, which was once the waterfront road before land reclamation, is a hill that rises precipitously from sea level. The original island of Hong Kong, before reclamation, was simply a huge mountain. For this reason, Hong Kong was considered worthless when first taken over by the British, with Foreign Secretary Lord Palmerston famously dismissing the territory as a "barren rock". Ironically, the higher up one gets on this "rock", the more desirable the property and the higher the rents – a pattern established in the early colonial years, when the higher slopes were considered less prone to malarial mosquitoes than those closer to sea level.

From Queen's Road Central, climb up either Ice House Street or Wyndham Street until they meet. The old, triangular-shaped ice-storage building (circa 1911) is now the home of the Foreign Correspondents' Club and the hip, ragtag, live-music Fringe Club. Wyndham Street is lined with small antique and crafts shops and leads to the nightlife areas of SoHo and BoHo.

Another worthwhile climb is D'Aguilar Street, lined with chic, modern boutiques and restaurants. Stanley Street, just off D'Aguilar, has some excellent antique shops and stores specialising in camera equipment. Continue up D'Aguilar, cross Wellington Street and proceed through the tiny flower market.

Map,
page 139

TIP

Wandering the convoluted roads and side streets of Mid-Levels, that area between Central and the higher slopes of The Peak, requires patience and a little stamina.

BELOW: Legislative Council Building.

The popularity of Lan Kwai Fong has given rise to high rents and high prices – this is now one of the most expensive areas in the world to eat, drink and be merry. But it doesn't seem to deter the crowds.

Farther along, the street branches out into two lanes. The one on the left is the L-shaped **Lan Kwai Fong ❽**, one of several busy nightlife areas for Hong Kong's young and trendy, where modern cuisine, funky bars, clubs, English pubs and tiny snack shops are found. Late-night revellers can get everything from pizza to sushi in the wee hours of the morning. Another drinking and dining area dubbed SoHo, an acronym for "south of Hollywood Road", is centred around nearby Staunton Street (*see* Western District).

These side streets wind upward to **Hollywood Road** (*see* Western District), packed with shops selling antiques, furniture, rattan and used books, and also to Glenealy Road. Glenealy is mainly residential and it snakes uphill and eastward onto Upper Albert Road and **Government House ❾**, the grand home of the former colonial leaders of Hong Kong. The long-term fate of Government House under the new Hong Kong government is still unclear, but it is currently being used as a state guest house and a place to host official banquets. The mansion was remodelled by the Japanese during World War II, including the addition of a tower with a vague Shinto look. There is a clear view of the building through the wrought-iron gates, which are opened to the public only a couple of times a year. Check with the HKTB for the dates.

The area surrounding Government House is one of the only remaining parts of Hong Kong Island that retains a genuinely colonial feel. If you go any further up, the pocket of exotic greenery is suddenly dwarfed by the high-rises of Mid-Levels; lower down, the area is engulfed by banks and office towers. Opposite Government House is the **Zoological and Botanical Gardens ❿** (open daily, 6am–7pm; free), a lush tropical area worthy of any urban retreat. The zoo and gardens house a variety of exotic wildlife, including an impressive collection of

red-cheeked gibbons. The zoo was opened in 1864 and still retains elements of its original Victorian gentility, with the added Eastern spirituality of elderly Chinese residents performing their *taijiquan* exercises each morning. From here it is just a short stroll to Hong Kong's other colonial crumbs. The Victorian-Gothic **St John's Cathedral** ⑪, inaugurated in 1849, is the city's oldest Anglican church, tucked away opposite the Citibank Plaza on Battery Path Road. The red brick **French Mission Building**, behind the Cheung Kong Center which replaced the old Hilton Hotel, is 150 years old and now serves as the Court of Final Appeal.

Another example of colonial architecture is **Flagstaff House**, home to the **Museum of Tea Ware** (open daily except Tuesday, 10am–5pm; tel: 2869 0690; free) and completed in 1846. It is reputedly Hong Kong's oldest surviving building. It was once the residence of the Commander-in-Chief of the British forces, when the area was Victoria Barracks.

Today, that vast expanse is **Hong Kong Park** ⑫, the site of, amongst other things, an aviary and botanical gardens. The structure resembling the tower of a mosque is an observation tower and a great place to photograph the area – if you can make it up the steps. Enter the park from Cotton Tree Drive or through Pacific Place shopping centre on Queensway.

The Peak

Hong Kong's most notable landmark, **Victoria Peak** ⑬, is also the residential aspiration of most of the population, not to mention the goal of more than three million visitors a year, equal to almost half the population of Hong Kong. But "The Peak", to those who have made it to the top of Hong Kong society, wasn't always regarded with such awe. A travel writer once described it as "beautiful in

Map, page 139

BELOW: St John's Cathedral.

Map, page 139

The latest model of the Peak Tram. The funicular railway uses the weight of the descending car to lift the ascending tram car to the top.

OPPOSITE: aviary, Hong Kong Park.
BELOW: Cafe Deco.

the distance, but sterile and unpromising upon more close examination". Indeed, during the first six years of Hong Kong's history, hardly anybody travelled to those inhospitable heights. It wasn't until 1888, when the **Peak Tramway** (actually a funicular railway) was opened, that the area atop the hill became The Peak, one of the most sought-after places to live in Hong Kong. Before the tram, sedan chairs transported lucky colonials to the top. Such coolie-powered transportation died long ago, but palanquins are still used during charity races once a year.

The impossibly steep Peak Tram, which takes local residents up and down the hillside, is more than just a tourist attraction. The tram runs from 7am to midnight, and hasn't had a single accident since it began operating in 1888. It still has only two cars, each carrying 72 passengers and one driver, and is pulled up and lowered by 1,500-metre (5,000 ft) steel cables wound on drums.

The most affluent residents on The Peak compete for the best chefs and stage the city's most sparkling dinner parties. Its best flats and houses are rented by banks and corporate giants for their top executives at astronomical sums. Swimming pools have been installed in lieu of verandas, but the area's wilderness, beautifully juxtaposed with stately residences, graciously survives. It is one of the few areas of Hong Kong that actually feels as if it's situated in a tropical climate. Cicadas buzz in the dense woods, wild birds and monkeys hop from tree to tree, and it is not uncommon for residents to have poisonous snakes removed from their gardens.

For nature-lovers, The Peak is the perfect place for a walk. On a clear day, you can wander through forests of bamboo and fern, stunted Chinese pines, hibiscus and vines of wonderful, writhing beauty. Ornithologists go to log sightings of blue magpies, crested goshawks and kites. The best way to see The Peak

is by walking around Lugard Road, which begins just opposite the Peak Tram's upper terminus at 395 metres (1,300 ft) above sea level.

From the top, visitors can marvel at some of the world's finest vistas sprawling all the way to China and Macau. At Lugard Road where it intersects with Harlech Road, you can first see the harbour, then Green Island and Peng Chau to the north, Lantau and Macau to the west, Cheung Chau further west, Lamma Island to the southwest, and finally the great masses of junks and sampans at Aberdeen to the south. This hike takes about 45 minutes round-trip from the Peak Tramway.

There are a number of restaurants clustered around The Peak, but for the best views book a window table at the glitzy Cafe Deco in the shopping mall next to the **Peak Tower**. In 1997, the building was completely redeveloped to incorporate new tourist attractions, such as a Ripley's Believe It or Not! Odditorium and a virtual-reality ride called "Peak Explorer". It is the first computer-operated entertainment ride in Hong Kong; an entertaining and educational journey through evocative scenes of the territory's early history.

While descending on the tram, stop at Barker Road and indulge in some of the finer views and footpaths through The Peak's mountainous forests. This road leads to the exclusive Plantation Road. The next stop is May Road, where the tram negotiates one of the steepest passenger-vehicle gradients in the world. ❑

THE STAR FERRY: A CENTURY OF VIEWS

Costing a couple of Hong Kong dollars, the crossing of Victoria Harbour aboard one of the Star ferries is a visual feast that is over in just seven minutes

From ancient to modern, from Rolls-Royce to rickshaw, Hong Kong offers every mode of conveyance for rich and poor. But the territory's quintessential transport is the Star Ferry. Shunting back and forth across Victoria Harbour, these green-and-white ferries link the community together in a way that is both symbolic and endlessly practical.

Of course, there's less of the harbour to cross now, thanks to massive reclamation projects, than when the inaugural ferry started running in 1870. The first of the current "Star" fleet made their maiden voyages at the turn of the century, in 1898.

Until Hong Kong Island was connected to Kowloon by road tunnels beneath Victoria Harbour and the Mass Transit Railway, the Star Ferry was the prime way to cross the harbour, an essential link in busy Hong Kong.

Appreciated but few awards

The Star Ferry fleet would win few prizes for glamorous design. Even the grandly named *Celestial Star* (other names include *Morning Star* and *Twinkling Star*, for example) is just one of a dozen bulky green-and-white floating, juddering people-movers. But from the clanking gangways to the weather-beaten coxswains to the solid wooden decks with their seats, which – like the ferries themselves – swing backwards and forwards to face Hong Kong or Kowloon, they are imbued with timeless character.

Cheap, practical, and endlessly fascinating, the Star Ferry is Hong Kong's transport of delight. It takes seven to eight minutes to make the crossing between Central, on Hong Kong Island, and Tsim Sha Tsui, in Kowloon.

△ **SEVEN-MINUTE JOURNEY**
The Tsim Sha Tsui ferry terminal has a knock-out view of Hong Kong Island (seen here before the Convention Centre was finished). Within a minute of arriving at the terminal, passengers are on the streets of Kowloon.

▽ **TOURIST SIGHTING**
The tourists are easy to spot on the Star Ferry – they are looking at the scenery. Local residents, on the other hand, will be looking at the horse-racing news or reading a novel, looking up only when the ferry eases to the gate.

SIMPLICITY ▷
The ferry boats themselves are efficient and simple. Top deck is more expensive, while lower deck is more interesting. Seat backs flop back and forth, depending upon which way the ferry and the view are headed.

TWO-DECK SERVICE, FIRST-CLASS VIEWS

Whether on upper or lower class aboard *Twinkling Star*, *Shining Star* or *Morning Star*, the Star Ferry has to be one of the world's great travel bargains. Infinitely cheaper than going by the road or rail tunnels beneath Victoria Harbour, the journey not only affords a double-ended view of Hong Kong and Kowloon, but also a glimpse at its multi-layered social strata.

The upper deck, the more expensive deck, commands the better vistas and perhaps wealthier patrons: immaculately coutured office women, executives chattering incessantly on their mobile telephones, a batch of commuters in the early mornings or late evenings, bridging the gap between home and work. The upper deck is also where most tourists find themselves, thinking the view will be better.

At water level, the lower deck is often full of grizzled types scanning the racing pages, weary-looking fellows with heavy baggage, and possibly a posse of giggling children on their way to or from school. One may find the lower deck to be more interesting.

Ride the Star Ferry long enough – there are approximately 450 crossings of Victoria Harbour daily – and one appreciates the simplicity and reliability of the ferry boats. Nothing glamorous, nothing ritzy. But there is that timeless certainty of a ferry always just minutes away.

△ **NOT ONLY THE STAR**
Star Ferries only ply between Hong Kong Island and Kowloon, but ferries to Lantau and elsewhere offer deck-top views and longer cruises.

◁ **RELIABLE**
The deck and gate crews set their watches to the arrivals and departures of the ferries, barely paying attention to the hustle of passengers.

WESTERN DISTRICT

The skyscrapers of the world of business and commerce dominate Central, but the traditional Chinese way of life still manages to thrive in the Western District. Nothing glitzy, but there to be found

Map, page 151

There's a popular urban myth among expatriate residents of Hong Kong about the polyester-clad, middle-aged American tourist who approached them in Central and asked, "Could you tell us where Chinatown is?" The story is almost certainly apocryphal, but nonetheless, sympathising with their need to escape from the gleaming high-rises and fashionable European houses, one could do a lot worse than kindly directing them to the Western District.

Western District is located just to the west of Central but is worlds apart from the ultra-modern financial district. Despite its name, it is probably the least Western area of Hong Kong and provides a rare glimpse of the old traditional Chinese city. The area begins officially at Possession Street and sprawls west to Kennedy Town. But Western's atmosphere emerges around Central Market to the west of the Mid-Levels Escalator, near the fringes of busy Central.

One of Western's charms is that it is the last refuge of the Hong Kong Chinese artisan. Here one can marvel at craftsmen who create mahjong tiles out of low-priced plastic to high-priced hand-carved husks. Find the Chinese herbalist, with his aromatic concoctions of snake musk, herbs, ginseng and powdered lizards, all part of pharmacopoeial potions dating back 4,000 years.

OPPOSITE: Man Mo Temple. **BELOW:** father and daughter on the waterfront.

Exploring the area

Western District properly begins once you reach the vicinity of **Central Market ❶**, itself not very picturesque and hardly meriting special attention. Just west of the market is The Center which houses a branch of the Hong Kong Tourism Board in its basement. The 73-storey building blends in with the rest of the polished steel and glass towers during the day, but at night it comes alive in a hypnotic, pyrotechnic display. Bars of neon, girdling the whole structure, pulse through a wave of gradually changing colours.

One can begin a walking tour of Western with a ride on the **Mid-Levels Escalator** that goes up from Central (near Central Market) to Mid-Levels. The ride up provides a wide view of the narrow streets and Chinese tenement blocks that lead into Western from the Central District. This reversible escalator was completed in 1993, at a cost of HK$32 million, and at 800 metres is one of the world's longest. It was built to allow commuters from Mid-Levels to ride to and from work in Central and thus ease some of the congestion of the streets that zig-zag down the hillside to Central. The escalator moves in only one direction at a time: it goes down until 10.15am, after which it is switched to the "up" mode for the rest of the day. About 36,000 people use it each day. The escalator begins from near Central Market at Connaught Road and stretches halfway up Victoria Peak.

BELOW: antique stores may actually have real antiques.

The escalator ends at the top of the hill on the residential Conduit Road, but the best place to start a walking tour is around **Staunton Street**. Dubbed "Hong Kong's SoHo" because it is south of Hollywood Road, Staunton Street and nearby Shelley and Elgin streets have become the centre of Hong Kong's alternative cafe culture. Before the escalator was built, these narrow streets were rather rundown and seldom visited by Westerners. Now they comprise a gallimaufry of cafes, restaurants and bars, offering an eclectic mix of ethnic cuisine – Vietnamese, Nepali, Portuguese, Cajun and French. The airy Staunton's Cafe is a great place to hang out and people-watch in the area, and it is a last chance to get a dose of Western-style caffeine before heading off into Western District proper. The traditional Chinese grocery stores in the vicinity are suddenly doing a roaring business in wine for consumption in the neighbourhood restaurants. Some of these restaurants require customers to bring their own wine, since Hong Kong's complex liquor licensing laws make it difficult for them to sell alcohol in this previously residential area.

Further along Staunton Street is a red sign which marks the former headquarters of the Xingzhonghui, or Revive China Society, the revolutionary organisation established by Dr Sun Yatsen in 1895 and dedicated to the overthrow of the Qing dynasty in China. It is one of 13 sites of interest in the Central and Western districts that form the **Sun Yatsen Historical Trail**. Much of Dr Sun's revolution was in fact orchestrated from Hong Kong. Next door is the rather more contemporary House of Siren, which hires out and makes to order costumes for Hong Kong society's fancy dress parties.

Immediately below Staunton Street lies **Hollywood Road**, once best known for its pricey if well stocked antique shops. These still exist in profusion, but

Map
page 151

around the escalator and the police station (*circa* 1911) a score of bars and restaurants have sprung up. Known as **BoHo** (Below Hollywood) this has become the late night trendy hangout, neatly joining up SoHo and Lan Kwai Fong.

Follow Hollywood Road west to the corner of Ladder Street and the **Man Mo Temple ➋** (open daily, 9am–6pm), built around 1842 on what must have been a little dirt track leading up from Central at that time. Tourists regularly throng through Man Mo, but this doesn't inhibit the temple's regular worshippers from flocking here to fill the temple with thick, redolent clouds of smoke from their joss sticks. The immense incense spirals hanging eerily from the ceiling can burn for weeks. Man is the god of civil servants and of literature, and in Mandarin society, civil servants were the most well-educated and sophisticated group. Mo is the god of martial arts and war and is more popularly known by his worshippers as Kuan Ti or Kuan Kung. Statues of the legendary Eight Immortals stand guard outside the temple; inside, two solid-brass deer (representing longevity) adorn the main chamber. Near the altar, there are three sedan chairs encased in glass. Years ago, when the icons of Man and Mo were paraded through Western on festival days, they were transported on these chairs.

Man ("civil") wears green garments and carries a calligrapher's brush, while Mo ("martial") wears red and holds an executioner's sword in his hands.

Sections of this neighbourhood were used as backdrops in *The World Of Suzie Wong*, the film that starred Nancy Kwan and William Holden. Apparently, these corners of Central and Western looked more like old Chinese Wan Chai than Wan Chai itself, where the story was set.

While in Western, don't miss a cruise down one of the most fascinating of all local shopping areas: **Ladder Street ➌**. This road zig-zags down steep inclines from Caine Road to Hollywood Road and down again to Queen's Road Cen-

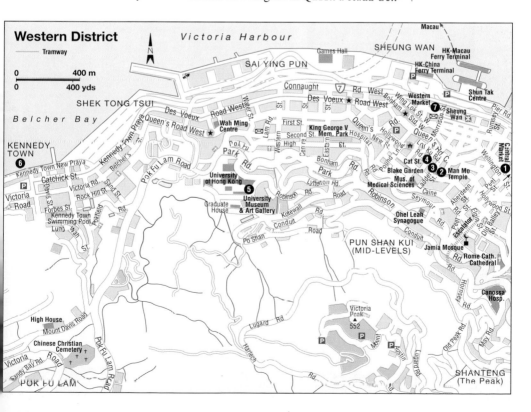

Chinese figurines to be bargained for in the streets of Western.

BELOW: Ladder Street, and Cat Street clutter.

tral. Nobody knows when its broad stone steps were constructed, but old records say that this 65-metre (118 ft) "street" was built so sedan chair bearers could more easily carry their human cargo from Hollywood Road to residential Caine Road. On Ladder Street are some of Hong Kong's oldest houses, including old shuttered buildings with wooden balconies and elaborate carvings.

Where Ladder Street meets Hollywood Road is a street officially called Upper Lascar Row but much more commonly known as **Cat Street ❹**, because the odds and ends you can buy here are known in popular Chinese as "mouse goods" and those who trade in them are known as "cats". The lanes here are filled with bric-a-brac, real and fake antiques, and more stalls than one can ever browse through. Bargaining is the rule here – whether for a safety pin, shoelace, or if you should be so lucky, a Tang-dynasty porcelain horse. The area was once famous for seamen's lodging houses and brothels, and it was a hangout for criminals and low-life characters of all kinds. In nearby Lok Ku Street are the Cat Street Galleries, which are devoted to artwork and antique reproductions from all over Asia.

After exploring the markets around Cat Street, keep going west to **Possession Street**, so called because it was here that Captain Edward Belcher landed on 26 January 1841 to plant the Union Jack and take possession of Hong Kong for Britain. At that time the island extended only as far as Queen's Road. However, land here has been reclaimed over the years, so no monument marks the exact spot where the British flag was planted. The only memento to the HMS *Sulphur*, whose crew was the first to step ashore, is Belcher Street, west of Possession Street, which was named after the *Sulphur*'s captain. Possession Street looks like a reversion to the 19th century because the road is barred to vehi-

cles. Rather than the noise of traffic, sounds and ambience here are generated only by people – the shopkeepers, street-side fortune-tellers and Chinese herbalists hocking their goods.

Map, page 151

Western backwaters

The deeper one goes into the Western District, the easier it is to forget the modern, Westernised Hong Kong. The district past Bonham Strand (a street lined with printing shops) looks more like a set for an old Chinese movie. City planners have classified this area as a slum, but architecturally, this district and its old four-storey buildings with ornate balconies and carved balustrades is more colourful and appealing than Hong Kong's more modern housing estates. And every little street has its own exotic specialities: ginseng and bird's nests, shark's fin and jade, funeral wreaths and snake wine, fortune-tellers and calligraphers and ivory and stone carvers.

Western was the first district to be settled by the British when they arrived in Hong Kong, in 1841. Malaria soon scared them away, leaving Western to the Chinese immigrants who arrived in the early 1850s.

Western District is for walking, for poking into little alleys and for getting lost in the web of side streets. Look for the key-cutters, tinkers, carpenters, cobblers and barbers in any alley. Their miniature factories operate in about six square metres (20 sq ft) of space. Shops may be simple upended crates, with the materials of their trade stacked outside. The craftsmen use drills and other tools of ancient design and timeless utility. Wander around and discover a veritable carnival of handicraft factories, teashops and restaurants.

From Western District one can walk up toward the residential district of Pok Fu Lam. The hilly upper region of Western (which is actually part of Mid-Levels) is completely different from Western District's lower region. Here the architecture is more Portuguese colonial than traditional Chinese – with tiled pitch roofs, stucco walls and projecting balconies. The **University of Hong Kong** has its campus here, and from various points along streets like Bonham Road which lead to the university, there is a splendid view of the harbour. Some of the structures on the university campus, including the Anatomy Building, the Government Bacteriological Building and the Vice-Chancellor's Lodge, were built before World War II.

BELOW: fish monger.

At the university, the **Fung Ping Shan Museum ➎** (open Monday–Saturday, 9.30am–6pm, Sunday 1.30–5.30pm; tel: 2241 5500; free), the oldest museum in the territory, is one of the best places in Hong Kong to see traditional Chinese arts and crafts. The museum houses a diverse collection of pottery and porcelain dating back to the seventh century. Its most prized possession is the world's largest collection of bronzeware from the Yuan dynasty.

Walking up to the university from Central via Bonham Road can be an exhilarating experience. There are no exceptional landmarks en route, but if you peek between the buildings from the road, you can see grand views of the harbour and the Western and Central districts below. The architecture of schools and mansions en route is also a glimpse into Hong Kong's colonial past.

Keep walking far enough to the residential district of Pok Fu Lam and finally to **Kennedy Town ➏**, one of Hong Kong's oldest Chinese settlements. Kennedy Town Praya, the main street, curves along the original

Chops, which have the legal authority of a person's signature, have been used in China for 3,000 years. Prosperous Chinese officials would often possess a variety of seals that charted their progress in the court.

OPPOSITE: jewelry market.
BELOW: commercial calligrapher.

footpaths bordering Belcher Bay, though some of the bay in front has now been reclaimed. Kennedy Town marks the western end of the Hong Kong tram route, but is otherwise of little interest to tourists. From outside the slaughter houses and squatter shacks close to the waterfront you can see the waters leading to Macau, and in the foreground, the grassy hump of Green Island. A former munitions dump, this small island is uninhabited, though there is talk of a project to build a bridge linking it to Kennedy Town.

Also here is the result of another huge land reclamation project – the new **Western Harbour Crossing**, Hong Kong's third cross-harbour tunnel to Kowloon, completed in 1997.

Whether you go all the way to Kennedy Road or just to the university, head back to Central by going down towards the harbour along Queens Road West or Des Voeux Road. These two streets are distinguished by their aromatic Chinese medicine shops, rice traders, traditional wedding dress stores, and merchants selling Chinese paper lanterns and incense. Take a look at the fascinating range of dried seafoods, including abalone, sea cucumber and shark's fin, which can sell for several thousand dollars a kilogramme.

Between the continuation of Queen's Road (which becomes Bonham Strand) and Des Voeux Road is colourful Wing Lok Street, with shops selling herbs, ancient medicines, preserved seafood and tea. Just one block above Bonham Strand is Jervois Street, another "speciality" street, this one devoted entirely to snake restaurants and Chinese wine shops. There are also jade-carvers, calligraphers, opera costumers, fan-makers and pottery-shapers in the area.

Man Wa Lane, on the opposite side of Bonham Street to Jervois Street, is lined with the chop-makers who carve elaborate name stamps from blocks of stone. These chops are not only practical instruments (formal documents in Hong Kong require a "chop", used as a signature), but works of ancient Chinese craftsmanship. Perhaps only the Arabs have as much respect for calligraphy as the Chinese. And watching a Man Wa chop-carver sculpt a customer's name out of a small block of stone, ivory, jade, or wood is quite an experience. There are male and female chop styles: when background material is carved out, the chop is male; when the characters are carved out, it's female. The chop is also important in other Asian countries such as Japan.

On Morrison Street, close to the harbour, stands a red brick Edwardian-style building called **Western Market ❼**. It was opened in 1906 and served for more than 80 years as a food market. Recognised as a historical landmark, its elegant architectural features were preserved and restored, and in 1991 it was converted into a shopping complex. Sometimes referred to as Hong Kong's version of London's Covent Garden, it offers a diversity of handicrafts, fabric and souvenir stalls, as well as a Chinese restaurant on the top floor. The comparison, however, is a little misleading and visitors will be disappointed if they expect as great a range and diversity of attractions as Covent Garden.

From Western Market you can take a walkway across Connaught Road West to the Shun Tak Centre, which houses the Macau Ferry Terminal. ❑

WAN CHAI AND CAUSEWAY BAY

Wan Chai's allure goes back to the times of Suzie Wong and sailors on the prowl. After years of dormancy, it's back, but classier. Adjacent is Causeway Bay, no longer much of a bay

Map, page 158

E ast of Central lie two lively districts in which to indulge in the hedonistic Hong Kong pleasures of eating, drinking and, of course, shopping. Wan Chai and Causeway Bay are, in general, architecturally undistinguished, but they are among the territory's most crowded and active districts, revealing the authentic flavour of modern Hong Kong.

Admiralty ❶, between Central and Wan Chai, used to be the site of a British naval station; now it is a combination of gleaming office towers and shopping malls. When the British first came to Hong Kong, they couldn't find a suitable site for a naval garrison, so the HMS *Tamar* was moored offshore just east of Central. It was many years later, after the Japanese occupation during World War II, that the Tamar naval compound was moved ashore. After Hong Kong's return to China in 1997, the Tamar compound was turned over to the Chinese People's Liberation Army. The jewel of Admiralty is **Pacific Place**, one of Hong Kong's ritziest shopping malls, showcasing the top names in fashion and housing three of Hong Kong's five-star hotels: the Conrad, Marriott and Island Shangri-La.

From Admiralty, it is just a few minutes' walk to Wan Chai itself, the legendary nightlife centre of Hong Kong that was immortalised in the film *The World of Suzie Wong*, about a Chinese prostitute with a heart of gold. By day, Wan Chai has a completely different personality than it does at night. Thanks to high rents in neighbouring Central, many companies have spilled into Wan Chai, providing a steady clientele for its many restaurants and shops.

Close to the waterfront, in an area sometimes known as Wan Chai North, are the **Academy for Performing Arts ❷** and the **Hong Kong Arts Centre ❸**, two of the most popular venues for theatrical and cultural performances in Hong Kong. The Arts Centre also has galleries, rehearsal rooms and a restaurant that provides views of the harbour. Right on the harbour is the futuristic **Hong Kong Convention and Exhibition Centre ❹**. Hong Kong's growing importance as a business centre in Asia made it necessary to upgrade and expand the territory's exhibition facilities. The HK$4.8 billion convention centre extension was completed just in time for the official ceremony for the handover of Hong Kong to China in 1997. The building extension sprawls over six-and-a-half hectares (16 acres) of newly reclaimed land (about the size of nine football fields). It adds an extra 38,000 square metres of function space to the existing convention centre. The complex is adjacent to the ritzy Grand Hyatt and the New World Harbour View Hotel and is linked by walkways to the 78-storey Central Plaza office tower, currently Hong Kong's second highest building at 374 metres (1,227 ft).

The Convention and Exhibition Centre is fringed on the harbourside by a **promenade** which hugs the

OPPOSITE: Central Plaza Tower.
BELOW: the lobby of the Grand Hyatt.

coastline all the way to Queens Pier in Central, albeit with a few short detours inland to skirt the heli-pad at Admiralty. Just outside the centre are two rather odd-looking statues. The black obelisk is the **Reunification Monument**, which was erected to commemorate the 1997 handover and signed in gold by former Chinese President Jiang Zemin. Just behind it is the golden Forever Blooming Bauhinia Sculpture, a favourite spot for mainland Chinese tourists to pose for a photo. The bauhinia flower is indigenous to Hong Kong and, as the territory's regional emblem since 1997, its five petals are printed on the Hong Kong flag.

Ahead, on the island across the channel, was Hong Kong... with the miniature skyscrapers in the centre and on either side the long waterfront, stretching for miles, wedged with sampans and junks; and behind rose the steep escarpment of the Peak, shedding the town and the lower social orders as it climbed...

THE WORLD OF SUZIE WONG
BY RICHARD MASON (1957)

The heart of Wan Chai

Elevated walkways lead south from the convention centre into the heart of Wan Chai around the MTR station and Lockhart Road, one of the busiest streets in the centre of the nightlife district. On the eastern end of Lockhart Road towards Causeway Bay, the road turns into an endless row of hardware and interior decor supply shops. The western end of Lockhart Road is a lively neighbourhood of bars, restaurants and old office buildings.

During the 1960s, Wan Chai was a favourite rest-and-recreation destination for tens of thousands of American, Australian and New Zealander soldiers and sailors fighting in the Vietnam War. It was during this period that the area earned its reputation as a tawdry but thriving red-light district. After a rather sad period in the late1980s and early 1990s, during which Wan Chai's nightlife seemed to be in terminal decline, the area successfully reinvented itself. Some of Hong Kong's trendiest bars and restaurants are here, packed out almost every night with a mixture of expats, locals and out-of-towners.

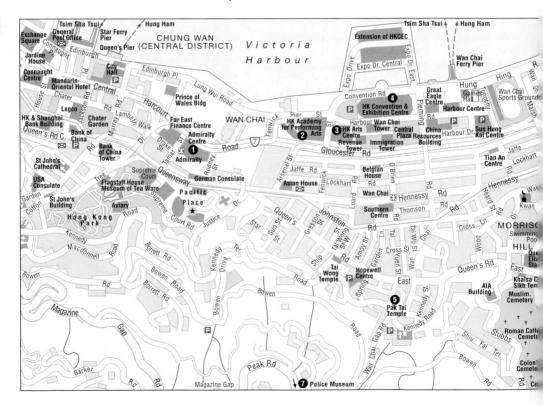

Map, page 158

There aren't many sailors roaming the streets of Wan Chai these days, so the die-hard "girlie" bars on Lockhart Road that are still in business have to fight hard for customers. If the reputation of some of these bars doesn't scare people away, the lack of charm and grace of the touts planted at the doors probably will. Few people other than groups of sailors and the occasional unsuspecting tourist venture into these bars. The women who work in these places are mostly Filipinas and Thais who have come to Hong Kong on temporary tourist visas. Modern-day Suzie Wongs stay away from Wan Chai because they earn far more being "hostesses" in the karaoke bars in Kowloon that cater to affluent Asian business executives. There are still a few old British-style pubs in the area, with names like The Old China Hand and The Horse and Groom, though they see far more Hong Kong Chinese after hours than old colonial "hands".

Three blocks to the south of Lockhart Road, **Queen's Road East** is famous for its rattan and rosewood furniture shops. This area also has two traditional Chinese temples that provide a glimpse of the old way of life in stark contrast to their modern surroundings. On Queen's Road East next to a narrow lane of steps leading up towards Mid-Levels is the tiny, dark **Hung Shing Temple**. Legend has it that this temple, built on top of huge boulders, was named after a Tang-dynasty official who was famous for his extreme virtue and his ability to make predictions that proved to be of great value to traders. Perhaps only by coincidence, several small banks in the neighbourhood are filled with groups of elderly "traders" who stare at computer screens to follow the share price movements of the stock market.

Much more impressive is the **Pak Tai Temple ❺** at the top of Stone Nullah Lane, a triple-halled temple noted for its three-metre-high statue, made in 1604, of the deity Pak Tai, who assures harmony on earth. The temple itself was not

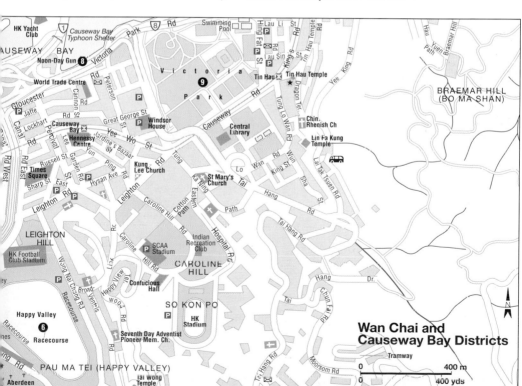

Wan Chai and Causeway Bay Districts

built until 1863. There are usually old men and women pottering around in the dark recesses of the temple, lighting incense sticks or laying out offerings.

Just before Stone Nullah Lane along Queen's Road East, you will encounter the circular, 66-storey **Hopewell Centre**, once Hong Kong's tallest building. There is a roof-top restaurant that offers an inspiring view of the city below but serves food that is far from inspiring. The Hopewell Centre also provides a short-cut to Mid-Levels, because you can take the elevator to the 17th floor and step out of the building onto Kennedy Road, which meanders around the lower part of the area known as Mid-Levels.

At the eastern end of Queen's Road East is one of the oldest settlements on Hong Kong Island. Western District had been the first Hong Kong suburb occupied by Europeans, but they soon deserted it because of malaria and moved to a spot said to be healthier. Optimistically, they named this second settlement east of Wan Chai and south of Causeway Bay, **Happy Valley**. It was relatively distant from the sea, somewhat deserted and, most important, didn't have as many unhealthy, malaria-ridden rice farms in its vicinity.

In 1840, shortly after Happy Valley was settled, the colony's residents created the greensward and edifice that has made Happy Valley world-famous amongst horseracing fans: the Hong Kong Jockey Club's **Happy Valley Racecourse ❻**. During the October-to-May racing season, it attracts up to 75,000 punters a race during weeknights and weekends. Night races under the bright lights are particularly exciting, the atmosphere is frenetic, and the rewards for picking the right horse can be huge. One of the best ways to experience the races is to join the Hong Kong Tourist Association's "Come Horseracing Tour", which provides transport to the racecourse and entry to the Members' Enclosure.

BELOW: classic Wan Chai architecture.

Map, page 158

The racetrack itself is state-of-the-art. Gigantic 20x5.8-metre (66x19 ft) video screens show the races in progress as well as all manner of betting, racing forms and other relevant data. The total amount wagered every season is staggering – the highest of any racing establishment in the world – but most of the course profits are donated to charitable causes. If you can't make it to the actual races, visit the **Hong Kong Racing Museum** (open Tuesday–Sunday, 10am–5pm, tel: 2966 8065; free). This tribute to one of Hong Kong's favourite pastimes was opened in 1996 at the Happy Valley Stand inside the racecourse. The museum has eight galleries and a video presentation that tell the history of horseracing in the colony, providing background on the obsession that racing has become in Hong Kong.

Happy Valley's would-be happiness begins on Queen's Road East, at the corner of winding Stubbs Road. There are several places from which to enjoy panoramic views of the area. One is the Stubb's Road Lookout, which offers breathtaking, uninterrupted views of the harbour, the Kowloon Peninsula and the Central Plaza building, with the Happy Valley Racecourse just down to the right. Another is Lovers' Rock, at the hillside above Bowen Road near Shiu Fai Terrace. In addition to the tourists who come to enjoy the views of Wan Chai and Happy Valley, local men and women (mostly women) flock to the site on the 6th, 12th and 26th days of each lunar month to light joss sticks, hang wine bottles on strings to the tree opposite the rock and pray for harmonious marriages. Like Stubbs Road, nearby Wong Nai Chung Gap Road also offers superb views of the city (don't confuse Wong Nai Chung Gap Road with Wong Nai Chung Road, adjacent to the race course). Also on this road, which leads to Repulse Bay Beach, is the Hong Kong Cricket Club, founded in 1851.

The Hong Kong Jockey Club has an annual turnover of HK$835 billion. Most of its earnings go to charity and civic projects. The annual per capita amount spent on gambling is HK$13,900.

BELOW: a busy Causeway Bay waterfront at night.

Map,
page 158

Views of the harbour are also good from the former Wan Chai Gap Station, which now houses Hong Kong's **Police Museum** ❼ (open Tuesday, 2–5pm, Wednesday–Sunday, 9am–5pm; tel: 2849 7019; free). The museum traces the history of the Hong Kong police force, with an occasional oddity on display such as the stuffed head of a tiger that was shot in 1915 after it killed a policeman.

Causeway Bay

Down Tai Hang Road toward the harbour to King's Road is **Causeway Bay**, bounded on the east by Victoria Park, on the west by Canal Road, on the south by Caroline Hill and Leighton Road, and on the north by the harbour. Causeway Bay really was a bay until the 1950s, when it disappeared into a great land reclamation project. What was then Causeway Bay is now Paterson Street. The present-day "bay" is occupied by the Hong Kong Yacht Club on Kellett Island (no longer an island since land reclamation) and the **Typhoon Shelter**. Yet this in turn is due to be reclaimed to make more building space in this highly congested area.

*In Hong Kong
They strike a gong
And fire off a noon-
day gun
To reprimand each
inmate who's in late.*

— NOEL COWARD

MAD DOGS & ENGLISHMEN

This part of Hong Kong's waterfront also features a unique genuflection to the musical genius of Noel Coward: the **Noon-Day Gun** ❽. Nobody knows for sure why the gun is fired at noon everyday, but according to a century-old legend, this ritual, now a Hong Kong tradition, began one day in the mid-1800s when one of the Jardine's opium boats sailed into the harbour and a willing minion gave the boat a 21-gun salute. The Hong Kong governor was incensed that a mere purveyor of "foreign mud" should receive the same greeting as a government official, so, as penance, he ordered that the gun be fired at noon everyday in perpetuity. One would have assumed the gun would fire its last in July 1997, but despite the end of the colonial era the Jardine-owned Noon-Day Gun tradition looks likely to continue just as long as Jardine's keeps loading.

*Until 1960, a
6-pounder was used
for the Noon-Day
Gun. People com-
plained it was too
loud, so Jardine
replaced it with a
3-pounder bought
from the Hong Kong
Harbour Police.*

Causeway Bay's modern history began in 1973 when the **Cross-Harbour Tunnel** was opened. This underwater freeway is one of the largest tunnels in Asia. Its four lanes cross two kilometres (1.25 mi) of harbour water between Hong Kong Island and Kowloon. There are now three cross-harbour tunnels, but this one is still the busiest.

With this tunnel came the transformation of Causeway Bay into a thriving urban area. Deluxe hotels such as the Park Lane and the Excelsior opened their doors to tourists. The World Trade Centre, next to the Excelsior, offers 42 storeys of offices, restaurants, bars and shops. Causeway Bay is best known as a busy shopping district, with large department stores, many of them Japanese. Retail rents in the area are among the highest in the world, and the streets are crowded to the point of being uncomfortable, even by Hong Kong standards. Pollution levels are notoriously bad. Movie theatres and scores of electronic and camera shops are packed along Hennessy Road down to Canal Road which was once a canal when there was a scheme to make Causeway Bay a mini Venice – a project sadly doomed to failure. Windsor House has two floors of shops devoted to the latest technology in computers and accessories. Times Square, a few blocks south of the main crossroads of Causeway Bay, is a huge modern building with restaurants, shops and a cinema.

OPPOSITE: Filipinas, the housekeepers of Hong Kong, socialise on Sundays.

Two blocks east is **Victoria Park** ❾, named after Queen Victoria, whose statue can be seen surveying the activities of her former subjects. This welcome chunk of expansive parkland in the middle of Causeway Bay has a public swimming pool, jogging tracks and tennis courts and is very popular with tai chi devotees in the early morning, and has become a tranquil idyll for many. Tens of thousands of people gather here on special occasions, such as Chinese New Year and the Mid-Autumn Festival. ❑

THE SOUTH SIDE

The southern part of Hong Kong Island reveals a totally different character to the built-up north. Except for the busy spots of Aberdeen and Stanley, much of the coast here is relatively pristine and uncrowded

Map,
page 134

nlike the northern part of Hong Kong Island, which has changed almost beyond recognition in recent years with successive land reclamation, the rocky coastline of the south side has changed very little. The character of this relatively unspoilt and tropical side of Hong Kong provides a complete contrast to the heavily urbanised north. Fishing villages, beaches and mountain scenery make this a particularly popular area for visitors to explore.

The harbour town of **Aberdeen ❶** can be reached from Kennedy Town through the residential districts of Pok Fu Lam and Chi Fu Fa Yuen and past the Wah Fu Estate. But most visitors take a more direct route south from Wan Chai through the Aberdeen Tunnel along Stubbs Road and Magazine Gap Road. There are buses or minibuses to Aberdeen from Exchange Square in Central District, or one can take a taxi. The tunnel route is generally the fastest, but you miss the sweeping views of Hong Kong Island from Stubbs Road.

Aberdeen has a character unlike any other town in Hong Kong, with huge numbers of floating vessels bobbing in the water along its shoreline. Its charm, though, is questionable, because this naturally ideal typhoon anchorage is home to what remains of Hong Kong's "boat people" and their raggle-taggle collection of junks and sampans.

Hong Kong's traditional boat people are fisherfolk who have been living on boats in local waters for thousands of years. They consist of two main groups: the Tanka (literally, the egg people, because they used to pay taxes with eggs rather than cash) and the Hoklo. Other Chinese have never accepted them (pre-Communist China wouldn't even permit them to settle on land), but the Hong Kong government has encouraged most of them to leave their boats and settle on land reclaimed from the harbour. Most of the fishing people have been lured to work in factories. Romantics might bemoan this loss of traditional life, but these hot, metal-roofed boats are more like floating slums, with unsanitary and unsafe living conditions.

At any rate, tourists are still seduced by the colourful 30-minute ride through **Aberdeen Harbour**. They enjoy the chaotic atmosphere, the incredible collection of sea life, and the dynamism of this city upon the water. They also enjoy the flamboyant Chinese floating restaurants moored in the "yacht basin" of **Shumwan**, across from the Aberdeen Marina. Reputed to be the world's largest floating restaurant complex with seats for over 4,000, the gaudy extravaganza captures the atmosphere of a traditional grand-scale Chinese restaurant.

What, though, does the southern Hong Kong area of Aberdeen have to do with that Scottish town of the same name? Nothing. The village wasn't named after the Scottish city, but for the Earl of Aberdeen, the 1848

PRECEDING PAGES: Stanley windsurfing rentals. **OPPOSITE:** floating restaurant. **BELOW:** Aberdeen.

Tin Hau, the goddess of the sea, is revered throughout Hong Kong. In Macau, she is known as A-Ma.

BELOW: Tin Hau Temple, Aberdeen.

Secretary of State for the Colonies. The Chinese call Aberdeen Heung Gong Tsai, or Little Hong Kong.

For the best overview of Aberdeen, begin with the town's **Tin Hau Temple**, built in 1851. The temple is rather shabby most of the year, but during April's Tin Hau Festival, it is alive with ceremony. Tin Hau is the goddess of the sea and traditionally important to the fishermen of Aberdeen. At festival time, thousands of gaily-decorated boats converge on Aberdeen's shores. During the festival, the temple is decorated with paper shrines and lanterns, and lion dances are performed outside. It's an event not to be missed.

Along Aberdeen's main street there is a teenage youth and cultural centre called the Warehouse, housed on the site of the former Aberdeen Police Station. The Warehouse is set in an atmospheric tropical garden that comes to life with the not-so-tropical sounds of live rock music during concerts performed there by local teenage bands.

A bridge links Aberdeen to **Ap Lei Chau**. This island, just two minutes away from Aberdeen, houses Hong Kong's prolific boat-builders. They make ferries, sloops, cruisers, speedboats, yachts and steel lighters, as well as traditional sampans and junks. Ap Lei Chau is also the site of a huge residential complex called South Horizons and an extensive collection of "factory outlet" stores.

Towering above Aberdeen Harbour on the hillside is the **Chinese Permanent Cemetery**, which is entered through a Chinese pagoda-style gate. From the cemetery there is an excellent view of the town and shoreline below; up higher still is the scenic **Aberdeen Reservoir**. Opposite the cemetery is the **Aberdeen Wholesale Fish Market**, which is set for redevelopment to make it a tourist attraction instead of the unsightly local market that it is now. Whatever the

aspirations may be for transforming the market into a Fish Market Complex, with a Festival Market Place for tourists, for now it remains a rather dull, long tin shed full of fish and other edible seafoods, resounding in the early morning with the shouts of fishermen haggling for the best price for their night's catch.

Map, page 134

Ocean Park to Stanley

From Aberdeen, go east past the Police Training School at Wong Chuk Hang to one of Hong Kong's biggest tourist attractions. Opened in 1977 at a cost of HK$150 million, **Ocean Park** ❷ (open daily, 10am–6pm; entrance fee) is the world's largest oceanarium. Located on 70 hectares (170 acres) of land, the park actually consists of two sections: a lowland site and a headland site, the two linked by a 1.4-kilometre cable-car bridge.

The headland site is at the end of the spectacular cable car ride overlooking the South China Sea. On the headland, Ocean Theatre is the largest marine mammal theatre in the world, with a seating capacity of 4,000, a giant pool large enough for dolphins and occasional visiting diving shows. Wave Cove simulates a rocky coastline with a machine that generates waves up to one metre high. At two different levels, sea lions, seals, dolphins, penguins and sea birds may be seen diving or skimming along the cove's surface. There is also the Atoll Reef, the largest aquarium in the world with about 30,000 specimens of sea creatures and two million litres (500,000 gallons) of seawater on three different levels of viewing galleries. The park is also home to two giant pandas.

Also on the headland is an amusement park with various rides, including The Dragon, one of the world's longest roller coasters at 840 metres (2,500 ft), which seems to whip out over the beautiful South China Sea at each pass.

Back in the lowland section, Film Fantasia is a high tech theatre containing 100 hydraulic seats that tilt forward, backward, left and right to make you feel part of the space voyage. It is advisable not to go right after a meal. Discovery of the Ancient World is an adventure trail with special lighting, sound effects, interactive displays and artificial fog to recreate seven scenic zones of the primeval equatorial rain forests.

The underwater viewing tunnel at the Shark Aquarium allows you a sprat's eye-view of more than 250 sharks and rays from some 35 different species. Ocean Park also carries out its own in-house shark breeding programme.

Beyond Ocean Park is a region of rocky coasts and smooth white sands. No office buildings or factories are anywhere in sight. But on summer weekends, it seems every office, factory and farm worker in Hong Kong descends on these shores. Hong Kong has 36 beaches, and 14 of them are on the south side of the island. A few, like Rocky Bay on the road to Shek O, have virtually no public facilities, but they offer unparalleled views and uncrowded stretches of sand and sea. Others, like Repulse Bay, feature bus loads of tourists, fast-food restaurants and about as much peace and quiet as a carnival. Repulse Bay and Stanley are also home to several residential developments that command some of the highest real-estate prices and rents in the world.

BELOW: dolphin star at Ocean Park.

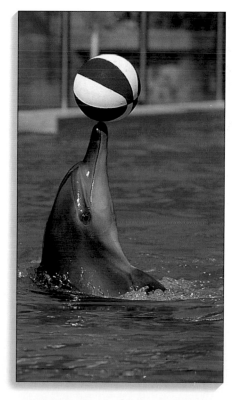

Deep Water Bay, the first beach beyond Aberdeen and Ocean Park, has some beautiful mansions, including the house where *Love Is A Many-Splendoured Thing* was filmed. It also has a nine-hole golf course managed by the Hong Kong Golf Club (open weekdays to the public). Farther along the road is the exclusive Hong Kong Country Club. The long stretch of beach here offers a quiet place to soak in the sun or go for a swim.

A popular destination on the south side of Hong Kong Island is **Repulse Bay ❸**. Now widened to several times its original size and developed into a playground for tourists as well as urban Hong Kongers, Repulse Bay Beach has everything except peace and quiet. It once had one of the finest resort hotels in the East, the Repulse Bay Hotel, but the structure has been replaced by a large pink apartment building with a big square hole in the middle called The Repulse Bay. Some say the hole is a passageway for the heavenly dragon to come down from the mountains; others say it was put there to generate good *feng shui*; still others say it was just the architect's attempt at being funky. It looks like a giant, square, pink donut from afar, but despite its unorthodox design, the building has maintained a bit of the dignity and grandeur of its predecessor – the terrace and verandah, with its staircase, fountain and lawns, are a replica of the old Repulse Bay Hotel. The building houses a number of excellent restaurants.

On the waterfront at Repulse Bay, there are a beachside restaurant, hamburger and noodle stands, luxurious high-rises and a beach that gets filthy on weekends due to an invasion by thousands of visitors. The aftermath of the weekend invasions has earned the beach the moniker "Repulsive Bay" among Hong Kong's expats. But the bay didn't get its name from the Monday morning

BELOW: The Repulse Bay and its hole.

garbage cleanups; it was named after the battleship HMS *Repulse*, which took an active part in thwarting pirates who plundered here in the early days of settlement in the territory.

The hills further inland from the shoreline have a sad history. It was over those hills that invading Japanese troops came pouring down at the end of 1941 during World War II. The Repulse Bay Hotel was a military target because British and Canadian troops used it as a base to keep open the road between Stanley and Aberdeen. After three days of fighting, the hotel was taken, and Commonwealth prisoners were marched to Eucliffe Mansion (this castle has also been demolished), about half a kilometre from the hotel. Most of the prisoners were executed, and survivors were put into the Stanley Internment Camp.

Just beyond Repulse Bay are two beaches that are a bit more quiet than the main beach. Middle Bay and South Bay are favourite hangouts for the more serious beach bums eager to tan their toned bodies away from the crowds.

Fifteen minutes' drive farther southwest leads to a popular tourist magnet, **Stanley ❹**. Despite the English name (it was named after Lord Stanley, a 19th-century Secretary of State for the Colonies), Stanley was the largest indigenous settlement in Hong Kong when the British first set foot here in 1841. In fact, a Tin Hau temple here documents that the town of Chek Chu (Stanley's Chinese name) was founded in 1770 by the pirate Cheung Po Tsai, who had taken control of the island.

Stanley Market, the main attraction on Stanley Peninsula, draws thousands of visitors on weekends – locals in search of a bargain as well as tourists looking for souvenirs to take home. A few steps from New Street, where the buses stop, is a large area with shops selling fashionable clothes (factory over-runs or

Map, page 134

In 1942, a tiger weighing 240 pounds and nearly six feet long was shot by an Indian policeman in front of the Stanley Police Station.

BELOW: Stanley village.

Map, page 134

During World War II, noncombatant Brits were herded by the Japanese into Stanley's ramshackle internment camp. Chinese civilians, however, were sent to China – over 20,000 every month.

TIP

What the No. 6 bus from Central to Stanley lacks in comfort and speed it makes up for in scenery – fine seascapes, a roller-coaster ride and some momentarily breath-less moments.

OPPOSITE: waterfront dining at Stanley's Oriental.

seconds), rattan, fresh food, ceramic jugs, budget art, hardware, brass objects, Chinese crafts, vases – almost anything.

Hong Kong residents come to Stanley for its excellent restaurants and sea-side feel. A modern shopping mall occupies a site at the end of Main Street, directly opposite one of the SAR's most amazing modern achitectural projects. Murray House (*circa* 1848) – formerly a British Army officer's mess – was moved stone by stone from Central and the stylish conversion now houses restaurants and boutiques.

East of the bus station is the **Old Stanley Police Station**, one of only 30 pro-tected historic buildings in Hong Kong. The early British settlers regarded a posting to Stanley Police Station (built in 1844) as highly dangerous. Only a small dirt track connected the town to the city of Victoria (now Central) and pirates frequently attacked and robbed the garrison. Stanley was all but aban-doned throughout the 1850s, until the original police station was replaced by the building which stands today. Old Stanley Police Station is also thought to have been the last point of resistance to the advancing Japanese forces in the battle for Hong Kong during World War II. On Christmas Day 1941, the town's commanding officer refused to believe that the British had surrendered and so the town fought on for a day after troops elsewhere had laid down their arms.

Down the road is **Stanley Prison**, which is still in use, while the two-storey building topped with a mock guard tower next to its parade ground houses the quirky Correctional Services Museum (open Tuesday–Sunday, 10am–5pm; free; tel: 2147 3199). Its nine galleries chart the history of Hong Kong's penal sys-tem, with creepy exhibits like a mock gallows and fake cells. To the right of the prison is the **Stanley Military Cemetery**, a quiet reminder of Stanley's part in World War II. It was also in Stanley – at both the prison and at nearby St Stephen's College – that the Japanese interned British prisoners of war. Near the cemetery is St Stephen's Beach, a cleaner and more pleasant place for relax-ing than Stanley's main beach.

Beyond Stanley

The beaches past Stanley are a little less accessible and therefore less crowded. To reach them, head north along Tai Tam Road past the **Tai Tam Reservoir**. Though the Tai Tam is the largest of the three reservoirs on Hong Kong Island, with a storage capability of 6.2 million cubic metres, the reservoir could only meet Hong Kong's water consumption needs for three days. In fact, most of Hong Kong's water supply comes via huge pipes from across the border in China. The area around the reservoir is hilly and picturesque and includes the Tai Tam Country Park, a popular picnic and hiking spot.

Tai Tam Road eventually leads up to the eastern town of Chai Wan, or you can head back south along Shek O Road, skirting Mount Collinson on the left and Tai Tam Harbour to the right for Hong Kong's most southerly beaches, Shek O and Big Wave Bay. At a fork in the road, you can go right about six kilometres to Big Wave Bay, a beautiful beach with no public transport to it. The Shek O beach and village, about the same distance from the fork, can be reached by pub-lic bus, and Big Wave Bay's beach is a 30-minute walk from Shek O.

The marketplace at **Shek O Village ❺** is a modest collection of shops selling beach paraphernalia. There are also some restaurants with seats outdoors and places to rent bicycles. What the market and beach hide, though, are some truly luxurious homes. Stroll out to Shek O Headland, facing the islands of Tai Tau Chau and Ng Fan Chau. To the right is the southernmost point of the island, **Cape D'Aguilar**. Up until the early 1990s, Vietnamese refugee boats could be seen around here as they drifted toward shore and what they hoped was freedom. ❑

Kowloon

0		400 m
0		400 yds

KOWLOON

The peninsula of Kowloon is one of the most densely populated places on earth. It feels as Hong Kong should

Kowloon means "nine dragons". In the 13th century, China was overrun by the Mongols from the north, and the boy-emperor Di Ping of the Song dynasty (960–1279) fled to Hong Kong. Ping counted eight mountains in the area now called Kowloon, and as Chinese believe dragons reside inside mountains he called them the Eight Dragons. His chief minister pointed out that an emperor is considered to be a dragon, thus there were nine dragons. At Sung Wong Toi Park, near the former international airport at Kai Tak, is a rock with the inscription "Sung Wong Toi", or "Emperor Song's Terrace". This is where Ping's chief minister, to avoid capture by the Mongols, took the young emperor into his arms and jumped into the sea, thereby bringing an end to the Song dynasty.

Much of Hong Kong exists on reclaimed land, and as the government's answer to Kowloon's shortage of usable land is to grind down mountains and push this earth into the sea, so the eight dragons are rather less visible than they used to be.

The southern tip of Kowloon Peninsula, stretching as far north as Mong Kok, was ceded to the British "in perpetuity" in 1856. In the 1860s, Russia, Germany, France and Japan began carving out spheres of influence for themselves in China, and the British, determined to make Kowloon more secure, forced China to lease the New Territories and what's called New Kowloon to Britain for 99 years.

Kowloon itself is just a few square kilometres or so in size, but it is one of the most crowded and developed areas in the world. At the tip of the peninsula is Tsim Sha Tsui, once a sharp, sandy point that is now a sprawling shopping district. Further north are the more traditional districts of Yau Ma Tei and Mong Kok, where street markets and old buildings have escaped demolition. On the eastern side of the peninsula are Tsim Sha Tsui East and Hung Hom, both built on reclaimed land, and almost exclusively a succession of luxury hotels, shopping centres, expensive restaurants and nightclubs.

Kowloon proper ends at Boundary Street in Mong Kok, which originally defined the frontier between Hong Kong and China. Although officially part of the New Territories, the districts immediately surrounding Boundary Street are more commonly known as New Kowloon. Most of the area is crammed with densely populated housing estates and shopping malls, strangely juxtaposed with historic architecture, temples and archaeological ruins.

The closure of Kai Tak Airport in 1998 initiated the redevelopment of Kowloon City and Kowloon Tong, where height restrictions had preserved old tenements for decades. ❑

PRECEDING PAGES: all that glitters in Tsim Sha Tsui.

KOWLOON

Lacking the towering high-rises of Hong Kong Island across the harbour, Kowloon's Tsim Sha Tsui, Yau Ma Tei, and Mong Kok nevertheless define the chaos and bustle of Hong Kong

Map,
page 176

Kowloon is one of the world's most densely populated urban areas, both with residents and perhaps with tourists shopping until they drop. Save for the waterfront, it is not an especially attractive place. But few can deny the electricity that charges life here, especially at night. The districts of most interest to travellers are Tsim Sha Tsui, Yau Ma Tei and Mong Kok.

Tsim Sha Tsui

Traditionalists will start their wanderings through Kowloon's Tsim Sha Tsui district at the **Star Ferry Pier ❶**, from where the Star Ferry makes the quick crossing from Victoria Harbour to Central, on Hong Kong Island. An obvious landmark and reference point is the adjacent **Railway Clock Tower**. Dating from the early 1900s, the tower is the final vestige of the historic Kowloon-Canton Railway Station, once the Asian terminus of the *Orient Express* to London. In the mid 1970s, it was replaced by a new station to the east, at Hung Hom.

Immediately behind the tower is the in-your-face **Hong Kong Cultural Centre ❷**, a minimalist structure with a sweeping concave roof spoilt by ugly tiles, not to mention its spoiling of the harbour view. Its construction caused a great deal of controversy in 1984, as it was designed without windows on what is perhaps the best harbour location in Hong Kong.

Nonetheless, it is there to stay and to be used. For example, during the Hong Kong Arts Festival in January and February, the centre stages local and international opera, classical music, theatre and dance.

This complex also houses the **Hong Kong Space Museum ❸** (open Monday, Wednesday–Friday, 1–9pm, weekends, 10am–9pm, closed Tuesday; tel: 2721 0226; entrance fee, but free on Wednesday), with daily showings of Omnimax movies on space travel and exhibitions of Chinese astronomical inventions. The **Hong Kong Museum of Art ❹** (open Friday–Wednesday, 10am–6pm, closed Thursday; tel: 2721 0116; entrance fee, but free on Wednesday) displays traditional and contemporary calligraphy and painting, along with historic photographs, prints and artifacts of Hong Kong, Macau and Guangzhou. Other galleries exhibit Chinese antiquities and travelling exhibitions of fine art.

On a less cultural note, the **Teddy Bear Kingdom** (open daily, 10am–10pm; tel: 2130 2130; entrance fee), just north of the Space Museum, provides a fun display of teddy bears from around the world, including the world's smallest bear and the most expensive one encrusted with diamonds and plated with gold. For an extra charge you can pick fabric, clothes and accessories and stuff, stitch and dress your own bear.

One of the unfortunate losers to suffer from the construction of the Cultural Centre was the venerable

PREVIOUS PAGES: concert rehearsal. **OPPOSITE:** Nathan Road neon. **BELOW:** the Railway Clock Tower and Cultural Centre.

Peninsula Hotel ❺, directly across Salisbury Road. Its exquisite rooms lost their classic harbour view; a new tower wing, however, rises above the blocked view. Built in 1928, the Peninsula was where people stayed before boarding the train. A sumptuous gilt-corniced lobby is accented by a string quartet on the balcony.

Situated immediately north of the Star Ferry Pier is **Star House ❻**, where *cheongsams,* porcelain, and what appears to be almost every conceivable kind of Chinese handicraft available, may be purchased at the huge Chinese Arts and Crafts store. Adjoining Star House on Canton Road is the mammoth **Harbour City ❼** complex, encompassing **Ocean Terminal** and **Ocean Centre** and filled with hotels, antique stores and designer boutiques.

From the Star Ferry Pier eastward along the harbour, a waterfront promenade extends past the Cultural Centre and Intercontinental Hotel towards **Tsim Sha Tsui East** and **Hung Hom Bay**, a stretch of reclaimed land packed with hotels, offices and shops. This provides a great vantage point for viewing one of the most spectacular cityscapes in the world. In Hung Hom, the **Kowloon-Canton Railway Station ❽**, built in 1975, is where trains depart for China and the New Territories. The **Cross-Harbour Tunnel** between Hong Kong Island and Kowloon emerges immediately west of the station. Ten minutes' walk from the station is **Hung Hom Ferry Pier ❾**, with services to Central, Wan Chai and North Point.

Behind Hung Hom Ferry Pier is **Whampoa Gardens**, a commercial and residential project built around the old Kowloon Dockyard, which operated from 1870 to 1984. With added landfill, the dock now has a 100-metre-long concrete "ship" filled with shops, restaurants and gardens.

The Cross-Harbour Tunnel took three years to construct and cost US$427 million. Of the harbour's three tunnels, it remains the busiest with over 150,000 vehicles passing through it every day.

BELOW: on the waterfront promenade.

The unusual-looking inverted pyramid situated on the harbour side of the railway station is the **Hong Kong Coliseum ⑩**, a huge 12,000-seat indoor stadium that features sell-out concerts by Canto-pop idols. Millions of dollars are spent on staging spectacular floor shows with dancers, elaborate costume changes, and hi-tech lasers and lights darting around the place. Seeing one of these concerts could be one of the more fascinating sights a traveller might encounter in Hong Kong, giving a different perspective on the local lifestyle.

West along Cheong Wan Road is the **Hong Kong Science Museum ⑪** (open Monday–Wednesday, Friday, 1–9pm, weekends, 10am–9pm, closed Thursday; tel: 2732 3232; entrance fee, but free on Wednesday), displaying more than 500 scientific and technological interactive exhibits, including robotics, computers, phones, a miniature submarine and a DC-3 airplane engine. Just opposite is the **Hong Kong Museum of History ⑫** (open Monday, Wednesday–Saturday, 10am–6pm, Sunday and public holidays, 10am–7pm, closed Tuesday; tel: 2724 9042; entrance fee, but free on Wednesday). The museum documents the 6,000-year story of Hong Kong from neolithic times right up to the 1997 handover. There are some fascinating displays including lifelike mock-ups of old-style tea houses, cinemas and a Cantonese opera stage. West of the Science Museum across Chatham Road, the **Rosary Church ⑬**, completed in 1888, is one of Hong Kong's most historic Catholic churches. Morning and evening masses are conducted in Cantonese and English.

Tsim Sha Tsui East has numerous hostess bars where wealthy men pay an extortionate sum for the company of a hostess. During the mid-1980s, one of them reluctantly changed its name from Club Volvo to Club Bboss after a long drawn-out lawsuit filed by Volvo, the Swedish car manufacturer, over the name.

Map, page 176

TIP

If you are a rambling male and roaming the streets of Tsim Sha Tsui East, give serious thought before entering a place of drink and pleasure. You may not have enough cash on hand to pay the bill for services not rendered.

BELOW: Nathan Road, electrified.

Up Nathan Road

At the bottom of **Nathan Road**, where it intersects Salisbury Road next to the Peninsula Hotel, begins myriad dazzling neon signs jutting out of buildings for as far as the eye can see. Tailor shops, jewellers, camera and stereo stores, hundreds of them, are crammed along Nathan Road and the surrounding maze of streets. The experience of joining the tide of window-shoppers through these streets amid dripping air-conditioners, blasting Canto-pop, honking cars, pavement hawkers and the relentless touts' offers of "Copy watch, massage, suit, madam/sir?" is one that few travellers forget. For those still hankering after Suzie Wong, only a few retro girlie bars are left. The classic topless bar and tourist trap Bottoms Up, on Hankow Road, is where James Bond was filmed sipping a martini in *The Man with the Golden Gun*. It's a time-warp that takes you back to the 1970s with its plush red-velvet seating and curtains and circular counter bars.

There are hundreds of excellent restaurants hereabouts, ranging from haute cuisine in five-star hotels to inexpensive stands dishing out noodles and rice. Try local delicacies such as *daan tart* (egg custard tarts), baked fresh daily, with a glass of iced soya milk for a typically Chinese afternoon snack.

Tsim Sha Tsui is also home to a series of run-down mansion blocks, oddly wedged in amongst the shops and luxurious hotels, the most infamous being **Chungking Mansions** ⑭, a teeming labyrinth of cheap guesthouses, curry restaurants, sweat-shops and *sari* stores. Reviled by many as a haven for lowlife, it is also the scourge of property developers, who are powerless to evict the residents, many of whom come from Pakistan, India, Nepal and Africa. For a number of years, Chungking Mansions has also been the temporary abode of the most thrifty of budget travellers.

A few minutes' further north along Nathan Road is **Kowloon Park** ⑮, offering a Chinese garden with lotus ponds, a chess garden, and an aviary (open daily, 6.30am–8pm) housing a colourful collection of rare birds. The Sculpture Walk displays work by local artists.

In the southeastern corner of the park is **Kowloon Mosque** ⑯, with its four minarets and large, white-marble dome gracefully standing out from the clutter of shops and restaurants. Built in 1984, it serves the territory's 50,000 Muslims, of whom about half are Chinese. The original mosque building, built in 1894, served the British army's Muslim Indian troops.

Yau Ma Tei

From Tsim Sha Tsui, Nathan Road slips into Yau Ma Tei. In the neighbourhood where it intersects Jordan Road, Canton Road – which begins at the Star Ferry Pier and runs north towards Yau Ma Tei – has jade and ivory shops selling *mahjong* sets. Shanghai Street still has shops selling red Chinese wedding dresses, embroidered pillow cases and other items for a Chinese bride's *trousseau*. Where Shanghai Street intersects Saigon Street is Tak Sang Pawn Shop, a World War II-vintage building where for decades gamblers have pawned their worldly possessions to pay off loan sharks.

Ning Po Street and Reclamation Street are famous for paper models of houses, cars, and notes from Hell Bank that are burnt at funerals, so as to assure that the deceased

Hong Kong has been the chief watching point (of the Cultural Revolution) for the outside world. Last week the British Crown Colony suddenly lost its spectator status. From the colony's teeming Kowloon district, thousands of pro-Maoist Chinese poured into the streets to harass Hong Kong's British rulers...

– TIME, 26 MAY 1967

BELOW: night chef.

will be well-off in the after-life. At the junction of Kansu and Battery streets is the **jade market** (open daily, 9am–6pm), packed with stalls selling jade objects. Dealers offer jade in every sculptable form, from large blocks of the raw material to tiny, ornately carved chips. Unless you are an expert, take along a Hong Kong Tourist Board information leaflet on jade, and spend wisely as not all the artifacts on offer are genuine. The best time to go is in the morning.

Shanghai Street continues north into an area once famous for its temples, now renowned for the **night market** ⓲ that lights up after dusk. Palmists, physiognomists, and a fortune-teller whose trained bird selects slips of paper to predict the future vie to reveal your destiny. This area has countless open-air restaurants, where oysters, prawns, clams, lobsters and fish are laid out on beds of ice from which diners choose.

Over a century old, the **Tin Hau Temple** ⓳ complex (open daily, 7am–5.30pm) is in Public Square Street. This is Hong Kong's main Tin Hau temple (there are scores throughout the territory), originally built closer to the harbour. Land reclamation forced it to move inland to here. Locals still visit it regularly to worship Tin Hau, the protector of fisherfolk and whose image is draped in intricately embroidered scarlet robes. To the right of the altar are 60 identical deities that represent every year of the 60-year lunar calendar. Worshippers place Hell Bank notes under the god dedicated to the years of their birth. Another temple in the complex was built to honour Shing Wong, the local city god, and the Ten Judges of the Underworld, depicted with human torsos and animal heads. The Fook Tak Temple is dedicated to Fook Tak, an earth god, and Guanyin, the goddess of mercy. Shea Tan Temple is dedicated to a protector of the community.

Map, page 176

Shanghai Street is full of shops that specialise in wedding attire. In the old days, Chinese brides wore red – the colour of good fortune. White, the Western bride's colour, is a sign of mourning in China.

BELOW: the night market.

**Map,
page 176**

Mong Kok

Mong Kok, north of Yau Ma Tei, is one of the most crowded, noisy and lively districts of Kowloon. In the early days of British rule, *gweilos* – foreign devils – seldom ventured past Yau Ma Tei and even today, Mong Kok is notorious for triad gangs, illegal gambling dens and assorted sleaze. Nevertheless, this predominantly Chinese neighbourhood has retained many characteristics of old Hong Kong – markets, small shops and food stalls that have long since disappeared from other areas.

After extensive land reclamation along the harbour front, low-class prostitution moved from the floating sampans of the **Typhoon Shelter ㉑** to triad-run karaoke bars, sauna and massage parlours around Nelson and Portland streets. Yellow signs in Chinese advertising "one-woman brothels" or "one-floor, one phoenix" are continually being torn down by the police, who nonetheless are fighting a losing battle, as prostitution in private flats – where many of these sleaze joints are located – is not strictly illegal.

On the east side of Nathan Road, on Tung Choi Street, the so-called **ladies' market ㉑** (open daily, noon–10.30pm) sells everything from fake designer accessories and clothing to cheap cosmetics and toys. It is also a popular area for late-night snacks; restaurants and takeaway carts display delicious noodles, seafood and congee. Tai Wo Restaurant (No.105) has desserts and herbal teas to revitalise health.

Hundreds of colourful song birds in beautifully crafted cages can be seen at the famous **bird market ㉒** (open daily, 10am–6pm), on the other side of Nathan Road on Yuen Po Street, about ten minutes' walk from the Prince Edward MTR station. ❑

BELOW: bird market.

Jade

Jade can be found everywhere in Hong Kong: street markets, antique stores, department stores. But jade was formerly the preserve of China's elite. Belief in the powerful essence of jade in China is nearly as old as Chinese civilisation itself, and its prominence in Chinese art and literature attests to its long-standing value. The ancient Chinese prized jade objects for the aesthetic beauty of the stone, the skill needed to carve it, and for the magical properties that it was believed to possess.

Most jewellery was made from jade, favoured over gems and precious metals, and some people held that the stone glowed with the vitality of the owner or became tarnished if the wearer fell ill. The Chinese have long believed that wearing jade ornaments imparts good health, good luck and protection from evil spirits. According to early ritual texts, jade jewellery was thought to exhibit the character of a gentleman, and the sound of jade clinking together as he walked required a balanced and dignified pace.

Jade carving was one of the earliest art forms to attain a degree of refinement. Jade probably reached its early zenith as central objects used in the ostentatious burials of the Han dynasty (206 BC to AD 220). Subsequently, jade work was eclipsed by other art forms until a mini-revival championed by the Qing emperor Qianlong (1735 to 1796), who prized jade carvings.

There are two types of jade: jadeite and nephrite. Early jade objects were carved from nephrite, a softer form of jade that can be worked with primitive tools.

One of the earliest known jade artifacts is known as a *bi*, a carved jade disk with a hole in the centre. There is no way of knowing the bi's origin, but its circular shape later came to represent the harmony between heaven and earth. The jade bi is one of China's most enduring ritual symbols; its use continued through the imperial era, becoming more fanciful in later periods, often with dragons crouched in vivid stance on the circumference of the bi.

RIGHT: pieces of jade at Hong Kong jade market.

The jade centrepiece of the Shang era is most definitely the gold-threaded jade burial shroud. It was believed that jade could preserve the body, and the suits were made of hundreds of square pieces of jade sewn together at the corners with thread of either gold, silver or bronze. The entire body was covered and usually there were additional jade pieces for all body orifices; a jade cicada was often placed on the tongue.

The best jade artifacts were crafted from the more valuable and harder jadeite. The hardness of the stone contrasts with the patient technique and dexterity needed to carve it; finished pieces appear as if shaped from something as soft as butter rather than one of the toughest minerals on earth, making jade artifacts true treasures.

The most well-known single piece of jade is Jade Mountain of the Great Yu Taming the Flood. According to records, the uncut stone was discovered in Xinjiang province and weighed more than five tons, requiring more than three years to transport to Beijing and six years for a team of artisans to carve. ❏

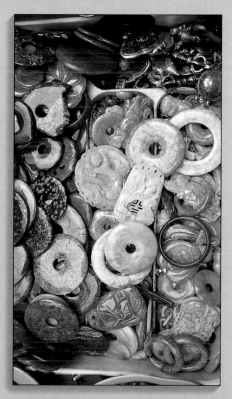

CHINA

Hong Kong

NEW KOWLOON

*Once anchored by Hong Kong's international airport,
the districts at the upper end of Kowloon Peninsula are off the
beaten tourist track, but they are worth exploration*

Kai Tak opened in 1936, and was expanded by the Japanese during World War II. Because of Kai Tak's proximity, building heights in Kowloon were restricted, and no flashing signs or lights were permitted in the area.

BELOW: Kowloon City, near the old Kai Tak Airport.

Situated at the centre of what's commonly called New Kowloon is the sad-looking site of Kai Tak, Hong Kong's former international airport. The runway was built so close to the apartment blocks of Kowloon City and Lok Fu that those of a nervous disposition were advised to avoid looking out of the window when coming into land. The airport site is slated for redevelopment beginning at the end of 2003, when it will be transformed into a massive housing estate and parkland.

Around Kowloon Tong KCR (Kowloon-Canton Railway) Station, and on Waterloo Road and Dorset Crescent, are the infamous Kowloon love motels. These motels are discreetly situated behind high walls and security cameras, and cars of guests are covered up to hide the license plate numbers. Tinted windows and curtains hide luxurious rooms rented by the hour, and the rooms themselves are kitted out with circular beds, jacuzzis, and twin tub baths.

Kowloon City ㉓ is best seen on foot, starting at Lok Fu MTR Station. Walk up Wang Tau Hom East Road as far as Junction Road, then turn left and continue west. Along Junction Road, the **Chinese Christian Cemetery** on the left is a stark reminder of the lack of space in Hong Kong, with graves stacked up like sardines on concrete terraces.

Map, page 176

Next door to the cemetery is the tiny **Hau Wong Temple** (open daily, 8am–5pm) with traditional roof tiles and incense spirals hanging from the rafters. Built in 1730, the temple is dedicated to Yang Liang Jie, a loyal and courageous general of the exiled Song dynasty's (960–1279) boy-emperor Ping. The general's birthday is celebrated on the 16th day of the sixth month on the lunar calendar. The temple keeper acts as a medium interpreting the advice of Hau Wong by means of *kay fook* – praying for the god's blessing.

Continue past the temple for 10 minutes until the junction with Carpenter Road, then turn left and head past Kowloon City Plaza on the left towards **Kowloon City Walled Park** ㉔. Before the British arrived in 1841, the old – and still infamous – **Walled City** was already governed by a Manchu magistrate, and therefore it was excluded from the treaty that granted Britain the New Territories on a 99-year lease. At first, Qing dynasty (1644–1911) officials continued to be posted in the City. In 1899, however, British forces were dispatched to invade the city, and the Qing officials and troops were expelled.

In the early days of colonial rule, British law was never fully implemented in the confines of the Walled City, and the area deteriorated into a "City of Darkness", a semi-lawless enclave which was left to its own governance. After World War II, low-rise blocks built without authority and completely lacking proper foundations sprang up on the site, resulting in a multi-storey squatter area with unauthorised electricity and water supplies. By the 1950s, the dank alleyways of the city became a notorious haven for drug addicts, triad gangs, illegal immigrants, and unlicensed doctors and dentists.

The Walled City remained a thorn in the side of the British. Beijing and even Taiwan vehemently opposed plans for its demolition during the 1980s, as both countries regarded the Walled City as Chinese territory. However, in 1987, with China's consent, 35,000 residents were gradually resettled in housing estates, with several tenants forcibly removed by the police, and the entire block was bulldozed to the ground. Fortunately, several remnants of the infamous Walled City – the foundation of the former wall, the foundations of the south and east gates, and a flagstone path next to the drainage ditch running along the foot of the inner wall – have been preserved in the Kowloon City Walled Park.

This beautiful park, modelled on the Jiangnan garden style of the early Qing dynasty, features a chess garden as well as the Mountain View Pavilion, from which **Lion Rock** can be seen looming in the distance. Near the southern gate, an information centre also houses a photo exhibition showing the history of the Walled City and the construction of the park, plus many relics used or found within the Walled City. Two old cannons and a stone couplet from Longjin Free School, which was once a feature of the Walled City, are displayed outside.

Kowloon City is known for cheap, rough-and-ready restaurants that serve dishes within minutes of ordering. If you do not mind noise or sharing a table with strangers, then the area has an enormous range of inexpensive and highly-rated Chinese, Vietnamese, and especially Thai restaurants. There is a growing Thai immigrant community which has opened up scores of

Public cemeteries permit bodies to stay for only seven years, then they must be dug up and cremated, or buried in an urn. The private Chinese Christian Cemetery, however, offers a permanent spot for upwards of US$80,000.

BELOW: working face, Kowloon.

Thai supermarkets, restaurants, fast-food hole-in-the-walls and dodgy karaoke bars – there's even a Thai baht exchange booth here. Farther east, massive housing projects and the Lung Cheung Road contrast with the scenic hills of Lion Rock in the distance.

A Lucky Temple

One of Kowloon's most colourful and popular places of worship, the **Wong Tai Sin Temple** ㉕ (open daily, 7am–5.30pm), sits opposite an MTR station in the neighbouring district bearing the same name. Wong Tai Sin, the Daoist god of healing, is said to have discovered the secret of transforming cinnabar (vermillion, a red mercuric sulfide) into an elixir for immortality. A painting of the god was brought to Hong Kong from China in 1915 and was first placed in a small temple in Wan Chai, before being moved to Wong Tai Sin. Backed by the formidable Lion Rock and facing the sea, geomancers agreed that this new site had favourable *feng shui*.

So much money was raised from the temple's donation boxes that the old site, built in 1921, was demolished and a new temple was constructed in 1973. The bright yellow roof tiling is from China's Guangdong province, and the main temple has a ceiling of panelled pinewood from Burma, with bold red pillars supporting the roof and ceiling. The rear of the temple's main altar is carved to show, both pictorially and in calligraphy, the story of this great god. There are two Chinese gardens surrounding the temple and a Confucian hall next door.

Since Wong Tai Sin is also the god of good fortune, the Chinese, who are too cautious to rely solely on luck, flock to the temple to ask him for advice on all matters, including horseracing tips and stockmarket trends. The sound of rat-

Chim, or fortune-telling sticks.

BELOW: Wong Tai Sin Temple.

Map, page 176

tling *chim* – a container holding dozens of fortune sticks – resounds all day long, as people shake them until a single bamboo stick falls out of the container. These sticks each have a number that is later interpreted by a fortune-teller at one of the rented stalls.

The **Chi Lin Nunnery** (Diamond Hill MTR Station, 5 Chi Lin Drive) is the largest Buddhist nunnery in Southeast Asia, bringing to life the artistic and architectural achievements of the Tang dynasty (618–907) from more than 1,000 years ago. Built on an area of 33,000 square metres (355,000 sq ft), the nunnery comprises a number of Buddhist halls serving various religious functions and a tranquil garden with lotus ponds in front of the main entrance. The Hall of Celestial Kings houses a statue of the Maitreya Buddha (Milefo), the Buddha of the Future and a heavenly being who will descend to Earth to save humanity. Guardians of the Four Directions surround him. On the left is a hall commemorating the goddess of mercy, Guanyin, who sits inside a grotto. On the right is Baishiyaja Guru (Medicine Master) accompanied by the Sun and Moon *bodhisattvas,* Buddhist redemption deities. The Sakyamuni Buddha rests on a lotus altar in the Main Hall. The Wan Fo Pagoda has a cast-bronze weather vane and wind chimes, and its seven tiers symbolise a gradual process of ascent in the eventual purification of the mind.

An ingenious project of "one wish, one tile" raised millions of dollars for fired-clay tiles imported from Japan. Rich and poor alike contributed at least HK$100 to have their wishes for good fortune, longevity, health, and world peace painted under the tiles before they were placed on the roof. The proceeds helped pay for the new roof. The complex includes a nursing home and clinic for the elderly, the nuns' living quarters, a Buddhist library and research centre,

BELOW: burning incense at Wong Tai Sin Temple.

Map, page 176

After the Communists took control of China in 1949, Hong Kong witnessed confrontations between refugees from China and Communist supporters. In 1967, four months of riots broke out, centred in Kowloon and initiated by labour unions sympathetic to Mao and the Communists.

and a special school for students with learning difficulties. A souvenir shop sells Buddha images, charms, beads, and books.

Sham Shui Po and Cheung Sha Wan

The old districts of Sham Shui Po and Cheung Sha Wan are situated to the east of Mong Kok, and even today, they remain areas that are off the beaten track. However, they provide a challenging alternative to the tourist spots of Hong Kong Island and Tsim Sha Tsui, and are of significant interest for discovering the turbulent history of the territory.

At **Sham Shui Po** ㉖ one can see the development of Hong Kong's architecture from grim H-block resettlement estates hastily constructed in the 1950s to clean, modern apartment blocks erected in the 1980s. Sham Shui Po Police Station, at Lai Chi Kok Road and Yen Chow Street, is one of Kowloon's remaining colonial pre-war buildings. During World War II, the station was occupied and used by the Japanese to interrogate prisoners-of-war, and nowadays residents report a ghostly British soldier wandering around at night.

If looking for a drink and a bite to eat, try the Garden Bakery and Restaurant, located at the intersection between Yen Chow Street and Castle Peak Road. This was the site of the 1956 riots that broke out at the nearby **Lei Cheng Uk Housing Estate** when pro-Communist union members set fire to a Nationalist flag and burned down the original Garden Bakery.

The Nationalist Party (Guomintang) had overthrown the Qing dynasty in 1911, but after suffering defeat by Communist forces in civil war (1945–1949), Chiang Kaishek, the Nationalist Party leader, fled to Taiwan, taking with him the entire gold reserves of the country and some two million supporters. Thousands of refugees flooded into Hong Kong to escape persecution at the hands of the Communists, increasing the territory's population by 2.5 million. During the 1950s and 1960s, periodic outbreaks of violence flared up between these newly arrived immigrants and Communist Party sympathisers, who blamed Chiang Kaishek and his Nationalists, now living on the island of Taiwan, for the tragic events of World War II.

Lei Cheng Uk Housing Estate is also home to amazing archeological discoveries made in 1955 by workers flattening the hillside upon which the estate was built. The **Lei Cheng Uk Tomb** (museum open Monday–Saturday, 10am–1pm, 2–6pm, Sunday, 1–6pm, closed Thursday; Tonkin Street; free) is a Han dynasty burial vault over 2,000 years old. It dates back to between AD 100 and 200, when Kowloon was under the administrative control of the Wu Empire, which took control of southern China (including Hong Kong) in the period immediately following the collapse of the Han empire. Four barrel-vaulted chambers form a cross under a domed vault, and there are a few funerary exhibits on show.

Interior of the vault of the Lei Cheng Uk Tomb.

Sham Shui Po is undoubtedly the best place in Hong Kong for computer software and hardware, and most arcades and stalls can be found on Yen Chow Street and Apliu Street (Sham Shui Po MTR Station). The police carry out frequent raids in these computer arcades to confiscate illegal Chinese-made software and video games, but the next day, these pirated goods resurface and it's business as usual.

All along Apliu Street, there is an open-air market selling loads of cheap electrical goods from secondhand stereos and computers to electric fans and clocks. Many of the latest compact disc and DVD players, Walkmans and television sets are *sui foh* – goods imported directly from Japan instead of through an agent and therefore available at much lower prices. Rip-offs do occur though, and it would be advisable to check all items before parting with too much of your cash. ❑

OPPOSITE: fond greetings.

NEW TERRITORIES

*Just the name suggests a frontier. Indeed, the New Territories
long served as a buffer between the British colony and China*

As anyone who has ever been to the New Territories (Sun Gaai in Cantonese) soon finds out, the glittering harbourside shopping malls of downtown Hong Kong are really just a glossy cover illustration masking a richer, deeper interior. The New Territories' 794 square kilometres (304 sq mi) encompass deserted beaches, winding trails stretching across empty hills, and stone-house villages that move to a rhythm centuries removed from modern Hong Kong. While much of the agricultural land has disappeared – either for industrial use or absorbed by new towns – some seven percent of Hong Kong is farmland, producing a quarter of the vegetables consumed here each year.

The New Territories is by no means a rural idyll, however. From the tops of the high hills beckon the skyscraping housing blocks of the New Towns, huge dormitories that have metamorphosed from what were once country markets or little fishing villages.

The New Territories became a part of Britain's colonial empire in 1898 when the British leased the area for 99 years from China, an arrangement that came to an end with considerable fanfare in 1997. However, the area's name remains unchanged. Officially, the New Territories included the area right down to Boundary Street in Kowloon, but since Kowloon has spread its tentacles out in all directions, nobody considers anything south of the Nine Dragons – the mountain peaks from which Kowloon takes its name – part of the New Territories.

It's worth noting that just as the New Territories is physically separate from Hong Kong and Kowloon, its long-time residents regard themselves as a race apart. The British had to put down armed uprisings by the locals after the lease was granted, and there is still a feeling of tradition and respect for the old ways and values here.

Recent development has divided the New Territories into three distinct segments. The western side, which has always been the most industrial, is being transformed by infrastructure projects connected with the new airport at Chek Lap Kok, on Lantau Island. The centre, dominated by new towns like Sha Tin and Tai Po, is the main route by road and rail up to China. The east around Sai Kung and Clear Water Bay is where the New Territories' most traditional character endures. All these areas are well covered by public transport, so it is simply a matter of deciding which area to explore first. ❑

PRECEDING PAGES: a misty winter's morning on the KCR rail line.

NEW TERRITORIES: CENTRE

Taking the Kowloon-Canton Railway right up the centre of the New Territories leads to the rest of China. Along the way are Hong Kong's largest shopping mall, nature preserves, and old traditions

Map, page 196

The most logical route to the central part of the New Territories is to take the Kowloon-Canton Railway (KCR) from Kowloon straight up the middle of the New Territories, through the Sha Tin Valley, past the coastal town of Tai Po and up to Sheung Shui, within sight of the border with Guangdong province. Passengers can get off the train at any of the stations along the route, then hop onto a bus or a taxi to explore farther afield.

As the train pulls out of Kowloon, the city seems to thin out a little before the track is suddenly engulfed by the tunnel under **Lion Rock**. At the other end of the tunnel, the carriages burst out into a valley that once grew rice specially for the emperor of China's table. Although there is not much chance of seeing rice paddies today, the scenery makes it obvious that the dense urban metropolis has been left behind.

Sha Tin ❶ is one of Hong Kong's fastest-growing New Towns, but it also offers plenty of recreation. Massive housing projects occupy what were once rice paddies, while the New Town Plaza, an extensive shopping and entertainment complex, offers cinemas, designer boutiques and a musical fountain that never fails to draw astounded crowds.

The Sha Tin Valley has several places of worship, three of which are especially worthy of note. First is the **Temple of 10,000 Buddhas ❷**, which can be reached by climbing 431 steps flanked by gold-painted effigies of enlightened beings up the hillside above the Sha Tin Railway Station. The temple's main altar room actually has 12,800 small Buddha statues along its walls. The temple is guarded by huge, fierce-looking statues of various gods, and by similarly fierce watchdogs that are chained up in the daytime. Also in the complex is a nine-storey pagoda of Indian architectural design, commemorating a Buddha who was believed to be the ninth reincarnation of Prince Vishnu.

A further 69 steps up the hill is the **Temple of Man Fat**, where visitors can see the preserved remains of the man who created this temple and pagoda complex: Yuet Kai, a monk who spent a lifetime studying Buddhism and living a meditative life. His greatest concern was to achieve immortality.

After his death, he was buried, but, according to Chinese custom, his body was later exhumed to be reburied in its final resting place. When the body was dug up for reburial, it was found to be perfectly preserved and radiating a ghostly yellow glow. Since there was obviously something supernatural about Yuet Kai, it was decided to preserve his body in gold leaf for posterity.

From the Temple of 10,000 Buddhas, you can look across the valley at the **Amah Rock**, so named because it looks like an *amah*, or nanny, with a baby on her back.

PREVIOUS PAGES: farm workers. **OPPOSITE:** light-rail station. **BELOW:** altar of Temple of 10,000 Buddhas.

Legend has it that a local fisherman once went to sea and did not return with his fleet. His wife waited patiently for his return day after day, but he did not appear. After a year the gods took pity on her and turned her into stone. Today the rock is a place of worship for Chinese women and stands as a symbol of women's loyalty and faithfulness.

Sha Tin and Tai Po

From either Amah Rock or the Temple of 10,000 Buddhas, one can look down on a third place of worship, one much more in tune with the present-day spirit of Hong Kong. This shrine is dedicated to Instant Wealth, or The Fast Buck, and it is the Hong Kong Jockey Club's (HKJC) **Sha Tin Racecourse ❸**. Thousands of punters (the grandstands hold 75,000) faithfully go there every September–June horse-racing season to bet money on the ponies and pray for good fortune. There is really only one winner in every race, however, and that is the many charities supported by the HKJC, which is a not-for-profit organisation.

The newest addition to Sha Tin's cultural scene is the **Heritage Museum** (open Monday–Saturday, 10am–6pm, Sunday, 10am–7pm, closed Tuesday, tel: 2180 8188; entrance fee, but free on Wednesday), opened in 2000, which includes a gallery of Chinese art, an exhibition entirely devoted to the New Territories, and another outlining the history of Cantonese Opera.

Another place of interest is the **Tsang Tai Uk ❹** (Mr Tsang's Big House), a walled village built in the mid-19th century by a wealthy quarry owner. As you emerge from the Lion Rock Tunnel from Kowloon, the village is on the right, just a stone's throw from the motorway. Actually, most of Tsang's progeny have moved elsewhere, and the fortress is now rented out to more distant relatives of

BELOW: shopping mall in Sha Tin.

his family. However, this remnant of the colony's opulent early days has been preserved despite the pile-driving march of high-rise development.

The village is rarely visited by tourists – making a trip all the more worthwhile – but the people here are hospitable and pleasant, and the whole complex is less commercially oriented than the more frequented Kam Tin walled village. Apart from a television aerial or two, some air-conditioning units and a soft-drink dispenser, one could imagine that there have been very few changes here in recent centuries.

From Sha Tin, the route along the Kowloon-Canton Railway heads north past the **Chinese University of Hong Kong**, with its highly respected art museum up on the hill, to the small market town of **Tai Po ❺**, which means "buying place". The town certainly lives up to its name, serving for many years as a place for farmers and fishermen to meet and exchange goods. But like many of the old market towns, it too has been developed.

The old town lies at the northeastern end of Tolo Harbour where the highway crosses the Lower Lam Tsuen River. On the northeast side of the river is Tai Po Market, with a huge fish section and dozens of vegetable stalls. Fu Shing Street will give the visitor a good idea of market town life in the New Territories; it is packed with shops selling everything from rattan furniture to the so-called thousand-year-old eggs.

The **Hong Kong Railway Museum** (open daily except Tuesday, 9am–5pm; tel: 2653 3455; free), complete with vintage train carriages, is housed in the former station. Not far away, but with its own railway station, is Tai Po Kau. From here, or from the train, you can see the departure and return of the fishing fleet. Like all the New Towns, Tai Po is undergoing the transition from an old market town to a modern city; its current population is more than 250,000 and rising.

The call of the wild

One of the greatest surprises of this very urban enclave is the **Tai Po Kau Nature Reserve ❻**, a 20-minute walk from the car park near the 14-mile stone on Tai Po Road. The oldest of Hong Kong's reserves, planting began in 1926 as part of the government's attempt to reforest the New Territories. Today, it is a prime example of the flora and fauna here. Spread over 460 hectares are native species such as litsea, giant bean, sweet gum and *Castanopsis fissa*, which was once used to make agricultural implements, as well as the more exotic camphor, acacia and paperbark. The joss-stick tree (*Aquilania sinensis*) was used for making fans and joss sticks, and it is thought to be behind Hong Kong's meaning of "fragrant harbour".

One of the real delights of the reserve is that some of the native species change colour in the winter. At Christmas time, some of the dark-green foliage turns yellow and orange, but by the spring they have turned light green again as the new leaves break into bud.

Animals, while rarely spotted, do live here in some numbers. At least a dozen species of birds – from bulbuls to magpies – make the reserve their home, while barking deer, civet cat, pangolin and porcupine have been sighted in the recent past. More visible is the population of langur monkeys, who often make their presence known if you

Map, page 196

Hardworking Hakka women dressed in samfoo (black pyjama-like suits), their faces framed by black curtains around the brims of their wide hats, work alongside men on construction sites. These women come from a traditional matriarchal society and think nothing of labouring at jobs that outsiders consider to be fit for men only.

BELOW: Hakka woman.

are having a picnic. They can be aggressive, and to combat this and their increasing numbers, giving food to wild monkeys was banned in 1999.

The reserve is well-kept, with colour-coded signposts guiding visitors along easy trails that range in length from one to 10 kilometres (6 mi). To guard against fire, there are no barbecue pits within the reserve, so a stroll through the woodland glades is a very peaceful and litter-free outing.

To the east, the coast around **Tai Pang Wan** (Mirs Bay) is largely undeveloped because it's well off the beaten track. Its population clings to traditional ways of earning a living such as fishing and vegetable farming. At one stage, this area was notorious for smuggling and as a point of entry for illegal immigrants swimming over from China. Nowadays the underground activity seems to have diminished and beautiful scenery has taken its place as the area's claim to fame.

Ting Kok Road leading round to the Plover Cove Reservoir, Bride's Pool and Starling Inlet must rank among the most picturesque routes in Hong Kong. At weekends and on public holidays, the roadside barbecue areas are teeming with noisy groups on cook-outs in the countryside, but even then, a five-minute walk away into the hills brings peace and solitude. The area around Bride's Pool, with waterfalls and woodland glades, is especially beautiful, while the village of Luk Keng to the north still has several fine old houses inhabited by cackling ancients. The nearby village of Nam Chung marks the northern end of the **Wilson Trail**, a 78-kilometre-long (49 mi) walking route that runs from Stanley on Hong Kong island to the northern end of the New Territories.

The road from Luk Keng meets up with Sha Tau Kok Road, which runs back to **Fanling ❼**, the next major stop on the railway line after Tai Po. Fanling and its neighbour Sheung Shui are New Towns with close to a quarter million resi-

BELOW:
old-fashioned
mailboxes.

dents. Nearby is Luen Wo, the region's traditional marketplace. While elsewhere in Hong Kong the mall and council-built marketplace are the norm, here shoppers make their way through a maze of stalls and side alleys, stepping around produce laid out on the ground, surrounded by the loud cries of merchants.

Fanling is also the site of one of the New Territories' least-visited temples, **Fung Ying Sin Koon**, or Temple of Paradise. There is an intricate system of pathways and steps leading to the altar, and its grounds include many waterfalls and shady benches suitable for meditating. On a more earthly level, the Hong Kong Golf Club just outside Fanling has three exceptionally good 18-holers, known as the Old, the New and the Eden. It is the site of the Hong Kong Open Tournament every February.

While **Lo Wu** ❽ is the last stop in the Special Administrative Region on the KCR line before it crosses into China, it is off limits to casual tourists, and you may only go there if continuing to the mainland. So **Sheung Shui** ❾ is the northernmost stop permitted on the KCR, and in many ways it is much more China than Hong Kong. Rather than specific sightseeing spots, everywhere here is worth seeing for a sheer, gritty, down-to-earth glimpse of what life is like away from the glitz of coffee-table books and tourist brochures.

Bypass the Metropolis Plaza near the KCR station, which is just another air-conditioned shopping centre, and plunge into the food market off San Hong Street in the part of town known as Shek Wu Hui. Just about everything is up for sale here, from produce that was harvested from fields across the border a few hours ago down to live crabs and frogs. Among the other stalls nearby are traditional medicines for sale, cheap clothes and bags, and even the odd gentleman letter-writer who, for a small fee, will take dictation.

The other interesting part of Sheung Shui is Po Sheung Tsuen, a short walk away to the west. This old village with its 18th-century ancestral hall – still the focus of local life – is a conglomerate of a few shiny new houses and scores of dilapidated old ones, connected by narrow, twisting alleys. It is a fascinating example of what life is like for the "other half" in Hong Kong.

All around the New Territories, you'll see clusters of what appear to be huge pickle jars with wooden lids, sometimes six or eight parked on a hillside. These pots contain the bones of dead Chinese. These people were buried long ago, but several years later, their bones were exhumed and placed in jars here to await consignment to their final resting place. This process takes a long time, because the exact geographical arrangement of a grave is tremendously important.

Permanent graves, shaped like concrete armchairs, can be huge. They can be seen on hillsides, and if you stand by one the view is usually of the sea or a pleasant valley. The placement follows the principles of *feng shui*, the ancient Chinese art of geomancy. The departed relative is going to be stuck on that hillside forever, so to keep him or her happy, the descendants bury the body where it can enjoy a good view and favourable breezes – conditions that are increasingly difficult to find in Hong Kong, even for the living. The other reason for the long wait before a proper burial is that these graves cost a fortune. Like everything else in Hong Kong, death isn't cheap.❑

Map, page 196

BELOW: duck herder.

CHINA

Hong Kong

NEW TERRITORIES: WEST

Once a sleepy part of the New Territories, the western half is increasingly undergoing a transformation, mostly because it is the mainland's link with the new international airport on Lantau

For years, the Castle Peak side of the Kowloon Peninsula was cut off from the heart of Hong Kong by its inaccessibility. But Hong Kong's newest transportation link (opened in late 2003) – the 30.5km (20-mile) overland West Rail, linking north Kowloon with the whole region has changed all that. A few years earlier, huge reclamation and construction projects changed the map almost daily as road and rail links were built for the new airport. The most striking new arrival was the **Tsing Ma Bridge** ⑩, sometimes referred to as Hong Kong's "Golden Gate", which in 1997 linked Lantau Island (and its airport) to the mainland for the first time. Some 2.2 kilometres (1.4 miles) long, the bridge's 200-metre-high (650 ft) twin towers are visible along much of the highway in the New Territories that leads to Kwai Chung, an extensive complex of container terminals, and the industrial community of Tsuen Wan, an example of Hong Kong's New Town developments. This urban sprawl, home to one million Hong Kongers, is at the end of the Tsuen Wan MTR line.

The Chinese presence in **Tsuen Wan** ⑪ seems to have begun about the second century AD. In the 13th century, the Chinese empire stretched to this area because the Chinese emperor was being driven south by invading Mongols. In 1277, the emperor and his entourage arrived in Tsuen Wan. Later, in the mid

In addition to being the world's longest road-and-rail suspension bridge at 2.2 kilometres long, the Tsing Ma Bridge is also the world's heaviest at 55,000 tons.

BELOW: local neighbourhood alley.

Map, page 196

1600s when the Formosan pirate Koxinga was building his empire, the Manchu government ordered a mass evacuation of coastal areas to save the populace from the marauding buccaneer. Koxinga's forces demolished the vacated settlement of Tsuen Wan and it was not repopulated until the late 17th century. It's difficult to believe that only 100 years ago this now-sprawling urban centre's industry consisted of only 24 factories, producing incense powder and powered by waterwheels turned by streams running down the mountainside. The container terminals you see now were built entirely on reclaimed land.

Tsuen Wan is worth the long MTR journey if only to poke around the **Sam Tung Uk Museum** (open Monday-Sunday, 9am–5pm, closed Tuesday; free), a beautifully-restored Hakka walled village of some 200 years whose name means three-beamed dwelling. The narrow alleyways trace a path past a central ancestral hall, an exhibition room and rows of tiny rooms stocked with period furniture and farming tools.

Beyond Tsuen Wan, the Tuen Mun Highway that leads to Castle Peak suddenly opens out into the countryside, leaving behind all traces of the industrialised urban community of Tsuen Wan. From this road you'll see more of the New Territories' farmland, mainly growing produce such as lettuce, cabbage and carrots for the urban market. While traditional methods of agriculture are harder to see than in years gone by, a few farmers still plant rice by hand and till fields with ploughs pulled by water buffalo. Farther along the highway is the new town of **Tuen Mun** ⑫, connected by the West Rail and Light Rail Transit (LRT) system to the old market town of Yuen Long.

Near **Castle Peak** ⑬ itself, adjacent to the LRT station, is a huge temple called **Ching Chung Koon** ⑭, which also serves as a home for the elderly who have no relatives or means of support. In addition, it is a repository for many Chinese art treasures, including lanterns more than 200 years old and a jade seal more than 1,000 years old. The library, which holds 4,000 books, documents the history of the Daoist religion. This temple is dedicated to Lui Tung Bun, one of the so-called Daoist Immortals. He was born in AD 789 and became a Daoist missionary after he was inspired by a dream known in Chinese mythology as the Rice Wine Dream.

Whatever caused his inspiration, Lui was set on the path of good works and he spread the Daoist faith rapidly, helping to rid the earth of many evils. He also had the help of magic weapons, such as a devil-slaying sword and magic fly-switch that are displayed alongside his statue in the temple. At the front of the altar is the 1,000-year-old jade seal kept in a glass case. The altar is protected by two statues that were carved from white stone about 300 years ago for a temple in Beijing. Inside the temple are a number of rooms filled with small photographs of people who have died. Their relatives pay the temple's keepers to have these pictures placed in special numbered slots, and forever after, living progeny can visit to pray to their ancestors.

Near Tuen Mun, on the slopes of Castle Peak, is a temple that is much smaller but no less intriguing. Although it is fairly high up the slope, there is a paved road that runs almost to its entrance. **Pei Tu Temple** ⑮ is dedicated to Pei Tu, a famous monk in Chinese

Over half of Hong Kong's population lives in public housing. The largest single housing project is Yau Oi Estate, in Tuen Mun. It has 9,153 units housing over 35,000 residents.

BELOW: figure at Ching Chung Koon.

mythology. Pei Tu was not a completely honest monk and he was forever getting into trouble and mischief. One night, he was given shelter at the home of a local farmer and in the morning took off with a prized golden statue. The perturbed host and his friends pursued him on horseback to a bend in the river. The monk then called upon one of his magic skills, took out his wooden bowl, stepped into it and pushed off across the stream. All the horsemen could do was watch because they couldn't risk their horses or lives in the deep, fast river. From that time on, the rascal monk was known as the "Cup Ferry", which in Chinese is Pei Tu. When he was finally driven south as far as Castle Peak, then called Green Mountain, he stopped running and established his monastery on this hillside. Hence it is called Pei Tu Shan, or Cup Ferry Hill.

A good stop-off on any trip around the New Territories is **Lau Fau Shan**, a huge fishmarket near Yuen Long. There is a restaurant here with an entry way and walls decorated with thousands of oyster shells, each about 13 to 15 centimetres (5–6 in) long. A narrow street passes by dozens of small, open-air eating houses as well as smart, air-conditioned places. Here merchants sell dried and salted fish, live shrimp, prawns and other edible creatures of the sea. Visitors can pick out a fish, pay for it, then take it to one of the nearby restaurants and have it cooked. Steer clear of raw oysters, which are sometimes contaminated.

Yuen Long ⓰ is another redevelopment project. It began as a traditional market town set in the middle of the largest flood plain in the New Territories. Its population, before development, was 40,000, and that figure is expected to grow to over one million when all the residential and commercial land in this area has been developed as planned. Formerly a place where farmers came to sell produce, the town is rapidly taking on a labour-intensive, light-industrial role expected to absorb up to 20 percent of the area's workers.

North of Yuen Long, next to a low-rise housing estate called Fairview Park, lies **Mai Po Marshes ⓱**, a stopping point on the migratory routes of more than 400 different species of birds. Bird-watchers and ornithologists can make arrangements to visit by calling the World Wide Fund for Nature, which manages the marshes.

Until the 1980s, the view from the lookout point at Lok Ma Chau Police Station towards China was all rice paddies and little villages. Nowadays the rural landscape has been replaced by the rapidly expanding city of **Shenzhen**, a standing testimony to what can be achieved by free-market forces. As one of China's foremost Special Economic Zones, Shenzhen is home to many of the factories and light industrial projects that moved north of the border in search of cheaper labour and land. This lively city has a raw energy all of its own, and many Hong Kongers visit on a regular basis in search of shopping bargains and inexpensive nightlife.

Also a quick trip from Yuen Long are the walled villages of **Kam Tin ⓲**. The most popular for visitors is the Kat Hing Wai village, which stands rather incongruously across the road from a supermarket. There are 400 people living at Kat Hing Wai, all with the same surname, Tang, because only descendants of the Tang clan are permitted to live here. Built in the 1600s, it is a fortified village with walls six metres (18 ft) thick, guard-houses on its four corners, arrow slits for fighting

On one side of the gateway of Pei Tu Temple is an inscription that reads: "There is no gate in this gateway because we do not want to keep people out".

BELOW: monastery at Tuen Mun.

Map, page 196

off attackers, and a moat. The authenticity may seem spoiled by some of the modern buildings inside, which peep over the old-time fortifications. There is still only one entrance, guarded by a heavy wrought-iron gate. Visitors can enter the village for a nominal admission fee, but in ancient times, the gate was used to keep out undesirables. Something else that's only allowed by permission, and with payment, is photographing the elderly folk sitting around the gateway. The commercialism continues inside, where at least one street is lined with vendors.

From Kam Tin you can take a scenic route via **Shek Kong** ⑲, which used to be the British military garrison and airfield but is now home to a skeleton force of the Chinese People's Liberation Army. The far end of Shek Kong village marks the start of Route Twisk, one of the most panoramic drives in Hong Kong. Within minutes you are high up in forested mountains, seemingly far from all human habitation. Route Twisk (which stands for Tsuen Wan Into Shek Kong) twists and turns for miles and then suddenly plunges right into the techno-industrial modernity of Tsuen Wan.

From the top of Route Twisk near Hong Kong's highest point, **Tai Mo Shan** ⑳ (957 metres/3,140 ft), one can look over to China and down to Hong Kong Island. This is the only part of Hong Kong ever to experience frost. Alternatively, rather than making the ascent on Route Twisk, continue on Lam Kam Road to Pak Ngau Shek in the Lam Tsuen Valley, where the **Kadoorie Experimental and Extension Farm** is located. The farm is an agricultural experiment associated with the University of Hong Kong. It provides farmers with specially developed high-yield crops and livestock. To avoid disruption of work, and to ensure the safety of visitors on its precipitous stepways, the farm limits the number of visitors admitted. ❏

BELOW: one of the New Territories' walled villages.

CHINA

Hong Kong

NEW TERRITORIES: EAST

*Few visitors to Hong Kong consider heading out to the eastern
shores of the New Territories. Here the seafood is the freshest and
the golf the finest – and the sharks are occasional visitors*

Sai Kung and **Clearwater Bay** ㉑, located on the eastern edge of Hong
Kong, are arguably the most attractive areas of the New Territories. Beyond
the old Kai Tak Airport – replaced in 1998 by Chek Lap Kok international
airport – Clearwater Bay Road snakes around the side of the Kowloon mountain range, then down the peninsula past smart villas and compact villages to
the aptly named bay itself. In summer the bay is dotted with revellers on company junks, and the beach is jam-packed with sunbathers. Swimmers are pro-
tected from sharks by a net that stretches across the bay.

On the way to Clearwater Bay, the road leads past the **Shaw Brothers Movie
Studio** ㉒, a cornerstone of the local film industry. The stars of the films shown
here are all Chinese celebrities who enjoy a following to rival that of any of the
Hollywood elite, and Western actors' roles here are limited to playing the bad
guys or dubbing the soundtrack.

At the far end of the road is the exclusive Clearwater Bay Golf and Country
Club, easily recognised by its landmark pyramid-shaped clubhouse. Non-mem-
bers can play here, but green fees are high. An indentation in the shoreline forms
Joss House Bay, which comes to life once a year on the birthday of the sea goddess Tin Hau. Hundreds of fishing junks and sampans head for the **Tin Hau
Temple** here to pay their respects to the Queen of
Heaven and Goddess of the Sea. This temple was built
by two brothers who allegedly were saved by Tin Hau
after their junk was destroyed by a typhoon in the 11th
century. While they were lost at sea, the brothers held
onto a statue of Tin Hau, prayed for her help and eventually reached nearby Tung Lung Island alive.

Years later, after the brothers had earned a fortune,
they built a temple on the island and dedicated it to the
sea goddess who had saved them. Later, another
typhoon wrecked the temple, but in 1266 descendants
of the two brothers built its replacement at this site.

Sai Kung

Hiram's Highway branches off Clearwater Bay Road
just before the University of Science and Technology,
and leads down to the town of **Sai Kung** ㉓. The road is
named after a brand of sausage made by Hiram K. Potts
that the highway's builder, John Wynne-Potts, was especially fond of. While the fringes of Sai Kung have fallen
prey to development, this town and its neighbouring villages still retain a strong seaside flavour.

City dwellers like to come here for a breath of fresh
air or to sample the restaurants that serve international
cuisine and extremely fresh seafood. Golfers and wind-
surfers also flock here, while on Sundays thousands of
Filipino residents in Hong Kong come to worship at the
main Catholic church. Stroll along the seafront and

BELOW: Tin Hau,
goddess of the sea.

you'll be treated to the twin and pleasurable sights of junks at anchor in the harbour and every imaginable and edible sea creature – alive – in the tanks in the quayside restaurants.

Map, page 196

The most interesting part of the town is hidden behind the Tin Hau temple off Yi Chun Street. A maze of narrow alleyways leads past traditional herbalists and noodle shops interspersed with ordinary family homes housing several generations under one roof. Stroll about for a genuine glimpse of village life, and nobody will give you a second glance.

Back on the seafront, if you fancy going around the harbour, you need only gaze out to sea for a few minutes before an old Chinese woman with a gold-toothed grin approaches, squawking "Sampan!". Bargain hard – prices are always for a one-hour trip – and check your watch when you set off. Or wander east along the seafront, where you can catch the ferry to Kau Sai Chau public golf course.

While it is not immediately apparent, the Kau Sai Chau golf course has created something of a social revolution in Hong Kong. Very much the game for rising executives, many avid golfers and would-be golfers were kept away from practising by the high membership fees of other private clubs. Kau Sai Chau was Hong Kong's first public course, inexpensively priced and offering a few good holes to anyone who wished and a route up the corporate ladder for the most ambitious. Previously part of the country park, the proposal to build a golf course here initially caused some environmental concerns, but the design has included excellent facilities and landscaping and has turned what really was "a barren rock with nary a house on it" into one of the most popular and beneficial recreation spots in the whole of the territory.

BELOW: simple transportation.

Map, page 196

Near Clearwater Bay is Silverstrand Beach. In spring, the waters offshore are a feeding area for sharks returning to northern waters. Many sightings are reported each year, with two gruesome deaths occurring in the late 1990s.

The road from town runs out to **Sai Kung Country Park ㉔**, the starting point of the **MacLehose Trail**. The trail stretches for 100 kilometres (60 mi) through mostly open country, from one side of the New Territories to the other, across the beautiful grassy hills as far as Tuen Mun. The trail is well marked, and there are places to camp along the way. Some parts are extremely steep and hard going, but anyone who is used to hiking should have no problems tackling the shorter sections or any of the other walks in this area. At the very end of the road into the country park, **Hoi Ha** provides a small stretch of sand on the edge of a marine reserve.

The beach that is the jewel in Sai Kung's crown is **Tai Long Wan ㉕**. Getting there involves an hour's trek, either around the High Island Reservoir or by cutting across the hills along the MacLehose Trail from the road at Pak Tam Au. Either way, it's more than worth it. There are two long swathes of very pale and powdery sand, and enough surf to make it worth lugging a surfboard over the hill. There are also a few shops selling cold beer and hot noodles, and enough open space to romp far and wide. The one downside of Tai Long Wan is that there is a strong undertow, so don't swim out too far. A day of rest and relaxation here makes it extremely difficult to believe that this is part of Hong Kong.

Wong Shek and beyond

Beyond the crest at Pak Tam Au, the road swoops down through woods and little villages to Wong Shek pier, but from just below the top it's worth pausing to admire one of the most pristine views in Hong Kong. You don't need to be familiar with Cantonese to work out that Tai Tan Hoi Hap must mean Long Harbour, which is stretched out below.

At **Wong Shek ㉖** itself, the Jockey Club water sports centre has dinghies and windsurfing boards for hire, and most Saturdays and Sundays the harbour is dotted with small sails. This is also a popular picnic and barbecue site – perhaps because it's seen as the "end of the line", just about as far away from the city as it's possible to get by road. So if those who have made the trip here are not out on the water, they will be gathered around the barbecue pits swathed in smoke and noise and all the paraphernalia – including live fish in specially oxygenated containers – that are the prerequisites of a good Hong Kong al fresco meal. On weekdays, however, the place is practically deserted, and enjoyment of this serene and very atypical Hong Kong place is all the easier. If you fancy more adventure, bargain with one of the local boat owners on the pier – the price should be no more than a few dollars a head – to make the trip around the point to Chek Keng.

The fisher folk at Wong Shek are all Hakka, and before the road was built the only way to get around was by sea, so they are still fiercely independent and a little off-hand with outsiders. Thoroughly at home on the water, they handle their craft like true seafarers and the ride across the water, past fish farms and a few hamlets, is exhilarating.

Chek Keng ㉗ is nearly deserted nowadays; one or two old black-clad crones run a shop selling soft drinks, but otherwise it's fascinating to wander round the old buildings and paddy fields and imagine the time when Hong Kong's New Territories were a land apart, with inhabitants living on what they could earn from the land and the sea, rather than "The Land Between", as the Hong Kong Tourist Board now dubs the area. You can walk on from here, using the MacLehose Trail to get over to Tai Long Wan or simply go back along the well-marked and maintained paths to Wong Shek. Either way, this is a gloriously empty part of Hong Kong that even most Hong Kong residents know little about. ❑

OPPOSITE: shipping lane to the east of the New Territories.

THE OUTLYING ISLANDS

Few travellers know of the many islands – rustic, often
inhabited, and accessible – that await in Hong Kong

There are over 230 islands in the territory – or Special Administrative Region, as it's now officially called – and it is regrettable that so few visitors make time to see them. Archaeologists believe that people have been living in this area for close to 6,000 years. Whether Hong Kong's original inhabitants were the forerunners of those here today, no one really knows, but the ancient tribes who left their marks on Hong Kong – as rock carvings found on Lantau, Po Toi, Tung Lung, Cheung Chau, and Kau Sai Chau – have probably long since moved on.

Apart from these ancient stone-carving people, those who have made their homes on the islands in the last thousand years have traditionally been fisherfolk and farmers, the Hoklo, Tanka and Hakka people. Older descendants of these agrarian tribes have managed to maintain traditional lifestyles, but their children are now among the great number of contemporary Chinese who have sought financial and material prosperity in the urban areas.

Twice the size of Hong Kong Island, Lantau has accelerated beyond its traditional standing as a bedroom retreat for commuters into the site of Hong Kong's international airport, opened in 1998. With the airport came a highway and rail link to Kowloon, making the ferry an option rather than a necessity. Still, outside of the few pockets of high-rise condominiums, Lantau's rustic ambience prevails over much of the island. Its neighbour, Cheung Chau, is so small that it has no cars, but there are plenty of fresh seafood restaurants.

Lamma, third-largest of the islands, is rugged and has little agriculture. Located south of Hong Kong Island's Aberdeen, Lamma can be reached in around 20 minutes by fast ferry, making its excellent and exceedingly fresh seafood worth the short trip.

Few travellers make it to Lantau (save for the airport) or Lamma. Even fewer still venture to one of the dozens of other smaller islands, most of which are nearly deserted. South of Hong Kong Island is Po Toi, a group of islands scarcely inhabited. Reached by either *kaido* or hired boat, Po Toi offers simple restaurants and beaches for those who make the voyage.

Most of the other islands that can be visited are off the New Territories' eastern coast. These include Tung Lung Chau, Tap Mun Chau, Kat O Chau, Ap Chau, Ma Wan, and Kwo Chau Kwan To. All can be reached with a little boat and leg work, and all offer something of Hong Kong's rural magic that long ago evaporated from populated areas such as Kowloon and most of Hong Kong island. ❏

PRECEDING PAGES: the easy animal life on Lantau. **LEFT:** the construction and overhauling of fishing vessels is a significant industry on outlying islands.

LANTAU AND CHEUNG CHAU

A new international airport has not only given Lantau a greater importance, it has cost Hong Kong US$20 billion to build it. Still, away from its north coast, Lantau hasn't changed much

Map, page 221

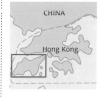

O f all the outlying islands, the greatest in size, and perhaps in atmosphere, is Lantau, which has a land area twice that of Hong Kong Island. On Lantau, it is still not too late to experience rural village lifestyles that have endured almost unchanged since the days of early colonisation.

The relative quiet and sheltering serenity of the island not only provide a peaceful getaway for harried urbanites, but also an appropriate setting for the Christian and Buddhist monasteries here. It is hardly surprising then, that there are mixed feelings about the impending arrival of Mickey Mouse to these green pastures. Hong Kong Disneyland will occupy a hunk of land at Penny's Bay, on Lantau's eastern peninsular, and Phase 1 will include a Disney theme park, a Disney-themed resort hotel complex, and a retail, dining and entertainment centre. Because Lantau is twice the size of Hong Kong Island but supports a population of about 35,000, there is space and peace here that is sorely lacking on the more populated island. Ironically, this tranquillity can sometimes be disrupted on busy weekends and holidays by the many urban residents who flock here seeking respite from their workday pressures.

Lantau means "broken head" in Cantonese, perhaps because its rugged dignity is dominated by the ragged Lantau Peak, which rises 933 metres (3,086 ft) above sea level. Once a quiet commuter's island for many Hong Kong professionals, Lantau's profile was again-raised in the late 1990s when plans for the new international airport, located off its northern coast on a tiny islet called **Chek Lap Kok ❶** and the reclaimed land connecting Chek Lap Kok to Lantau, were announced. New housing blocks have also been built in northern Lantau to house over 15,000 airport and airline employees, and bridges now connect the airport to Kowloon and Hong Kong. Despite this massive development on Lantau's northern coast, Lantau proper has escaped much of the onslaught of new construction, and most of the island fortunately remains rural, for now.

Lantau is accessible by both ferry and hovercraft to **Mui Wo ❷**, also known as **Silver Mine Bay**. Buses travel from this village along Lantau's southern resort coast and across its mountainous centre to the island's towns and monasteries. On the northern side of Lantau, in addition to the international airport, is **Tung Chung**, a massive New Town built from the ground up next to Chek Lap Kok. On a hill overlooking this little harbour is an old fort built in 1817. The fort's thick ramparts still stand, as do six old cannons, much as they did during the 19th century when they guarded the town and bay from smugglers, pirates, scoundrels and unexpected "outer barbarians".

Lantau is cobwebbed with wandering pathways and dusty trails that spiral up, down, and around its scenic

OPPOSITE: seafood market, Cheung Chau. **BELOW:** Lantau windsurfer downs a beer.

BELOW: ascending
to the sitting
Buddha, and
inside the Po Lin
monastery temple.

mountains. The 70-kilometre (43-mi) Lantau Trail and other intersecting side trails, for example, are good for a short stroll, a day trip, or overnight trek. A particularly good trail circles the blue **Shek Pik Reservoir**, on the western slopes of Lantau Peak. This 20,900-million-litre (5,500-million-gallon) reservoir gathers most of the freshwater carried by streams and rivulets from Lantau's heights.

Monastery in the clouds

Up on the mountainous central spine is Lantau's best-known attraction, its largest temple and monastery – the red-orange-and-gold **Po Lin Monastery** ❸ (open daily 10am–6pm; free). The world's largest outdoor bronze statue of a seated Buddha, at 24 metres (79 ft) high, was completed here in 1990. After a stroll through the grounds, visitors can treat themselves to a vegetarian meal served by Po Lin's resident monks in a large dining hall. For those who wish to break up their Po Lin area tour with a local-style high-tea hour, there is a tea plantation and teahouse called the **Lantau Tea Gardens** just a short walk away from the Po Lin Monastery compound. The teahouse has rooms for rent, barbecue facilities and a free camping area.

West of Po Lin, in the direction of Tai O on Lantau's northern coast, is an excellent walking path that traverses mountain ridges, canyons and streams en route to Lantau's **Yin Hing Monastery** ❹, a haven rich with traditional Buddhist paintings and statues. The monastery sits on a slope and commands a fine view of the surrounding mountains, farmland and the blue South China Sea.

Anyone who has seen a junk up close has to marvel at the fact that such a rough and tumble collection of timber, barrels, poles and rough-hewn planks can cope with Hong Kong's typhoon-ridden seas. But they do, and when a nasty

storm hits the area, the biggest of these junks go out to sea to do battle with nature, rather than risk being battered into splinters near shore. These junks dot the waters off Lantau's principle town, **Tai O ❺**, on the west coast.

Here, the island's Tanka "boat people", who traditionally lived on their boats near shore, have become semi-land dwellers. Some of their larger junks have been turned into three-storey permanent living structures. Further up at Tai O Creek, they have also built rickety homes on stilts over parts of the creek where the water rises during tide changes. Tai O used to be well-known for the rope-drawn ferry that carried people back and forth from the narrow tidal creek that separates Tai O island from Lantau. Alas, modernisation has arrived even at this traditional outpost, and a new hand-raised drawbridge carries the traffic now. But old women still hang around the bridge landings, offering short boat rides up and down the picturesque canals. A short stroll on both sides of the tidal creek is worthwhile for a look at the boat people and their unique way of life.

A hideaway that beckons people interested in peace and quiet is the **Lantau Mountain Camp**, at about the 770-metre (2,540 ft) elevation of **Sunset Peak** (870 metres/2,870 ft). This camp consists of 20 small stone houses, built before World War II as a rest haven for the British colony's Christian missionaries taking time off from their work in China. The houses can also be rented by laymen who book in advance.

Lantau is also understandably famed for its many long, smooth and often empty beaches. The finest sandy sweeps are on the southeast coastline that arcs from Cheung Sha south of Silver Mine Bay to Tong Fuk. The most popular and crowded beach (probably because it is the easiest one to reach) is **Silver Mine Bay Beach** and a beach resort of the same name near the Silver Mine Bay ferry

Map, page 221

At one time Tai O exported salt to China. Fishermen later flooded the salt pans to create fish ponds.

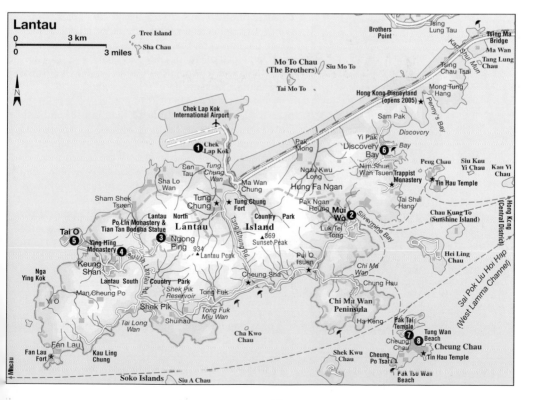

landing. Beware: the water is often too polluted to swim here. A clutch of bars and restaurants has opened in Mui Wo, roistering affairs that become extremely busy at weekends; try the China Bear, nigh-guaranteed to make you miss your return ferry. The bus route from Silver Mine Bay to Tai O passes **Pui O Village** and Cheung Sha, one of the best beaches on the island and home to an excellent South African-themed restaurant, The Stoep.

Away from the rest of the island is a major real-estate development called **Discovery Bay ❻**, a well-planned and uncrowded, if rather characterless, housing/resort complex that includes a golf course. "DB" or "Disco Bay", as it is known locally, has its own rapid-ferry system to and from Central on Hong Kong Island and is linked to northern Lantau by a tunnel.

Cheung Chau

Cheung Chau ("long island" in Cantonese) is the smallest of the inhabited outlying islands, but it's the most populated and busiest. It is urbanised in a charming Old China way, with the distinctly Chinese junks and sampans crowding the island's small, curving harbour.

Cheung Chau is a fishing island, its harbour filled with fishing boats of all sizes, shapes and colours. They compete for space with the ubiquitous, round *kaido*, the small boats used as water taxis to whisk passengers back and forth between Cheung Chau's "dumbbell" knobs, or ends.

The island is shaped like a dumbbell, with hills at the northern and southern ends and a village nestled in a connecting rod of land in between. The thin, middle part of the island is narrow enough that one can walk from Cheung Chau Harbour on its west side to Tung Wan Harbour on the east in a just a few minutes.

Below: village of Cheung Chau.

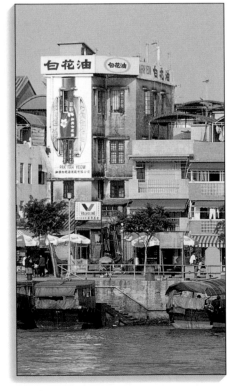

The village of **Cheung Chau**, near the ferry dock, is a tangle of alleyways. There are no cars apart from a bonsai fire engine and ambulance on the island, a Hong Kong phenomenon that gives the place an automatic serenity. Head off in any direction from the ferry terminal and you will pass both modern and traditional shops and restaurants.

A short distance to the left of the ferry dock, up the main road, is **Pak Tai Temple ❼**, built in 1783 and dedicated to the god Pak Tai, protector of fishermen and who is credited with saving the island from plague during the late 1700s. Inside, in front of the altar, are statues of two generals, Thousand-Li Eye and Favourable Wind Ear, who were said to be able to see or hear anything at any distance.

Scattered about the island are several temples dedicated to Tin Hau, Queen of Heaven and Goddess of the Sea. In fact, the entire territory is peppered with temples to Tin Hau, and these many temples dedicated to her reflect her importance not only to Cheung Chau's residents, who make their living from the sea, but to many in Hong Kong (in Macau, the same deity is known instead as A-Ma).

The island was once the haunt of pirates. The most notorious of them all, Cheung Po Tsai, used to hide out here. As on the other outlying islands, "Family Trail" walks are well-marked and lead to Cheung Po Tsai Cave as well as other scenic spots on the tiny island.

Each year in late April or early May (depending on where it falls on the lunar calendar), the island hosts a giant celebration for a four-day Bun Festival. The festival, known as *Ching Chiu* in Cantonese, originated many years ago after the discovery here of a nest of skeletons, believed to be the remains of people killed by pirates.

After this discovery, the island was plagued by a series of misfortunes, and the islanders eventually called in a priest, who recommended they placate the restless spirits of the victims by making offerings to them once a year. How pastry buns came into this story is anybody's guess.

During the festival, giant bamboo towers covered with edible buns are erected in the courtyard of Pak Tai Temple. In the past, revellers climbed up the towers to pluck their lucky buns – the higher the bun was, the more luck it would bring. This amusing little ritual ended in 1978 when one of the towers came crashing down, bringing broken bones and bruises and smashed buns, rather than luck, to the eager climbers. Now the buns are handed out in a less interesting but more orderly – and safer – manner to participants.

Another attraction during the festival are the "floating children", colourfully-clad children hoisted up on stilts and paraded through the crowds. The four-day celebration also includes performances of Chinese opera, lion dances, religious services and other festive events to entertain the hoards that descend upon this little island from all over Hong Kong.

There are excellent beaches to be found on Cheung Chau. The main beach, but not the prettiest, is **Tung Wan Beach ❽**, on the other side of the narrow isthmus from Cheung Chau Harbour. Other beaches include those at Tai Kwai Wan and Tung Wan Tsai on the northern end. ❑

Map, page 221

Pak Tai Temple was visited by England's Princess Margaret in the mid 1960s.

BELOW: windsurfing beach, Cheung Chau.

CHINA

Hong Kong

LAMMA

Although it's the third-largest of the outlying islands, Lamma is blessed with but two villages and no cars. The contrast with Hong Kong Island, just 20 minutes away by fast ferry, is staggering.

The third-largest of the outlying islands, and relatively unknown both to visitors and to Hong Kong residents, is Lamma. Rich in grassy hills and beautiful bays, the rugged terrain means that there is only a very small area of farmland. Archaeologists have associated Lamma with some of the earliest settlements in the region.

Lamma is an island devoted to fishing, with a population of around 8,000 people. Among them are a surprising number of Europeans, who value the peace and quiet of the rural lifestyle; like several other of the outlying islands, Lamma has no cars. Although the island has a regular ferry service, which has expanded considerably in recent years, it has remained relatively undiscovered, much to the joy of those who have moved out to its peaceful ambience.

Yung Shue Wan ❶ (Banyan Bay), at the north end of Lamma, is one of two ferry gateways to the island. This village, popular with expatriates trying to get away from the noisy crowds of Hong Kong, has a number of restaurants and bars. Its narrow main street is lined with shops and seafood restaurants.

Following the main street through the small village, it is only a short stroll out into Lamma's empty countryside. On a side street just past the town's main intersection is Yung Shue Wan's **Tin Hau Temple ❷**, dedicated to the Queen of

BELOW: Lamma and South China Sea.

Map,
page 225

Heaven and the Goddess of the Seas. The 100-year-old temple is guarded by a pair of stone lions. Inside, behind a red spirit stand (to deflect evil spirits), is the main shrine with images of the beaded and veiled Tin Hau.

The most popular walk on Lamma is a well-maintained pathway running much of the length of the island to Yung Shue Wan's sister village of Sok Kwu Wan. The well-marked, hilly, concrete-paved track runs past neat vegetable plots and three-storey buildings (nothing higher is permitted, with the exception of the power station chimeys that loom behind the hill to the right of the path), then along **Hung Shing Ye Beach**, a long, clean stretch of sand. The path then follows the coast, ascending and descending like a rollercoaster ride.

The walk treats hikers to spectacular views out across the sea. A detour along one of the paths leading off to the left to the central ridge gives views across the Lamma Channel to the soaring skyscraper apartment buildings of Aberdeen and the south side of Hong Kong Island. The contrast between bustling, crowded Hong Kong Island and empty Lamma could not be more startling. The walk from one end of Lamma to the other can be completed in an unhurried hour and a half and can leave time for a fine seafood meal. Be sure to take a hat – the deforested hills provide virtually no shade.

Sok Kwu Wan ❸, which lies on the eastern shore of a long fjord-like inlet known as Picnic Bay, is the Lamma village closest to Aberdeen. It is the haunt of Hong Kong's "Weekend Admirals" or "Saturday Sailors", the nautical names given to the pleasure-junk captains. Picnic Bay is brimming with floating fish and shrimp farms, all tended by a picturesque fleet of assorted boats of various sizes and shapes. The nautical products, fresh as can be, of the seafood industry find their way to markets and tables throughout Hong Kong. As can be expected from a fishing village, Sok Kwu Wan bustles with a long string of seafood restaurants, even more beguiling in the evening when each establishment tries to out-do its neighbour with bright lighting displays and the marvellous aromas of freshly cooked fish, shrimp, prawns, lobster and other seafood. The village also has its own 150-year-old Tin Hau Temple.

Walkers wanting a final challenge might take the one-hour hike to the top of rugged **Mount Stenhouse** (Shan Tei Tong), which rises a steep 353 metres (1,158 ft) from the head of Picnic Bay. Or take a 30-minute walk to sandy **Lo So Shing Beach**, nestled in a small cove on the other side of the island.

Lamma is easy to get to by ferry from Hong Kong Island, with around 30 departures from Central to Yung Shue Wan daily and 12–15 to Sok Kwu Wan. Central-Yung Shue Wan takes approximately 20 minutes on a fast ferry, 35 minutes on the slower services. There is also ferry service to Lamma from Aberdeen on the south side of Hong Kong island. ❑

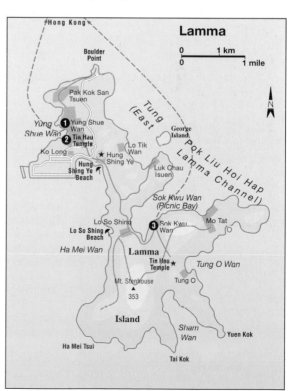

OTHER ISLANDS

If Lamma is visited rarely, imagine the paucity of tourists on Hong Kong's even smaller islands. Most are clustered off the New Territories. Be prepared to rough it, and to enjoy it

Most of the outlying islands seem deserted in comparison to the urban areas of Hong Kong. Many young islanders have moved away, attracted by the vibrancy of Kowloon and Hong Kong Island, leaving their homes to ageing parents and occasional visitors who come on weekends and holidays. While fishing used to be the major means of earning a living for the remaining islanders, the most profitable businesses now are restaurants and tourism. The weekdays often pass by quietly, but on weekends and holidays, the islands come to life with city dwellers looking to spend a day out visiting temples and combing the beaches. Some of these islands have hostels or camps for those who want to extend their stay overnight.

Po Toi and Tung Lung Chau

Po Toi Island is actually a group of islands located at the southernmost area of the territory of Hong Kong, southeast of Stanley on Hong Kong Island, and is inhabited by only a handful of people. The main island, Po Toi, is home to a large rock resembling a river snail. Under the rock is a cave with rock carvings shaped by wind and rain. Also on Po Toi are the Deserted House of Mo's Family and the nearby Coffin Rock, two curiosities for adventurous explorers. At the island's southern tip there are many strange rock formations, including the Calligraphy by Ghosts, Buddha's Hands Rocks and Monk Rocks. The open-air restaurants near the pier in the south serve delicious seafood. Most Hong Kong residents hire a junk or a boat to go to Po Toi on weekends. There are also *kaido*, small boats that ferry passengers from Aberdeen and Stanley on Sundays and public holidays for about HK$60 per person round-trip.

Also known as Nam Tong Island, **Tung Lung Chau** is located off the southern tip of the Clearwater Bay peninsula in eastern New Territories. The island's biggest attraction is the Buddhist Hall Fort built about 300 years ago and renovated in recent years. To find the fort, follow the path from the hamlet at the ferry pier over the rolling, open landscape of northern Tung Lung. The fort, perched on a low headland in the northeast, was abandoned in 1810. But its interior is reasonably well-preserved, with the bases of the partitions between the rooms visible.

On the north shore of Tung Lung Chau are some rock carvings on the cliffs depicting the daily lives of people who lived in this area several hundred years ago. It is a perfect place to enjoy the beautiful sea view, with waves rushing to the shore. The more adventurous visitor can hike along the cliffs and hills. Like most of the outlying islands, there is no regular ferry to Tung Lung, but *kaido* boats from Shau Kei Wan on Hong Kong Island operate on most weekends.

BELOW: windsurfing is an option most everywhere in the outlying islands.

Mirs Bay islands

Out at Mirs Bay northeast of Kowloon, **Ping Chau** (not to be confused with Peng Chau near Lantau) is one of the territory's most remote isles. From its hilltops, you can get a bird's-eye view of the mainland's Bao An area. Years ago, Ping Chau had a population of 3,000, but now, most islanders have moved to urban areas and only return on weekends and public holidays to run their restaurants or hostel businesses. City people like to come to the island to have picnics on holidays and to enjoy the silence surrounded by long white beaches of smooth sand scattered with seashells, starfish and spiked sea urchins.

The island is made of what locals call "thousand-layer rocks" in different shapes and colours. There are other natural attractions as well, including caves, rock formations and waterfalls with colourful names given by the locals: Kang Lau Shek (Drum Tower Rock), Lung Lok Shui (Dragon Fall Water) and Nam Ki Shui (Hard-to-Get-Over-Water). There are also old-fashioned stone houses with courtyards and winding passages.

Because of its proximity to mainland China, Ping Chau has become the first stopover spot for illegal immigrants from Guangdong province in recent years. To get to Hong Kong, people from the northern villages swim across the ocean to Ping Chau and then hire boats to move closer to urban areas.

There are simple village houses on the island that are available for rent, as are small bed-and-breakfast type places that provide food and lodging. To get to Ping Chau, take the ferry from Ma Liu Shui, near the University KCR station in the New Territories. However, the service only operates at weekends and on public holidays; contact Tsui Wah Ferry Service (tel: 2527 2513) for information.

To the northwestern part of Mirs Bay is **Tap Mun Chau** (also called Grass

Map, page 130

BELOW: in search of an isle.

Map, page 130

There's always a boat of some sort to just about anywhere in Hong Kong. For the more out-of-the-way places, the small *kaido* is often the primary option. Rarely on a fixed schedule, the seaworthy *kaido* makes short trips usually based on demand, especially on weekends and holidays.

Island), a thriving community of fishermen. The harbour at Tap Mun is usually crowded with fishing boats and other workboats, and along the edge of the inlet is a row of old cottages. The harbour is a central gathering point for fishermen from all over this region. There are terrific views of the sea from the northern point of the island, particularly from the top of the hills next to the 100-year-old Tin Hau temple. There are dozens of Tin Hau temples all over Hong Kong, but this one on Tap Mun Island has special importance because it is the last one before fishermen reach the open sea. Traditionally, fishermen visit the temple to make offerings and pray for a safe return from their voyages. There is one odd thing about this particular Tin Hau temple. When the east winds roar, their sounds can be heard in a crevice under the altar – this eerie howling is interpreted by fishermen as a warning of storms to come. Tap Mun can be reached by *kaido* from Wong Shek pier in the New Territories.

Such is the importance of this Tin Hau temple that former island residents who may have emigrated to all parts of the globe will make a special effort to come back for major festivals. Landing at Tap Mun leads past a couple of tasty seafood restaurants and some shops, but many of the village houses stand empty. A single path winds through the village, up past the island police station which looks like a little fortress, to a grassy plateau whose brisk winds make it very popular with kite flyers young and old. Parts of Tap Mun are covered with thick, impenetrable scrub, but in the upper reaches, much of it abandoned agricultural land, there are plenty of places to sit and relax over a picnic. The shore is rocky and what beaches there are lie covered in stones, but from here you can savour the views across the sea up to the China coast, which is gradually being filled with more and more construction projects. The islanders here have always been a hardy independent breed, with a dubious regard for authority. At one time the area was particularly busy at nights as unlit boats smuggled electronic goods over the border.

Island hopping from Sai Kung

Some of the most easily accessible outlying islands sit in the Inner Port Shelter (Ngau Mei Hoi) offshore from Sai Kung village, which at one time was a British military firing range. It's all peace and quiet nowadays though, and the harbour, home to more gin palaces than junks, makes a very photogenic start to the trip. Sampan owners will either make a one hour tour for about HK$100, dropping you off for a short stroll at whichever island you desire, or charge HK$300 to take you to your destination and then pick you up later. Negotiate the price briskly and synchronise watches before setting off! One of the nicest beaches is at Hap Mun Bay on **Kiu Tsui Chau** (Sharp Island), with fine sand and water that is usually clear. You can also camp overnight here, and there are barbecue pits for a cook-out. If recent visitors or perhaps a recent storm have left the beach in a mess, don't hesitate to move on round the harbour: there are other strands on **Pak Sha Chau** (White Sand Island) and **Cham Tau Chau** (Pillow Island). **Yim Tin Tsai** (Little Salt Field) Island is remarkable for its Catholic chapel, which sees little use now as many of the islanders have moved into town. Remember that whichever island you pick, you should take enough food and drink to keep you going, and sunscreen and mosquito repellent are also advisable.

Kwo Chau Kwan To (Fruit Islands), or Ninepin Group, to the east of Hong Kong is a paradise for diving and fishing. There is a small Tin Hau temple and some fabulous caves on Nam Kwo Chau (South Fruit Island). Fishing expeditions, either by day or night, complete with hire of rods and tackle, are available from several of the shops on Sai Kung seafront. ❑

OPPOSITE: rock with a view on an outlying island.

MACAU

An Iberian accent and a Chinese countenance give this small enclave one of the most unique moods in Asia

With its casinos, hotels and a distinctly Old World air mixed with an Asian ambience, Macau is nonetheless one of those places typically in the shadow of something bigger and usually overlooked by travellers. Yet the profile of this former Portuguese colony, hidden in the shadow of Hong Kong, has risen with the addition of its first international airport in the late 1990s. No longer does the international traveller need fly to Hong Kong in order to visit Macau.

As befits the first European settlement – established in the mid-16th century – on the southern China coast, Macau's antiquity is evident throughout its 16 square kilometres (6 sq mi), which doesn't include its neighbouring isles of Taipa and Coloane. It's a walkable city of just over five kilometres (3 mi) in length, and throughout are Iberian churches and fortifications that give Macau its unique textures.

After the media-saturated handover of Hong Kong to Chinese sovereignty in 1997, the return of Macau to China in 1999 was rather anticlimactic. But unlike the two years of acrimonious negotiations between England and China over Hong Kong's future, the 1987 agreement between Portugal and China went smoothly. As with the Hong Kong agreement, Macau is guaranteed a "one country, two systems" status as a Special Administrative Region for 50 years following the December 1999 handover. Thus Macau's existing economic, political, judicial, cultural and social systems are guaranteed (on paper) for the next half century.

Unlike the British, however, the Portuguese rarely had an adversarial relationship with China regarding its colony. Indeed, Portugal's former constitution defined Macau as a "Chinese territory under Portuguese administration. The present status... serves the interests of Portugal, China and the population of Macau". In fact, in the 1970s Portugal offered to return the colony to China's control, but the idea was rejected by the Chinese, who said that the time simply was not right. It was felt, apparently, that the right time would be after the return of Hong Kong to China's embrace. ❑

PRECEDING PAGES: old illustration of a funeral in Macau; 17th-century lighthouse at Guia. **LEFT:** Portuguese resident of Macau.

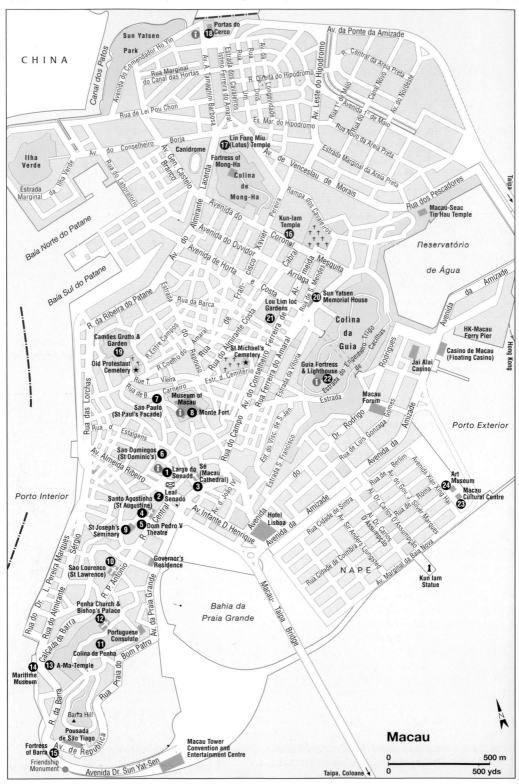

Macau

0 —————————— 500 m

0 —————————— 500 yds

MACAU

Often perceived as something of a second fiddle to Hong Kong, Macau is in fact quite different. Its ambience is Mediterranean, its gambling casinos are cash cows, and its attitude is low-key

Map, page 236

Macau's face has changed in recent years, but, thankfully, its complexion remains much as it has been for the past 400 years. A new bridge (Ponte da Amizade) now stretches across the Outer Harbour (Porto Exterior) to tiny Taipa Island, leading to its underused international airport, its runway on yet another massive landfill. The ferry terminal and helicopter platform reach out into the harbour on landfill. Two other landfills in the Outer Harbour support modern, high-rise districts and more reclamation work to the west has created the odd-looking artificial Nam Van lakes. Yet despite all the reclamation, towering skyscrapers and new infrastructure, the heart of Macau has preserved its colonial feeling with some beautiful period buildings and shady twisting lanes.

Macau, established in 1557, was the first European colony on China's shore and, until 1999, when it reverted to Chinese sovereignty, it was the last. The best place to start any foray into old Macau is **Largo do Senado ①** (Senate Square). It is the old city's main square and covers some 3,700 square metres. and has been repaved in a traditional Portuguese wave-pattern mosaic.

The pride of the square is the **Leal Senado ②** (Loyal Senate) building, regarded by most as the best example of Portuguese architecture in Macau. The Leal Senado was dedicated in 1784 and its facade completed in 1876. It was restored in 1939, with further internal restoration completed in the late 20th century. The title "Loyal" was bestowed on Macau's Senate in 1809 by Portuguese King John VI, who was Prince Regent at the time, as a reward for continuing to fly the Portuguese flag when the Spanish monarchy took over the Portuguese throne in the 17th century. An inscribed tablet here, dating from 1654, grants Macau its sacred title: "City of the Name of God, Macau, There is None More Loyal." Head up the staircase to the fine wrought iron doors and beyond. The library and council chamber show fine examples of Old World woodwork. Half the offices on the ground floor have been converted into a gallery for special exhibitions.

Nearby to the north is the **Sé ③** (Macau Cathedral). It was declared the mother church of the Macau diocese in 1850, which then included all of China, Japan and Korea. Its stained-glass windows are its main attraction.

Many of Macau's best sights lie south of Largo do Senado, across Avenida de Almeida Ribeiro, in a string all the way to the southern tip of the peninsula. The first of these is **Santo Agostinho ④** (St Augustine). The baroque-style church of St. Augustine is the largest in the region. Spanish Augustinians first founded a church here in 1586, but the present structure dates from 1814, and its ornate facade from 1875. Across Largo de Santo Agostinho sits the exquisite **Dom Pedro V Theatre ⑤**. Named after Portugal's most famous poet, Luis de

BELOW: reverting to Chinese sovereignty in 1999.

Camoes (1524-80), the renovated 18th-century building is now closed to the public, and there's a private members-only bar and restaurant next door. It was once the residence of the president of the select committee of the East India Company, the all-powerful firm that for centuries "ruled" the area from India to the South China Sea. The fully restored theatre has 350 seats. From the main road, Avenida de Almeida Ribeiro, the square runs up to the church of St Dominic and extends on to the ruins of São Paulo.

São Domingos (St Dominic's), with its Christian-Oriental motif, is one of the oldest of Macau's many churches. It dates from the 17th century, but the Spanish Dominicans built a chapel and convent on this site as early as 1588. From St Dominic's follow the pavement north to the ruins of **São Paulo** ❼ (St Paul's). Its towering façade and impressive grand staircase are, perhaps, the most striking of all Macau's churches. Historians often cite it as the finest monument to Christianity in Asia. Unfortunately, the site must have bad geomancy – what the Chinese call *feng shui*. The first church on the site was destroyed by fire in 1601, and construction of a new one was begun the following year. The classical façade you see now was crafted by Japanese Christian artisans who had fled persecution in Nagasaki. In 1835 another fire spread and eventually destroyed São Paulo, the adjacent college and a library reputed to be the best east of Africa. In 1904, efforts were made to rebuild the church, but little was done. Still, today the grand façade of São Paulo remains as Macau's most enduring visitor symbol.

Overlooking the façade of São Paulo, due east, are the massive stone walls of the **Fortaleza do Monte** ❽, simply called **Monte Fort**. The fortification was built in the early 1620s. When Dutch ships attacked and invaded Macau in 1622, the half-completed fortress was defended by 150 clerics and African slaves. A lucky

BELOW: colonial architecture, and the façade of São Paulo.

cannon shot by an Italian Jesuit, Geronimo Rhu, hit the powder magazine of the Dutch flag ship and saved the city. In 1998 the **Museum of Macau** (open daily except Monday, 10am–6pm; entrance fee) was opened on the site of the fortress. The museum documents the history of the enclave and its citizens, from its first settlement in 1557 through to the handover to the Chinese in December 1999.

Perhaps the starkest proof of the recent deterioration of both Macau and its once mighty Roman Catholic presence is the church and seminary of **St Joseph's Seminary** ❾. This Jesuit church was dedicated in 1728, and its sole purpose was to establish religious missions in China, a task it performed admirably. Today its vast halls, classrooms and living quarters are mostly empty, but its architecture and sculptures are worth viewing, and its beautiful chapel is open to the public. The mid-18th-century church of St Joseph's is reached through the seminary, or through the street if the front door is open. The church protects a sacred relic – a 13-centimetre-long (6 in) piece of bone from the left arm of St Francis (ardent Macanese and Portuguese Catholics believe the relic protects the city from natural disasters). The statues in the lovely chapel were salvaged from São Paulo in 1835.

Regarded as the most fashionable church in Macau, **São Lourenco** ❿ (St Lawrence's) was originally built in the 1560s of wood, replaced by *taipa* in 1618 and finally reconstructed with stone in 1803. It was again rebuilt in 1846, and then again in 1892. It is one of the most elegant of Macau's religious edifices and is open to the public. Its double staircase, iron gates, towers and crystal chandeliers are European, but the roof is made of Chinese tiles. It overlooks the pastel pink government buildings next to it.

The first stop on most tours of Macau is **Colina da Penha** ⓫ (Penha Hill), on top of which stands the magnificent **Bishop's Palace** ⓬, unoccupied for many years now but partly open to the public. From one vantage point there, it's possible to see across the Old City to Macau's Inner Harbour (Porto Interior), and less than a kilometre farther, China. The Bishop's Palace – larger than anything similar in Asia outside the Philippines – was, at one stage in early Eurasian history, the seat of Roman Catholicism in Asia. Macau was also the training and publishing centre for Roman Catholic missionary efforts in this part of the Catholic world.

One of Macau's favourite haunts, the Bela Vista ("nice view") hotel, closed in 1999 to make way for the new Portuguese consulate. The original 23-room hotel was built over 100 years ago by a sea captain; it later served as a health resort for French troops from Indochina, sanatorium, secondary school, Cantonese language school, home for Portuguese refugees from Shanghai and Hong Kong in World War II, British servicemens' club, and finally a hotel. Completely rebuilt in the early 1990s, the eight-suite inn, a gem of colonial architecture, was considered to be one of Asia's finest.

No sojourn to Macau would be complete without a visit to **Temple da Deusa A-Ma** ⓭ (A-Ma Temple). The temple squats beneath Barra Hill, at the entrance to Macau's Inner Harbour. It is the oldest temple in the territory, said to date back 600 years to the Ming dynasty. It was certainly there in 1557, when Macau was ceded

Map, page 236

Established more than three centuries before the colony of Hong Kong, which is just 65 kilometres (40 mi) away, Macau reverted to Chinese sovereignty in 1999.

BELOW: interior of the former Bela Vista.

to Portugal. The original temple was said to have been erected by fishermen from southeast China and dedicated to Tin Hau, the patron goddess of fishermen and called A-Ma in Macau. It was then called Ma Kok Miu (Ma Point Temple). The Chinese named the area A-Ma-Gao, or the Bay of A-Ma. The oldest surviving part of this temple is a lower pavilion to the right of its entrance. There is a coloured, bas-relief stone carving here said to be a rendering of a Chinese junk that carried the goddess A-Ma from Fujian Province through typhoon-ravaged seas to Macau, where she walked to the top of Barra Hill and ascended to heaven. Near the Temple is the **Maritime Museum** ⑭ (open daily except Tuesday, 10am–5.30pm; entrance fee, half price on Sunday), with displays tracing the history of shipping in the South China Sea. Next to the museum you can jump on a motorised Chinese junk for half-hourly tours of the Inner or Outer Harbour.

The large walls of the old **Fortaleza da Barra** ⑮ (Fortress of Barra) rise far above the avenue guarding the entrance to Macau's Inner Harbour. At a gap in the rampart, a cannon and crimson awning mark the entrance to the Pousada de São Tiago, a small hotel nestled within the walls of the old fortress of Barra. Furnishings and fixtures imported from Portugal grace this 23-room inn.

To get up to the quaint Pousada, pass through large hand-carved wooden doors into a cave-like staircase chiselled out of the thick stone walls. Water cascading down the back wall adds to its mystery as you turn up a second flight of stairs. A picturesque cafe and bar with a tree-shaded open-air terrace rim the top of the old fort walls and complete the panorama. The Pousada's stucco white walls and red tiled roofs are terraced into the hillside and rise up another two levels. Even the fort's chapel has been preserved much as it was when Portuguese defenders were fighting off the Dutch.

BELOW: children playing mahjong.

Macau's latest tourist attraction, at odds with its history-steeped churches, temples and buildings, is the 338-metre (1,110-ft) **Macau Tower**, a concrete blunder on the tip of the artificial lakes. Take the lift to the observation deck for a 360-degree views of Macau, and look through its glass floors (not recommended for vertigo sufferers). There are also balloon rides and climbing trips around the outside of the tower. Next door's Convention and Exhibition Centre houses some tacky shops, nice restaurants and a 500-seat cinema/theatre.

Near the southern foot of Colina de Mong-Ha sits **Kun Iam Temple** ⓰, dedicated to Quanyin, the Buddhist Goddess of Mercy. Some sub-temples in this complex are dedicated to A-Ma. The present temple dates back to 1627 and was built on the site of an earlier 14th-century temple. Foreign visitors, particularly Americans, will be interested to know that on a table in this temple's courtyard the first Sino-American Treaty was signed in 1844 by Ki Ying, China's viceroy in Guangzhou, and Caleb Cushing, who was the United States' "Commissioner and Envoy Extraordinary and Minister Plenipotentiary" to China.

Along the northern foot of Colina de Mong-Ha is the quaint **Lin Fung Miu** ⓱ (Lotus Temple), built in 1592. In the old days it served as a guest house for mandarins travelling between Macau and Guangzhou. Its most recent restoration was in 1980 and it is an excellent example of classical Buddhist architecture. Clay friezes over its entrances are some of the best examples of Buddhist art in the region. Beautifully garbed in silk robes and an opulent headdress, an image of the sea goddess Tin Hau stands tall over the main altar.

From the southern tip of the territory, head north about 4 kilometres (2½ mi) to the border with China. Macau's border gate, **Portas do Cerco** ⓲, was built in 1870. Not many years ago, the gate was closed to all foreigners (though Chinese

Map, page 236

In World War II, the Japanese invaded Hong Kong but honoured Portugal's neutrality and did not invade Macau. Consequently, many Europeans took refuge in Macau.

BELOW: Portuguese youth at play.

passed through it in both directions daily) and visitors were forbidden to photograph it. Today the gate is open from early morning to midnight, accommodating people going into China to resorts across the border. Protecting the other approach to the city is the Fortress of Mong-Ha, on Colina de Mong-Ha, constructed to provide a defence vantage to guard the Portas do Cerco. Built in 1849, the fort's barracks now hold a 24-room pousada for official visitors, as well as a hotel and tourism training school.

Picturesque **Camoes Grotto and Garden** ⑲ is where Luis de Camoes, the celebrated Portuguese soldier-poet, is said to have composed part of the national epic, *Os Lusiadas*. A bronze bust of Camoes rests in the garden's grotto. Above the grotto is an observatory built by a French explorer, Count de La Perouse.

Most tours make a quick visit to the **Dr Sun Yatsen Memorial House** ⑳. Sun Yatsen, the father of modern China, is revered in both Beijing and Taipei. Opened after he died, the memorial is near where he practised medicine at Kiang Vu Hospital. (He was one of the first Western-trained Chinese doctors in this area. His birthplace is across the Chinese border, in Zhongshan.) The memorial is not as old as you'd expect – in the 1930s it was used as an explosives depot until it accidentally blew up. What you are looking at is a new structure built near the original monument site. Close by is one of the best gardens in the territory: **Lou Lim Ioc** ㉑, a beautiful Chinese garden built in the Suzhou-style. Its walks twist amid ornamental mountains, resembling a classical Chinese landscape painting.

Colina da Guia rises east of the Sun Yatsen memorial and Lou Lim Ioc and is home to the **Guia Fortress and Lighthouse** ㉒, the first thing one sees when approaching Macau by sea. This 17th-century, Western-style lighthouse – the oldest on the Chinese coast – stands atop Colina da Guia and guards coastal

BELOW: from atop Guia Fortress.

approaches. It is the highest point in Macau and open to the public. Besides the views, it features a small art gallery and some notable tunnels.

To the south of the Avenida da Amizade lies a rectangle of reclaimed land that is one of the most up-and-coming areas in Macau. Known as The NAPE, the area is not only home to a growing number of restaurants and bars but also the state-of-the-art **Macau Cultural Centre ㉓**, which is located at the junction of Avenida Man Sing Hai and Avenida Dr Sun Yat Sen. It comprises the Auditorium Building, home to two auditoria, several gallery spaces, a conference hall, dance and music studios, a restaurant and a five-storey **Art Museum ㉔** (open daily except Monday, 10am–5pm; entrance fee), which houses a permanent collection of over 3,000 works. Further north along the seafront, **Dynasty Plaza** is Macau's new nightlife zone, with a range of close-knit bars, cafes and restaurants where you can drink, dance and eat till the wee hours. Visible from the waterfront is the beautiful bronze statue of Kun Iam, recently designed and crafted by Portuguese artist, Christina Reiria. The dome under her feet holds a small meditation centre and Buddhist library.

Casinos and gambling

Macau is sometimes known as the Las Vegas or Monaco of the East, and gambling is the main reason some eight million visitors each year, over 80 percent of them Hong Kong Chinese, land in Macau. Lady Luck – who lurks in eleven casinos – thrives on gambling-mad Chinese.

Those casinos that are located in hotels (in the Lisboa, Mandarin, Kingsway, Pousada Marina Infante, Holiday Inn, New Century and Hyatt Regency) are well-equipped and popular, but possibly the best place to get a feel for the mania

Map, page 236

The casinos of Macau maintain a dress code that is more permissive for women than for men. For example, men may not wear shorts, while women are allowed to do so. Neither sex, however, can wear flip-flops.

BELOW: casino lights in Macau.

Map, page 236

Casino gambling started in Macau in the 1930s. Today, about one-third of the government's revenue is derived from gambling.

OPPOSITE: barber shop on Coloane.
BELOW: St Francis Xavier Chapel.

that the Chinese have for gambling is on a moored floating barge in the Outer Harbour called the Macau Palace Floating Casino; other predominanly Chinese casinos are the Jai-Alai Place, the Kam Pek (specialising in Chinese games), and the newest, the Pharoah's Palace Casino. Almost every game known to gamblers can be played in Macau's temples of money, and the slot machines – hungry tigers, as the Chinese call them – are always hungry. Roulette and its cousin *boule*, played with a larger ball, are highly popular and use only a single zero on Macau tables. Blackjack is also very popular, and played with peculiar Macau rules.

Betting chips are available in all of Macau's casinos, but the Chinese prefer cash. Superstition always follows the Chinese gambler. Water is considered good luck and the Chinese word for water, *soi*, is also a slang word for money. Choi Sun is the god of luck and fortune in Macau, and visits only those he feels like – he can not be invoked. To a fellow player, just say *fat-la* (fortune is coming), the good-luck cry of Macau.

Taipa and Coloane

The "other" Macau is not on the peninsula that is generally regarded as Macau, but consists of the two outlying islands of Taipa and Coloane. Previously, access to these islands was by small ferry boats that, in the case of Coloane, could only approach at high tide. Today, Taipa is connected to the mainland by two arching bridges. Access is by taxi or bus.

Taipa has a number of high-rises, relieving some of the pressure on congested Macau. The island has historically been a centre for junk-building and firecracker manufacture, and in the early 1700s, became the busy centre for Western trade with China when an imperial edict banned English and French ships from Guangzhou, insisting they moor at Taipa instead.

The Portuguese ambience persists in a few places today, notably at the small *praia* just below Largoda Carma, which rivals its larger and more famous predecessor on the Macau peninsula for beauty, elegance and romance. Five old houses, painted mint-green, have been beautifully restored and converted to a string of three museums, a small art gallery and a piano bar and restaurant. You can poke around the **Macanese House**, the best of the set of museums, stocked with period furniture.

Coloane is almost twice as big as Taipa, and is popular for its beaches, golf course (next to the Westin Hotel) and the legendary Fernando's restaurant on **Hac Sa beach**, where lunches rarely finish before dusk.

One of Coloane's beaches, **Kao Ho**, is the site for Macau's deep-water port. Situated on the northern end of the island, Kao Ho was once a traditional haven for South China Sea pirates. Most of the islanders supported piracy, a major source of livelihood. But one day the pirates overstepped their watery bounds. After a mass kidnapping of Chinese children from Guangzhou, and a subsequent refusal of outrageous ransom demands by Coloane's buccaneers, Portuguese authorities went after the pirates and defeated them in a two-day battle, in 1910. A memorial to this incident is set into a tiny square in front of the **Chapel of St Francis Xavier**. ❏

GUANGZHOU

For centuries, Guangzhou was the West's gateway to China, a unique point of contact between two very different worlds

Many Westerners still call this city in southeastern China "Canton", and the cuisine that comes from here is still Cantonese. But to the Chinese this city is Guangzhou, although it was once known as Yangcheng, or Goat City. From the 16th century until the middle of the 20th, Guangzhou was the main centre of trade between Europe and China, and much of the time it was China's only international port by imperial decree. It is no longer China's main port to the world – Shanghai and Hong Kong far surpass it – but Guangzhou has been so long in the Western consciousness that it retains a certain nostalgic cast as China's connection with the world.

The nature of its interdependence with Hong Kong to the southeast has altered over the years. Hong Kong first gained value to the British because of Guangzhou's importance as a port, but in the twentieth century the roles reversed and Guangzhou gained economic, and even political, importance because of Hong Kong's proximity.

Guangzhou is cradled by the Zhu Jiang, or Pearl River, which skirts the city on its western and southern extents. For nearly a century, from 1861 until 1949, the British and French retained concessions on Shamian Island, on Guangzhou's southern flank where the Zhu Jiang bends to the east on its way to the ocean. But Westerners were not the first foreigners to call on Guangzhou. During the Tang dynasty, from AD 600 to 900, merchant ships from Arabia and Persia made regular stops in the city.

Although it has since yielded to economic aspirations, Guangzhou was a hot bed of Chinese nationalism during the 20th century. Dr Sun Yatsen, considered the founder of contemporary China, was born in a nearby village. Scattered throughout the city itself are many monuments to martyrs and uprisings. During the short time that the Nationalists and Communists were allies, Mao Zedong taught at the Institute of Peasant Movements, and Zhou Enlai instructed at the Huangpu Military Academy.

Today, Guangzhou – in common with other large Chinese cities – is a typical urban mess, rather grey and not especially attractive. Nevertheless, it is an energetic centre, and it is where most of what the world knows about China – Chinatowns around the world, not to mention cuisine, are Cantonese – originated. Indeed, this is where the West's affair with the Middle Kingdom took root and flourished. ❏

PRECEDING PAGES: retail sales drive the southern economy; with money to spend, young people troll in the evenings. **LEFT:** statue of Dr Sun Yatsen, Guangzhou.

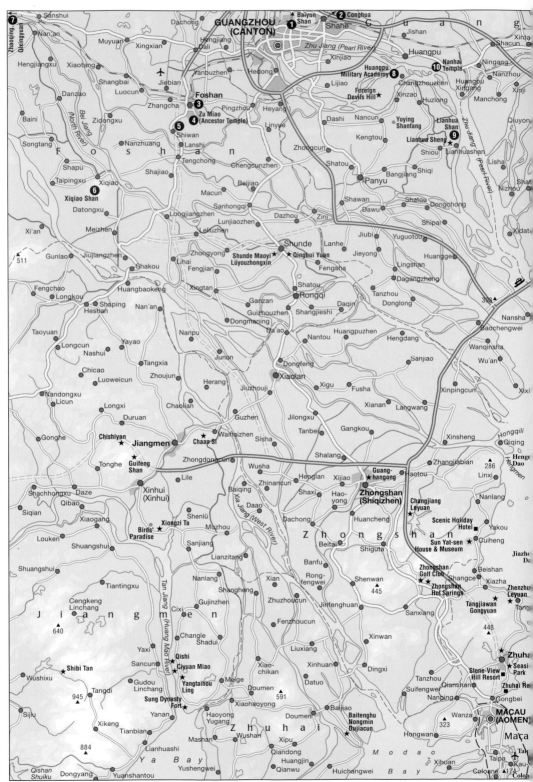

Pearl River Delta

GUANGZHOU

*For a long time one of the few Chinese cities open to travellers,
Guangzhou has long had economic modernisation as its goal. Still,
despite the usual urban bustle, some of old Canton remains*

Map,
page 257

The mythical origins of booming Guangzhou (Canton) are not the most auspicious. As legend has it, five celestial beings, riding on the backs of five flying goats, landed in the southeastern coastal region of China and founded Guangzhou. To the Westerner, goats may not do much for engendering civic pride in an economic powerhouse and gateway. Yet the name Yangcheng, or Goat City, was once affixed to this city. Even today, the evening newspaper is called *Yangcheng Wanbao*, the Goat City Evening News.

But goats are spunky and independent, and in Guangzhou, there is a palpable sense of China's energy and of its breakneck pace in transforming itself into an international player. Guangzhou is a boisterous urban centre with all the blemishes one equates with modern cities: air thick with pollution, streets crowded with cars and trucks, blocks of cramped housing overflowing with people, and an invigorating chaos.

Located in Guangdong province, Guangzhou lies at the mouth of the **Zhu Jiang** (Pearl River), 45 kilometres (30 mi) upriver from Humen (Tiger Gate), also called Bocca Tigris on old maps and where the Zhu Jiang enters the ocean. Around five million people live in the greater metropolitan area, with over two million within the city's boundaries. As with many of China's cities, Guangzhou's population is probably much higher than official figures indicate, in part because of the large numbers of rural men who come to Guangzhou in search of work (estimates of this roving work force are as high as 100 million people throughout the country).

Guangzhou has a temperate, subtropical climate. The Tropic of Cancer runs a few kilometres to the north, and for a few days in July, the sun lies directly above the city. The rainy season comes during the hot summer months, when daily afternoon showers are typical.

Flying goats notwithstanding, Guangzhou probably was founded in 214 BC as an encampment by the armies of the Qin emperor, Qin Shi Huangdi (221–210 BC). At first the town was called Panyu; the name Guangzhou first appeared during the period of the Three Kingdoms (222–280). During the Tang dynasty (618–906), the city was already an international port, but remained second to Quanzhou – Marco Polo's Zaytun – for centuries.

In 1514, a Portuguese flotilla reached Guangzhou. The province's name in the Cantonese dialect is Guangdong, from which the Portuguese somehow derived the name of Cantào. From Cantào came Canton.

From 1757 to 1842, Guangzhou held a trade monopoly in China, as it was the only Chinese port open to foreigners. Traders were obliged to cooperate contractually with Chinese merchant guilds, and this arrangement eventually planted the seeds for the subsequent *comprador bourgeoisie*.

OPPOSITE: serious air-pollution plagues the city. **BELOW:** one of many downtown high-rises.

After the overthrow of the Ming dynasty by the Manchu in 1644, nationalist ideas survived longer in Guangzhou than in other parts of China. Yet, at the same time, close contact with overseas Chinese (*huaqiao*) ensured the continuation of an openness to the world and a desire for reform in the city.

Openness, in turn, would eventually spawn revolutionary zeal. Trade with the British East India Company increased, particularly imports of opium. But the profits from the opium trade financed colonial expansion rather than benefiting the local Chinese population, and China's silver reserves were depleted to pay for the imports. This culture of dependency helped nurture revolutionary ideas and motivate secret societies amongst the Chinese, seeking to preserve the ideals of the Ming period and fostering a determination to restore this last Chinese dynasty to power.

In 1839, the Chinese commissioner Lin Zexu ordered the confiscation and destruction of 20,000 chests of opium, leading to military intervention by Great Britain in the First Opium War (1840–1842). The resulting Treaty of Nanjing – in Great Britain's favour – led to the opening of Guangzhou, Shanghai, Xiamen, Fuzhou and Ningbo to foreign trade, as well as Hong Kong's cession to Britain "in perpetuity".

In 1858, in a reactionary fit by the Chinese, foreign traders were required to limit their base of operations to the island of Shamian, along the Zhu Jiang in Guangzhou. After the Second Opium War (1856–1860), foreigners settled in other parts of Guangzhou and continued trading.

Following the overthrow of the Qing dynasty in 1912, Guangzhou became the centre of a movement led by Sun Yatsen (in Mandarin, Sun Zhongshan) and the headquarters of the Guomintang, or the Nationalist Party, the first modern

BELOW: dancing girls at school.

political party in China. During a rather brief period of cooperation between the Guomintang and the Communists, Mao Zedong worked and taught at Guangzhou's Institute of Peasant Movements, and Zhou Enlai and Lin Biao at the Military Academy.

The modernisation of Guangzhou began in the early 1920s, and most of the main streets defining the city today were built in that period; in addition the remainder of the old city wall was pulled down and a collection of junks on the river was removed. The period's feverish sense of urgency in construction – it took only 18 months to build 40 kilometres (25 mi) of road – persists today. Throughout the city, high-rises, hotels, bridges and new highways now seem to materialise overnight.

Urban personality

The personality of Guangzhou differs significantly from that of northern China. While a visitor can stand in the middle of Tiananmen Square in Beijing and feel the solidity and backbone of Chinese authority, in Guangzhou, he or she can easily stand on any street and feel the lack of order in the traffic and commotion. The language of Guangzhou, Cantonese, is incomprehensible to northern Chinese, who typically speak Mandarin (Cantonese has nine tones, instead of the four tones in the Mandarin dialect).

While it is urban, Guangzhou has been marked more by trade than industry, in contrast to Shanghai, although light industry is now an important part of Guangzhou's economy.

The area around Guangzhou was overcrowded even 200 years ago, and many peasants from the region emigrated to Southeast Asia, North America and

Map, page 257

Guangzhou is not a beautiful city, but it is a distinctly Chinese city. It was from Guangzhou that most of the world's experience with things Chinese – Chinatowns around the world and cuisine – has its origins.

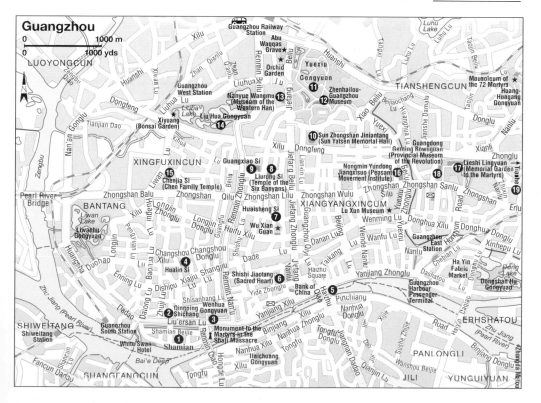

Europe. As a result, Cantonese is the most common dialect amongst overseas Chinese. Likewise, the same is true for Cantonese cuisine, which is the most varied of all Chinese cuisines but is often mocked by other Chinese.

There is a famous Chinese saying: In Beijing one talks, in Shanghai one shops and in Guangzhou one eats. Without a doubt, Guangzhou is best known for its eclectic food, from *dim sum* to dried rat meat. Dim sum – a varied collection of dumplings, small bite-sized pieces of meat and vegetables, and noodle dishes chosen from carts wheeled around the restaurant – is available almost everywhere in Guangzhou. The locals eat dim sum for breakfast and with evening tea. Restaurants serving over 2,000 dishes featuring local seafood delicacies are common in Guangzhou.

A new underground metro system connects most of Guangzhou's major sites of interest – look out for the red signs with the "y"-shape symbol. Tickets are inexpensive, but travellers might find it simpler and faster to take a taxi; fares inside the city shouldn't cost more than 20 yuan.

Old Guangzhou

The island of **Shamian ❶**, in the southwest of the city on the northern bank of the Zhu Jiang, is a preserved relic of the colonial past. Originally a sandbar, the small island was reclaimed and expanded, then divided in 1859 into several foreign concessions, primarily French and British. A canal was constructed, and after ten o'clock in the evening, two iron gates and narrow bridges kept the Chinese off the island.

Shamian is compact in size and feels very much like a resort area, in sharp contrast to the hustle of Guangzhou proper. A programme of gentrification in

BELOW: colonial architecture on Shamian.

recent years has renovated a number of old colonial buildings and nurtured restaurants and cafes, whilst former Catholic and Anglican churches have been reopened for worship. Many of the brightly-painted former trade and consular buildings, most of which were constructed by the French, are now used as government offices.

To the north of Shamian Island, on the mainland along Qingping Lu, is **Qingping Shichang ❷**, a market area that spills out into the side alleys around the main roads of Renmin Nan Lu and Nuren Jie. This was one of the first places to develop under China's gradual adoption of market economics and, as such, it was for a long time something of an oddity with its carnival-like atmosphere and crowds of shoppers. Today, Qingping is best known for selling every imaginable animal for food, including dogs, cats, owls and a variety of insects. Stalls lining Dishipu Lu and Daihe Lu sell jade, jewellery, old timepieces, Mao paraphernalia and reproductions of antique porcelain .

To the east of the market is **Wenhua Gongyuan ❸** (Culture Park), with roller-skating rinks, an open-air theatre, theatre halls, art exhibitions and performances by the School of Acrobats. Nearby is the well-stocked Department Store of the South (sometimes called Nanfang Department Store), on the corner of Renmin Nan Lu.

To the north of this area, follow Xiajiu Lu, a pedestrianised shopping street to reach Guangdong Restaurant; behind, in a narrow side alley called Shangxia Jie, is **Hualin Si ❹**. This temple is said to have been founded by an Indian monk in 526, although the existing buildings date from the Qing dynasty. There are 500 statues of *luohan*, pupils of the Buddha, in the main hall. A statue of Marco Polo, which once stood here, was lost during the 1966–76 Cultural Revolution.

Map, page 257

BELOW: Haizhu Bridge.

Sun Yatsen

If there is one political figure respected by people with different political opinions – whether in China, Taiwan, Hong Kong or overseas – it is Dr Sun Yatsen (1866–1925). A determined revolutionary, Sun devoted his life to bringing democracy to China.

Sun was born in 1866 in a coastal village in Xiangshan, in China's Guangdong province. Later he changed his name to Sun Zhongshan. Although he is often called Sun Yatsen by the Western world, most Chinese remember him as Sun Zhongshan.

Raised in a poor farming family, Sun learned the hardships of working life at an early age. Nevertheless, he received an extensive education. In 1878, he went to a church school in Honolulu and later studied medicine in Hong Kong and Guangzhou. The experience in the West helped him see the corruption and backwardness of the feudalist Qing dynasty, and he decided to devote himself to bringing about a democratic republic in China.

Sun founded the Society for Regenerating China, in Honolulu in 1894, and later established a branch in Hong Kong. After a failed uprising in Guangzhou, he fled overseas with some colleagues, but continued his work. He travelled to France to promote his revolutionary theory, and at the same time extensively studied the political systems of European countries and the United States.

After failing in several attempts to unite the Chinese in revolt, Sun finally succeeded with an uprising in October 1911, which eventually led to the overthrow of the Qing dynasty rulers and the establishment of the Republic of China. In January 1912, Sun was elected as temporary president, but he soon stepped down to concentrate on developing industries. Having realised the need to develop the country's infrastructure, Dr Sun first came up with a plan to build a 100,000-kilometre-long (62,000-mi) railway network in 10 years, which meant introducing foreign investment to finance the project. However, China was now ruled by unruly warlords who fought amongst themselves for territory, and Sun's dream was never realised.

In 1913, the next president of the Republic of China, Yuan Shikai, restored the monarchy by declaring himself the emperor, which shocked the country. Sun sent a punitive expedition against Yuan, beginning what historians call the "Second Revolution". But due to a lack of preparation and the fact that the participants, mainly warlords, had their own selfish aims, the revolution failed and Sun fled to Japan.

Without an army of his own, Sun finally realised that no warlords were reliable and decided to reform his Nationalist Party, or Guomintang, and set up a revolutionary government in Guangzhou. In 1924, the first national conference of the Guomintang was held in Guangzhou. The same year, Sun set up an army and a military school with the ambition of defeating the warlords.

However, Sun died in 1925 of disease, in Beijing. His funeral was attended by over 750,000 people, and his coffin, in accordance with his will, was buried in Nanjing's Zijinshan hill. His confidante, Chiang Kaishek, took over leadership of the Guomintang. ❑

LEFT: Dr Sun Yatsen in 1924.

Opposite the canal that separates Shamian from the city begins the **Bund** (Yanjiang Lu), which continues eastward along the waterfront to **Haizhu** ❺, built in 1933 and the oldest steel bridge across the Zhu Jiang. Just to the east of **Renmin**, the bridge that connects the eastern end of Shamian with the mainland, is a memorial to Chinese killed by foreign troops guarding the foreign quarters, in 1925.

To the north of Haizhu, the 50-metre-high (160 ft) double towers of the Catholic cathedral, **Shishi Jiaotang** ❻ (Sacred Heart), are visible. Built in the early 1860s, the cathedral was left to decay after 1949 and left to decay even more during the Cultural Revolution of the late 1960s and early 1970s. In the 1980s, it was restored and now holds services under the auspices of the Patriotic Catholic Church, which the government has banned from having contact with the Vatican.

Farther east along the river, past Haizhu Bridge and running north, is Beijing Lu, Guangzhou's main shopping street. Because of Guangzhou's proximity to Hong Kong, there are some classy boutiques and fashionable shops here. Department stores selling Western products and electronics can be found on Beijing Lu as well. Where Beijing Lu intersects with Zhongshan Lu, on the right hand side, is the Foreign Language Bookstore, where visitors can find maps and souvenir books as well as a variety of English classics at cheap prices.

Mosques and pagodas

Near the intersection of Renmin Zhong Lu and the sixth section of Zhongshan Lu (Sun Yatsen Street), in Guangtalu south of Zhongshan Lu, is the onion-shaped dome of **Huaisheng Si** ❼, a mosque dating back to 627 and founded by

Map, page 257

BELOW: downtown Guangzhou.

a trader who was said to be an uncle of the Prophet Mohammed. At that time, Arab traders visited China, so the legend may well have some truth to it, although it does not give sufficient evidence for an exact date of the foundation of the mosque. The 25-metre-high (82 ft) minaret, **Guang Ta** (Naked Pagoda), dominates the area, although new high-rises are competing to capture the skyline. Huaisheng Si is a cultural centre for Guangzhou's 5,000 Muslims.

To the north of Zhongshan Lu, a fairly narrow street leads to **Liurong Si** ❽ (Temple of the Six Banyan Trees). Its **Hua Ta** (Flower Pagoda), built in 1097, is a well-known symbol of the city. It appears from the outside to be nine storeys, each storey with doorways and encircling balcony, but inside the pagoda there are actually 17 levels, not nine. Visitors can climb to the top of the pagoda for a view of Guangzhou's sprawling streets, although some vantage points are somewhat marred by skyscrapers. Liurong Si, said to date back to the fifth century, was mentioned by the poet Su Dongpo in an 11th-century calligraphic tribute to six banyan trees that grew in its courtyard. The trees are gone now, but his inscription remains.

The main hall contains three brass statues of the Buddha, eight Luohan figures, statues of the Ggod of Medicine, and an image cast in 1663 of the goddess of mercy, Guanyin. The statues date back to the Qing dynasty. Old calligraphy steles mounted on the walls of the courtyard have been dated back to the Qing dynasty as well. Today, the temple is the local headquarters of the Chinese Buddhist Association.

A few hundred metres northeast is **Guangxiao Si** ❾, a temple preserved during the Cultural Revolution on orders from Zhou Enlai. The temple is believed to date back to sometime around AD 400, making it older than the city itself. Some of the present buildings were, however, built after a big fire in 1629, and

BELOW: the unemployed at the railway station.

most probably only after 1832. At the entrance is a brightly painted laughing Buddha, and in the main courtyard, a huge bronze incense burner fills the air with smoke. The main hall is notable for its ceiling of red-lacquered timber, and the back courtyard has some of the oldest iron pagodas found in China.

Dongtie Ta and **Xitie Ta** (Western and Eastern Iron Pagodas) date to the city's beginnings. There is a seven-metre-high (23 ft) stone pagoda behind the main hall with sculptures of the Buddha placed in eight niches. It is thought to date back to 967, but was only put in its present location at the beginning of Mongolian rule in the Yuan dynasty. The halls reflect several different eras.

Sun Yatsen memorials

To the northwest, in a formal garden near Jiefang Bei Lu, **Sun Zhongshan Jiniantang** ❿ (Sun Yatsen Memorial Hall) is easy to spot with its eye-catching blue roof tiles. The hall, built shortly after the death of Sun Yatsen in 1925 and completed in 1931, now houses a large theatre and lecture hall with seating for 5,000 people. The octagonal hall is made of steel and reinforced concrete and sits in a six-hectare (15-acre) park.

Guangzhou's largest park, **Yuexiu Gongyuan** ⓫ is beautifully landscaped with three artificial lakes, rolling hills, rock sculptures and lush greenery. Its centrepiece is **Zhenhailou** ⓬ (Tower Overlooking the Sea), built in 1380 and a memorial to the seven great sea journeys undertaken by the eunuch Zheng He to east Africa, the Persian Gulf and Java between 1405 and 1433. Today, the tower houses a museum showcasing the history of Guangzhou.

Nearby is the marble and granite **Sun Yatsen Monument**, which sits on a hill above Sun Yatsen Hall. Visitors can climb to the top for a great view of the city.

Map, page 257

For 40 years I have devoted myself to the cause of national revolution, the object of which is to raise China to a position of independence and equality among nations... we must associate ourselves in a common struggle with all the people of the world who treat us as equals.

— DR SUN YATSEN

BELOW: Sun Zhongshan Jiniantang, and train station.

TIP

Theft is a problem in Guangzhou. Be careful around bus stops and train stations. Because of its economic prowess, Guangzhou has long been a magnet for the rural unemployed, who often remain unemployed after arriving in the city.

BELOW: unemployed rural men entertain themselves.

Also in Yuexiu Park is the Sculpture of Five Rams, which tells the story of five heavenly creatures who flew over the city on rams – or goats – and relieved the people of famine. Yuexiu Park has facilities for recreational activities, including a golf driving range, bowling alley and swimming pool.

Across Jiefang Bei Lu from Yuexiu Park is a small, grassy area called **Orchid Garden**. The garden is filled with flowers in spring and summer, and offers a quiet patch of nature in which to rest after hours of hiking around the city.

Farther north and west past the teeming crowds of the railway station lies **Sanyuanli**, Guangzhou's Hui Minority district, with its Muslim-Chinese restaurants serving Chinese cuisine with Middle Eastern influences. Sanyuanli is also the city's red-light district.

The China Hotel dominates the major intersection on Jiefang Beilu and Liu Hua Lu, where the ambience of so-called Food Street has become a popular style of eating. It has been copied by others, but the original was opened by the China Hotel and still stands as an institution. Open kitchens in a long, narrow setting serve hotpot, dim sum and a variety of local favourites.

Farther south along Jiefang Bei Lu is the **Nanyue Wangmu** ⓭ (Museum of the Western Han), the tomb of the Nanyu emperor. In 1983, bulldozers clearing the ground for construction of the China Hotel dug up the tomb of the emperor Wen Di, who ruled southern China from 137 to 122 BC. The spot where the tomb was found is now the site of a museum, housing the skeletons of the emperor and 15 courtiers, including concubines, guards, cooks and a musician, who were buried alive with the emperor.

The museum recreates the setting of the tomb so that visitors can walk down stairs into the actual chambers. Archaeologists found that the tomb walls were

built from sandstone carved out of Lianhua Shan, about an hour east along the Zhu Jiang. Thousands of funeral objects from jade armour to bronze music chimes are displayed in adjoining rooms. The museum also features a rare collection of porcelain pillows from the Tang and Yuan dynasties, donated by a Hong Kong collector.

West of the China Hotel on Liu Hua Lu is **Liu Hua Gongyuan** park ⑭, which features Guangzhou's largest artificial lake. Built as part of the government's Great Leap Forward in 1958, the park provides rowboats that take passengers around the lake to view the spacious grounds surrounding it.

Chenjia Si (Chen Family Temple) ⑮, located on the western end of Zhongshan Lu, is one of China's more whimsical temples, built in 1894 and restored after the Cultural Revolution. The temple has six courtyards and a classical Chinese layout, and is decorated with friezes crafted in Shiwan, near Foshan to the west. The largest frieze depicts scenes from the epic *Romance of Three Kingdoms*, with thousands of intricate figures against a backdrop of ornate houses, grandiose gates and pagodas. There is a giant altar of gold-leaf plating and additional wood, brick and stone friezes along the rooftops. The name Chenjia Si recalls the descendants of the Chen clan, one of the most common family names in Guangdong Province, who provided the funds to build the temple.

Chenjia Si is also home to the **Guangdong Folk Arts Museum**, which was established in 1959. The museum displays arts and crafts from all over China but especially Guangdong Province. The collection includes embroidery, traditional dress of China's minority groups, porcelain figures and jade carvings. The displays are showcased in the temple's halls.

Map, page 257

BELOW: whimsical figures, Chenjia Si.

Map, page 257

Among those who taught at the Peasant Movement Institute were Zhou Enlai (above) and Mao Zedong.

OPPOSITE: service-industry workers are increasingly important.
BELOW: bicycle lane.

Eastern districts

In the eastern part of the city, on Zhongshan Lu, is the former Kongzi Miao, or Confucius Temple. The building lost its religious function during the "bourgeois revolution" in 1912. In 1924, **Nongmin Yundong Jiangxisuo** ⑯ (Peasant Movement Institute) was opened here as the first school of the Chinese Communist Party. The elite of the Communist Party taught here: Mao Zedong (his work and bedroom can be viewed), Zhou Enlai, Qu Qiubai, Deng Zhong, Guo Moruo and others. This is also where Mao developed his original theory of peasant revolution.

After the collapse of a workers' uprising in 1927, the Communists were forced to retreat for a time from the cities. A park and memorial, **Lieshi Lingyuan** ⑰ (Memorial Garden to the Martyrs), was created in 1957 in memory of the uprising and its nearly 6,000 victims. The temple is mostly of Ming-period style. Directly east of the temple is **Guangdong Geming Bowuguan** ⑱ (Provincial Museum of the Revolution), a reminder of the role of the Guomintang (Nationalist Party) and its predecessors since the First Opium War.

South of Zhongshan Gan Lu are the old buildings of Guangdong University, where China's first modern and highly respected author, Lu Xun, lectured in 1927. An exhibition there is dedicated to him. Until 1927, the All Chinese Trade Union Federation was located nearby. Liu Shaoqi, the revolutionary and later president of the People's Republic – and a victim of the Cultural Revolution – worked there.

In the northeast, near the zoo on Xialie Lu, is a memorial park built in 1918 for the 72 victims of an uprising in 1911. The large park features monuments symbolising democracy and peace. On the western side of the memorial park there is a small museum on Guangdong province's revolutionary history. To the southeast is the **Hai Yin Fabric Market** on Dong Hu Lu, one of the largest fabric markets in China. Over a thousand stalls in hundreds of rows sell wool, fine silk and locally made fabric at bargain prices. Nearby, Dongshan Hu Gongyuan borders a tributary of the Zhu Jiang.

Northeast lies Guangzhou's new financial and shopping centre, **Tianhe** ⑲. The giant Tianhe Sports Centre takes up at least five city blocks and features basketball courts, Olympic-size swimming pools, running tracks, soccer fields and other sports facilities. Across the street is Team Plaza, a six-storey shopping mall that features a Japanese department store on the bottom level and expensive shops spiralling upward. Just north of the stadium is the imaginatively named Times Square; it doesn't really compare to New York's or even Hong Kong's, but there are some good restaurants inside. New high-rises, hotels and expensive restaurants continue to expand the city eastward.

Now that China has, more or less, completely embraced market economics throughout most of the country, along with privatising nearly all state-owned industries, Guangzhou must compete as an entrepreneurial city with both Shanghai and Hong Kong, no easy task. Shanghai, for example, has been targeted by the government to become a regional competitor with Hong Kong and Singapore as a financial centre. ❑

OUTSIDE GUANGZHOU

Anyone spending any time in Guangzhou eventually seeks to escape the city. Fortunately, there are a number of options that can steady the urban nerves. Anything seems quiet after a week in Guangzhou

The sub-tropical climate of southern Guangdong province has made the land an ideal setting for the production of tea, lychees, bananas, oranges and pineapples, and as a holiday retreat for Chinese.

The north of **Guangzhou** itself is surrounded by the hills of the Dayu Ling mountain range, while the **Zhu Jiang** (Pearl River) cuts through Guangzhou itself, offering boat trips to travellers looking for small villages, towns and hilly areas to the east, west and south of Guangzhou. Monasteries and temples dot the river's course; many were built during the Qing dynasty to honour the Northern Emperor Zhen Wu, who warded off flooding of the Zhu Jiang.

Guangzhou's proximity to Hong Kong and the southern coast has made the area an industrial centre, and many of its urban areas are modernising into nondescript, ugly places. If visiting Guangzhou for a week, the traveller may find it pleasant – if not outright necessary – to escape the city at least once for some fresh air and quiet, a little exercise in the hills, or to recapture some peace of mind. Fortunately, the environs of Guangzhou offer numerous options for escape, whether to an amusement park and its inherent tackiness, rustic hills peppered with temples, or small villages with a slower pace of life and architectural remnants from the Ming and Qing dynasties.

BELOW: elderly woman surveys the street.

North of Guangzhou

An easy half-day trip to the north of the city leads to **Baiyun Shan ❶** (White Cloud Hills), a series of hills overlooking Guangzhou's increasingly fussy skyline. A cable car ascends to the top, where you can walk to several other peaks. Souvenir stands and teahouses are found at various peaks and precipices in the area, ideal places to sit back and take in the surrounding hills outside the city.

If skipping the cable car to walk up to the peak, there is a paved road as well as stone paths that wind up though through the trees. Nengren, an active Buddhist temple where many Chinese come to light incense and pray, is found half way up to the peak of **Baiyun Wanwang** (White Cloud Evening View). There is also an old swimming pool nestled among the trees where locals escape during the summer heat.

At the base of Baiyun Shan is the garden of **Yun Tai**, which features some well-manicured flower beds, rock sculptures, fountains and greenhouses. Although the park is reminiscent of a miniature golf course, it may be worth visiting for a quick escape from the city. If approaching Baiyun Shan from the heart of Guangzhou, you will pass **Lu Hu**, a lake that previously supplied water for the city. Today it is better known for an expensive golf course and restaurant, although it is a nice place for a walk along the water and to relax under the cooling trees.

Two to three hours northeast of Guangzhou is the town of **Conghua ❷** and **Conghua Wenguan**, a hot spring that has become a popular tourist destination for local and overseas Chinese. In addition to the hot spring, the area is known for its clean air and serene setting. Many long-term expats living in Guangzhou travel to Conghua to escape the city bustle and play golf. Unfortunately,

TIP

In the hills immediately north of Guangzhou are several amusement parks – including Nanhu and Dongfang – that are best missed, unless the children absolutely must have such an experience while in China.

BELOW: hot springs at Conghua.

expensive hotels have claimed as private property the area around the hot springs north of the city itself, so it is difficult for the traveller to meander around the aqua-green hot springs.

The land surrounding Conghua is extremely rural and is known for its production of lychee and tea. Tour groups run from Guangzhou to Conghua's lychee fields during summer and fall, when lychees are in season. The Conghua Tea Farm runs tours from Guangzhou, and one can sample various teas and go out into the fields with wicker baskets to pick leaves from the topmost branches and brew this tea oneself.

To the west

An hour by bus and 30 kilometres (18 mi) to the southwest of Guangzhou is the city of **Foshan ❸**, home to **Zu Miao ❹** (Ancestor Temple), a Daoist temple whose history dates back to the Song dynasty. Renovated in 1372, the temple houses a two-ton bronze statue of the Northern Emperor Zhenwu, the so-called Water God who watched over the Zhu Jiang, which was prone to frequent flooding. The temple itself is well-preserved, with many finely sculptured friezes made from limestone, ash of shells, paper, rice, straw and sand. The once colourfully painted friezes depict Chinese fables and scenes of Foshan's history. Many of the friezes have faded to an antique tone, which adds to the temple's charm.

The grounds of Zu Miao are fairly spacious, with courtyards and halls displaying antique weapons, iron bells and porcelain figures. In the main courtyard, the city has set up an exhibit of old carved-stone street markers from the Qing dynasty, when the streets were so narrow that the addresses were carved horizontally into the buildings.

There are at least a dozen hot springs at Conghua; unfortunately, none is outdoors. Water temperatures average 30–40°C (86–104°F), with a maximum of 70°C (158°F).

BELOW: portraits of local people.

One early Western traveller to the area wrote: "Foshan was like a forest of buildings without end. Thousands of stores dealing with various trades and workshops were dispersed in crisscrossing streets. The streets were so narrow only two people could walk down them at a time."

A 15-minute walk north of Zu Miao leads to **Renshou Si**, a pagoda built in 1935. An apartment complex crowds the seven-storey pagoda, and one can no longer climb to the top. Still, the pagoda is well-preserved, and a friendly elderly couple watches over it and are knowledgeable about its history.

The city of Foshan itself is quite busy, with its fair share of pollution and traffic. The smaller streets may remind the visitor of an older city, home to merchants and bankers in the 19th century. Today, shops sell handmade crafts and porcelain souvenirs all the way to **Shiwan ❺**, which is a half-hour walk away, about two kilometres (1¼ mi) to the southwest. In Shiwan there are many porcelain factories (not to mention porcelain toilet factories) that welcome tour groups. Shiwan itself does not offer much, and is only worthwhile for those with a serious interest in porcelain.

Further southwest of Guangzhou lies **Xiqiao Shan ❻**, a hilly area with villages that have retained some of their 19th-century ambiance. Xiqiao is one of the more charming towns outside Guangzhou that still thrives on its local produce and river trade. From the town, one can travel by cable car up to the peak of the nearby hills to walk along stone paths that wind through even smaller villages, rocky plateaus and waterfalls.

Feiliutian Chi, a waterfall that is the most famous in Xiqiao Shan, is said to fall 1,000 metres (3,000 ft), which seems a considerable exaggeration. Nearby is the Tianhu Hotel and a restaurant, providing a decent lunch break. Because of its

Map, page 252

BELOW: market porcelain.

proximity to the waterfalls and lakes, the eastern area of Xiqiao Shan has been built up for tourism. Further down the path from the hotel are caves and a lake at Baiyun, and a route back to the main road into Xiqiao.

Easily accessible by train and boat in a couple of hours and 110 kilometres (68 mi) west of Guangzhou, **Zhaoqing** ❼ is what the Chinese call "Little Guilin", with the same type of limestone karst formations found in Guilin, but on a much smaller scale. On the banks of the Xi Jiang, the city of Zhaoqing is not much to see in itself, as it has modernised into a heavily trafficked and polluted city; still, if staying over, there are many restaurants and hotels.

South of the city is the **Chongxi Ta**, a pagoda; further east along the river lies the **Yuejiang Lou**, a temple. Both were heavily damaged during the frenzy of the Cultural Revolution, but have been renovated and are famous sights in the city.

Zhaoqing's main attraction, **Qixing Yan** (Seven Stars Crag), is located north of the city and has been made into a large park. The crags take their name from the legend that the small hills are actually stars that fell from the heavens. The limestone hills are fairly low, covered by greenery and surrounded by artificial lakes and modern pagodas that float over the water. There are stone paths that lead through the park and make for a nice walk.

You can also glimpse people picking tea, and may very well be invited to join in the picking. Each of the crags is named after what its shape symbolises – a toad, stone house, jade curtain. There are plenty of souvenir and refreshment stands scattered throughout the park.

If visiting Zhaoqing, it may be worth your time to visit **Dinghu Shan**, 20 kilometres (12 mi) away to the north and famous for a Ming-era Buddhist temple, as well as many villages scattered over the mountain. Compared to Zhaoqing,

BELOW: bamboo rafts and rice fields.

Dinghu Shan is less touristy. You can glimpse Guangdong province's subtropical vegetation, walk through what the Chinese call a virgin forest and pass waterfalls. Atop the mountain is a lake that is well worth the hike.

Map, page 252

To the east

In 1995, Guangdong province opened the **Grand World Scenic Park** to spark local tourism. The park occupies an amazing 480,000 square metres to the east of Guangzhou and seems to have been built to rival nearby Shenzhen's theme park of world sites in both scale and investment. The Grand World Scenic Park features six theatres that were built as replicas of opera and music houses around the world, including in Japan, France, England, Saudi Arabia, Greece and New York. The park strives to present festivities representing the ecleticism of 98 countries and "the landscapes of 26 countries", creating an overwhelming aura of Disneyworld, Chinese style. There are well-landscaped gardens and displays of Guangdong's horticulture within the park, as well as a variety of tacky souvenir stands and restaurants. The entrance fee may seem a bit steep.

Further east lies the original site of the **Huangpu Junxiao ⑧** (Huangpu Military Academy). Zhou Enlai and other Communist Party officials were trained here; several prominent buildings constructed during the 1940s still stand. Today, the academy is a museum where one can learn about the history of the Communist Party. Unfortunately, much of the history is conveyed in Chinese. The academy has become a must-see for mainlanders.

Accessible by both bus and boat, **Lianhua Shan ⑨** (Lotus Mountain) lies about an hour southeast of Guangzhou on the Zhu Jiang. The mountain area was an important stone quarry 2,000 years ago, and today the mining caves and

Chiang Kaishek, who became leader of the Nationalists and later Taiwan, was once Huangpu Military Academy's president.

BELOW: hot chillies.

Map, page 252

Lin Zexu, the Chinese commissioner who ordered to put an end to the British opium trade in Guangzhou, bivouacked his troops in the quarry at Lianhua Shan during the Second Opium Wars.

OPPOSITE: tea plantation.
BELOW: market rooster.

carved rock formations have eroded enough to take on a natural look. Lianhua Shan is officially deemed a "tourist resort", with its fair share of theme park amusements, including a driving range, water slide, bumper cars and pricey restaurants. Fortunately, these new additions inhabit just one side of the mountain. Motorcycles will take you past this area to the top, where stands a pagoda built during the Ming dynasty.

Nearby, a statue erected in 1994 of Guanyin, the Goddess of Mercy, is made of 120 tons of bronze with pure gold plating and stands 41 metres (120 ft) high. The view from this spot takes in the extensive paddies of rice spread out below and the Zhu Jiang, or Pearl River, below that.

From the Guanyin statue, descend a long flight of steps to the mining area. Sturdy paths have been added that weave through the rocks and ponds, while Qing dynasty inscriptions mark the various mining spots. The path will finally lead out to the original and now remote district of Lianhua, where an active temple is nestled in the lush greenery. Bamboo huts and additional cave formations give this area a truly magical feel. Exiting the park here and walking back to the boat dock passes through a market area selling dried fish and snakes, as well as a variety of other seafood delicacies. There are many restaurants along the main road as well.

Panyu, a district to the southeast of Guangzhou, is home to the Nanhai Temple, built during the Sui dynasty. Today it sits among some spacious grounds, with cultural relics housed within its walls. The city of **Nanhai ⑩** itself is more like a Guangzhou suburb, and one can reach the temple from Guangzhou by taxi. Excavations of Nanhai show that merchants from the Qin and Han dynasties used the area as the starting point of the China's emerging maritime trade, which eventually replaced the overland Silk Road in importance. Indeed, people from Guangzhou often brag about how Guangzhou and the surrounding area were commercial and trading centres some 2,000 years ago, with silk, ceramics and tea as the three biggest exports for the region.

Most people who travel to **Dongguan ⑪** do so for business reasons. Few travellers to China will want to go there for any aesthetic reason. Still, for those of an entrepreneurial bent, it is considered the factory headquarters of China. Indeed, Dongguan is home to the world's largest shoe factory, and many of the Nike shoes and clothing distributed worldwide are made here. It is not necessarily a place to visit, but it still stands as a city that has made a name for itself in the world.

Increasingly, travellers may find themselves coming to Guangzhou and the surrounding Pearl River Delta region. With the return of Hong Kong and Macau to China's control, the Chinese government has plans to turn the delta area into an economic powerhouse. In early 1998 it was announced that a bridge would be built from Hong Kong across the open water to the mainland on the Macau side, no small feat. Such a bridge would make the transport of goods and people quicker and easier. In the end, Hong Kong and Macau will probably end up dragging Guangzhou and the rest of southern China into their orbit, rather than Hong Kong and Macau becoming more like China. ❑

INSIGHT GUIDES
Travel Tips

CONTENTS

Getting Acquainted

The Place

Hong Kong covers an area of 1,095 sq. km (423 sq. miles) and has a population of around 6.8 million. The population density is therefore 6,210 people per sq. km (16,075 per sq. mile), making it one of the most crowded places in the world.

Since 1 July 1997, Hong Kong has been a Special Administrative Region of the People's Republic of China, after being a British colony since 1841. The Hong Kong government, however, enjoys a certain degree of autonomy from the rest of China. The Hong Kong Basic Law guarantees (on paper) that the territory's capitalist system and ways of life will remain unchanged until at least 2047. Under the principle of "Hong Kong people ruling Hong Kong" the territory's chief executive must be a Hong Kong citizen. The legislature consists of a mixture of appointed and elected Hong Kong residents. Hong Kong also maintains separate customs regulations, laws and tax systems from the rest of China.

The term Hong Kong is both an administrative and geographical one. For convenience, Hong Kong is divided into three sections: Hong Kong Island, Kowloon and the New Territories. Kowloon refers to the mainland area on the other side of the harbour from Hong Kong Island. The New Territories is the area between Kowloon and mainland China that was leased by Britain in 1898 for 99 years. The area includes Hong Kong's 200-odd outlying islands. The original term Hong Kong referred to Hong Kong Island only, but has since come to refer to the combined Hong Kong Island, Kowloon and the New Territories.

A greater proportion of the population has gradually spread to the New Territories, reflecting the government's policy to develop new towns where there is much more space. Nearly 50 percent of the population is in the New Territories, 30 percent in Kowloon, and 20 percent on Hong Kong Island.

Time Zone

Hong Kong is eight hours ahead of London and thirteen ahead of New York. The difference is reduced by one hour from April to the end of October when daylight saving time is in effect in Europe and the US.

The Climate

Hong Kong has a humid subtropical climate. There are, however, four distinct seasons. The ideal time for travelling to Hong Kong is from the end of September to early December, when the weather is warm, the air is dry and it seldom rains. The average temperature is 23°C (74°F), with humidity around 70 percent.

In winter, from late December to early March, temperatures can be slightly chilly, especially in the rural areas, so it is advisable to bring light woollens and sometimes a

coat. The average temperature is 17°C (63°F), humidity 75 percent.

Temperatures and humidity rise abruptly in spring from March to mid-May when average temperatures reach 23°C (74°F). In summer, which lasts until early September, temperatures hover around 30°C (86°F) and humidity is consistently above 70 percent. Even when it doesn't rain you may quickly be dripping with sweat. Wear light clothes, but bring some long sleeves for the summer – not because it gets chilly in the evening but because many restaurants and shops have very effective air-conditioning.

The People

Most of Hong Kong's population, at least 96 percent, are ethnic Chinese, either born in Hong Kong or having migrated from mainland China during successive periods of political turmoil after the 1949 revolution and during the Cultural Revolution of the late 1960s and early 1970s. The majority originated from Guangdong province (Canton) to the north of Hong Kong, though many also migrated from Shanghai.

Hong Kong does have a significant expatriate population. In recent years, the largest expatriate group has been nationals of the

Typhoons

From June to early September, it is not uncommon for Hong Kong to experience tropical storms or typhoons. If you are there at the time when a typhoon hits, you will find that virtually everything comes to a complete standstill. The Hong Kong Observatory has standard typhoon warnings that vary according to how close a typhoon is to Hong Kong. Usually, this begins with a typhoon number one signal, which may shortly escalate to a number three. When the number eight signal is raised, it means Hong Kong may suffer a direct hit. Schools, offices and shops close immediately and everyone goes home. A rare

typhoon number ten is almost certain to mean serious damage, as the storm sweeps through the territory causing floods and sometimes deaths. Watching typhoon news bulletins can be dramatic and exciting but when everything closes you will be stuck for anything to do. Hotels, however, do continue to operate. In fact, locals often go to hotel restaurants as they are the only places likely to be open during a typhoon. You are not advised to go outside during a typhoon as fatalities have been known to occur in both urban and rural areas, mainly due to objects and structures that fall in the strong winds.

Philippines, who number around 142,500. Most of them work as domestic helpers and their conditions of stay only allow them to remain in Hong Kong for as long as their employment contract continues. Since the handover in 1997, a large community of expats remains in Hong Kong, of whom the highest number are not British, as you might expect, but Americans and Canadians. Many Hong Kong Chinese emigrated to North America in the 1990s, only to return with a new passport and pick up their former lives. Non-Chinese residents of Hong Kong cannot become Hong Kong citizens, but after seven years of continuous residence they can acquire the "right to land" and may not be deported from Hong Kong.

THE FAMILY

Family values are extremely important to the Chinese. In the old days before the current urban overcrowding, whole extended families would live together in one house. Even in large wealthy families where each member could afford several homes of their own, it is still a preferred way to live.

For most people, the excessive cost of housing adds to the imperative to live with parents until marriage and sometimes beyond. Young people or unmarried people in their twenties and thirties rarely think of moving out and living by themselves or sharing a place to live with friends. It would be considered unfilial and selfish.

Sunday is usually a family day, when the whole extended family gets together. Chinese restaurants are usually packed at lunchtime with noisy family groupings.

In business, the Chinese usually prefer to involve their family rather than strangers if at all possible and, generally speaking, they have a tendency not to trust strangers. Many of Hong Kong's wealthiest business empires are still controlled by families, with power handed down from father to son. By tradition the oldest son has a more

Lucky Numbers

Chinese people are incredibly superstitious about numbers. The number 8 is especially lucky, because the word for 8 sounds like the word meaning wealth. Similarly, 4 is to be avoided because it sounds like the word for death. No cars at the Hong Kong School of Motoring have any 4s on their number plates. A garment tycoon paid millions of dollars for the number 8 car registration plate. Prices, especially in Chinese restaurants, often end in an 8.

onerous duty to continue the family line and is under a lot of pressure to be successful and bring honour to his family.

Older people are treated with respect in traditional Chinese societies. Children will consider it their duty to look after their parents, and it is not at all uncommon to find executives in their early twenties giving most of their monthly income to their mother, who usually manages the family funds. It is rare for elderly people to be sent to old people's homes instead of being looked after by their children.

Familiar Chinese language terms of address for strangers give them family names, too. For instance, a young man is referred to as "older brother", but never "younger brother", even when addressing someone slightly younger, as it is considered insulting and resembles one of the (many) local slang terms for the male sexual organ. A man over the age of forty is referred to as "uncle" or over sixty as "grandpa". Female equivalents also exist.

NAMES

Chinese names are generally of three characters, with the family name being the first, followed by the given names. However, most Hong Kong Chinese are also referred to using the initials of their given name, and by adopted

Western first names, which have become much more common in recent years. For instance, Cheung Che Kwan could be C K Cheung or John Cheung. Obscure names can be entertaining sometimes, such as the clerk who adopted the name "Nothing Wong."

BUSINESS CARDS

If you're coming to Hong Kong on business, make sure that you have a good stock of business cards (usually called name cards in Hong Kong), preferably with your name and title written in Chinese on one side and English on the other. It is an old custom to offer and receive name cards with both hands rather than one. This gesture is not extremely important, but would show that you know how things are done. You should certainly treat someone's name card with respect – don't write on it.

BUSINESS ATTIRE

Despite the hot and humid climate, Hong Kong's business attire is still very formal: dark suits and ties are worn by men all year round, and women are usually quite conservatively dressed at the office – they rarely wear trousers. Many people work on Saturday mornings, and on this day everyone comes to the office in casual wear. On the whole, Hong Kong's people are very fashionable and well dressed both at work and at play.

Gifts

It is not as important to give gifts to business associates in Hong Kong as it is in some other Asian countries, but if you do give them, they should be wrapped in brightly coloured paper. If you are given gifts, do not open them in front of the giver. Certain gifts are considered unlucky and should be avoided – clocks, sharp objects and anything in black.

Planning the Trip

VISAS & PASSPORTS

Nationals of most developed countries do not need a visa to enter Hong Kong as a tourist. Conditions of stay vary according to nationality, but most nationalities may enter Hong Kong visa-free as tourists. For instance, US nationals and most EU nationals are given three months visa free on arrival. British nationals should note that the previous one-year unconditional visa on arrival with the right to work has now been replaced by a six-month tourist visa on arrival.

For those taking up employment in Hong Kong, it is necessary to obtain a work permit from the Immigration Department, usually in advance of entering the territory. Your company should be able to assist with the necessary paperwork. Hong Kong residents should carry a Hong Kong identity card, which is issued by the Immigration Department.

All other visitors are in theory supposed to carry photographic identity such as a passport with them, but it is unlikely that you will be stopped by police officers and asked to produce identification.

CUSTOMS ALLOWANCES

Hong Kong is a free port, so you can bring as many gifts as you like in and out of the territory. Cars can also be brought in for personal use without payment of duty. Firearms must be declared and handed into custody until departure. Duty-free allowances for visitors are 200 cigarettes and 50 cigars or 250g tobacco and one litre of wine or spirits.

DEPARTURE TAX

Hong Kong imposes a departure tax of HK$80 on all passengers leaving the territory (free for children under 12). This fee is usually included in the price of the ticket, but if not you will be issued a receipt, a portion of which will be retained by security staff at Immigration.

Electricity

The voltage in Hong Kong is 200/ 220 volts, 50 cycles. For a place of such international standing, it is surprising that Hong Kong still does not seem to have standardised plug fittings. However, hotels will certainly have adaptors to make any appliance work.

Health

No vaccinations are required for Hong Kong, though travellers planning to stay any length of time should be aware that Hepatitis A and B are prevalent across Asia, and precautions are therefore wise.

Tap water is best avoided in Hong Kong. Bottled water is normally provided by hotels and is readily available from convenience stores throughout the territory. Avoid eating food from street stalls to be on the safe side, as they tend not to have the same standards of hygiene as licensed restaurants.

Money Matters

The Hong Kong dollar is the standard unit of currency and comes in denominations of HK$1,000, $500, $100, $50, $20 and $10 notes plus HK$10, $5, $2 and $1 coins. The dollar is divided into 100 cents and there are coins of 50¢, 20¢ and 10¢ denominations. The dollar rate fluctuates against most major international currencies but it is pegged to the US dollar at approximately 7.8 Hong Kong dollars to the US dollar. This means that the currency is much more stable than most in the region.

There are three note-issuing banks in Hong Kong: HongKong Bank, Standard Chartered Bank and the Bank of China. Most high street banks will exchange foreign currency and generally display exchange rates on digital boards. They usually offer better rates than the money-changers in the major tourist areas, although there's usually a $50 charge for a single transaction. Cash machines are plentiful in the urban areas and allow the withdrawal of local currency with most major credit cards.

Chinese Festivals

Hong Kong has a year-round calendar of exciting traditional festivals, some of them also public holidays. Most of these are based on dates in the lunar calendar and therefore the dates vary from year to year by up to a few weeks.

Lunar New Year (January/February)

This is the single most important Chinese festival of the year, a time for visiting friends and relatives (often in mainland China). For Hong Kong's expatriate residents, it's a time to take a break. There are various things to see during the Lunar New Year. The highlight is the fireworks display, when Victoria Harbour lights up in a multi-million dollar pyrotechnic extravaganza. There is also a lively Flower Market in Victoria Park. In recent years, the Hong Kong Tourism Board has organised a New Year Parade in Central, which is amusing if stopping short of being dazzling.

Much more important to the pragmatic Hong Kong Chinese, Lunar New Year is a time of year when debts should be cleared. It is also a bad time for employers – staff are paid an annual bonus of at least one month's salary, and if they have performed well, they expect to receive more. People greet one another with *kung hei fat choi*, which is a wish for good fortune and prosperity. In return for the greeting, they expect to receive little red packets with *lai see* (lucky money) inside.

Shops traditionally close at Lunar New Year, but increasingly many of the larger ones stay open to attract extra trade.

Spring Lantern Festival (Yuen Siu) February/March

This is popularly referred to as the Chinese Valentine's Day. It is held on the 15th day of the Lunar New Year and involves the hanging of colourful traditional lanterns in homes, restaurants and temples.

Birthday of Tin Hau April/May

Since fishing and the sea have a special place in Hong Kong's history, Tin Hau – the goddess of the sea – has a special importance, particularly among the fishing communities. Fishermen decorate their boats in bright colours and flock to the Tin Hau temples around the territory to pray for a good catch in the coming year. The best places to join the homage to Tin Hau are at the Tin Hau Temple in Aberdeen and in the New Territories town of Yuen Long, where there is a parade with lion dancers and floats.

Cheung Chau Bun Festival May

The tiny outlying island of Cheung Chau is the only place in the world to hold a bun festival. Towering piles of sweet buns intermingled with effigies of gods are stacked up in the grounds of the Pak Tai temple. Figures in historical costumes parade on stilts or ride on floats across the island.

Dragon Boat Festival (Tuen Ng) June

It is said that the national hero Qu Yuan drowned himself over 2,000 years ago in protest against a corrupt government. Legend has it that while people tried to rescue him, they beat drums to scare the fish away and stop them from

Public Holidays

The fact that many Hong Kong residents work a five-and-a-half-day week and have short periods of annual leave is compensated by a relatively large number of public holidays every year – 17 in total. These are as follows:

- **1 January:** New Year's Day
- **January/February:** Lunar New Year (three-day holiday)
- **April:** Ching Ming Festival Good Friday and Easter Monday
- **May/June:** Dragon Boat Festival; Buddha's Birthday (May 11); Labour Day (May 1)
- **1 July:** SAR Establishment Day
- **September/October:** The day following Mid-Autumn Festival
- **1 October:** National Day (2 days)
- **October:** Chung Yeung Festival
- **25 December:** Christmas (2 days)

eating his body. In these enlightened times (and thanks to a few decades of intervention from Hong Kong's Independent Commission Against Corruption) such dramatic protests are no longer necessary and this event is purely a festival. To symbolise the ancient rescue attempts, elaborately decorated dragon boats race to the beat of loud drums. International dragon-boat races with competing national teams are held the week following the festival.

Mid-Autumn Festival September

If there's one festival in the year you should make an effort to see, this is it. Paper lanterns, in all shapes and sizes, are illuminated and taken out to public parks and high places. Many people go to Victoria Park, and it is a very beautiful sight to watch the throngs with their illuminated lanterns. At this time of the year, people also eat special sweet cakes known as mooncakes, which are made of ground lotus and sesame seeds. They are definitely an acquired taste, but all part of the fun.

Getting There

BY AIR

Hong Kong

Hong Kong is a major international air-traffic hub for the region, handling over 30 million passengers a year. Hong Kong's impressive international airport is located at Chek Lap Kok (CLK), on the northern shore of Lantau and about 34 km (21 miles) from Central. While the interior is rather bland and cold, CLK's Y-shaped terminal is at least highly efficient. Aircraft are received at a plethora of gates; moving walkways and an Automated People Mover speed arrivals to Immigration where queues are dealt with swiftly. Suitcases are usually circling the carousel when you reach the baggage hall, and there is a large shopping mall, left luggage office, post office, an adjacent 1,100-room hotel plus plenty of (rather pedestrian) food and beverage outlets. The terminal is also dotted with other facilities, such as smoking rooms, ATMs and international communications embracing phone, fax and the Internet. Enquiry hotline: 2181 0000; www.hkairport.com.

Transport to the rest of Hong Kong includes an express train service, buses, a ferry and taxis. See Getting Around, page 289, for details.

Guangzhou

Guangzhou's Baiyun Airport is 10 km (6 miles) and a 30-minute drive from the city. The domestic and international terminals are housed in separate buildings. Domestic flights operate between Guangzhou and Beijing and many other large cities in China. There are international flights from Guangzhou to Bangkok, Hanoi, Ho Chi Minh City, Jakarta, Kuala Lumpur, Manila, Singapore, Sydney and Vientiane. With the exception of Singapore Airlines, MAS and Garuda, which have offices selling tickets in Guangzhou, tickets for international flights on Chinese and foreign carriers must be purchased from the CAAC main office. Tickets for domestic flights are sold at the offices of the Chinese carriers and

Airline Offices in Hong Kong

Air Canada
10/F, Wheelock House, 20 Pedder St, Central. Tel: 2867 8111.
www.aircanada.ca

Air New Zealand
17/F, Li Po Chung Chambers, 189 Des Voeux Rd, Sheung Wan. Tel: 2524 9041. www.airnz.co.nz

American Airlines
10/F, Peninsula Office Tower, 18 Middle Rd, Tsim Sha Tsui. Tel: 2826 9269. www.aa.com

Asiana Airlines
34/F, The Landmark, Central. Tel: 2523 8585.
www.flyasiana.com

British Airways
24/F, Jardine House, Central. Tel: 2822 9000. www.ba.com

Cathay Pacific Airways
4/F, Swire House, Connaught Rd, Central. Tel: 2747 1888.
www.cathaypacific.com

Delta
25/F, Caroline Centre, 28 Yun Ping Rd, Causeway Bay. Tel: 2526 5875. www.delta-air.com

Dragonair
46/F, Cosco Tower, 183 Queen's Rd, Sheung Wan. Tel: 3193 3888.
www.dragonair.com

Emirates
11/F, Henley Building, 5 Queen's Rd, Central. Tel: 2526 7171 (flight info).
www.emirates.com

Eva Airways
9/F, Jardine House, Central. Tel: 2810 9251. www.evaair.com

Garuda Indonesia
15/F, Dah Sing Financial Centre, 108 Gloucester Rd, Causeway Bay. Tel: 2840 0000.
www.garuda-indonesia.com

KLM Royal Dutch
22/F, World Trade Centre, 280 Gloucester Rd, Causeway Bay. Tel: 2808 2111; www.klm.com

Korean Air
11/F, Tower Two, South Seas Centre, Tsim Sha Tsui East. Tel: 2733 7111.
www.koreanair.com

Lufthansa
11/F, Nan Fung Tower, 173 Des Voeux Rd, Sheung Wan. Tel: 2868 2313 (res.); 2769 6560 (flight info.). www.lufthansa.com

Malaysia Airlines
23/F, Central Tower, 28 Queen's Rd, Central. Tel: 2521 8181.
www.malaysia-airlines.com

Northwest Airlines
18/F, Cosco Tower, 183 Queen's Rd, Sheung Wan. Tel: 2810 4288. www.nwa.com

Qantas Airways
24/F, Jardine House, Central. Tel: 2842 1438; www.qantas.com

Singapore
17/F, United Centre, 95 Queensway, Admiralty. Tel: 2520 2233 (res.); 2216 1088 (flight info.). www.singaporeair.com

Sri Lankan Airlines
27/F, Tower One, Lippo Centre, Admiralty. Tel: 2521 0708.
www.srilankan.lk

Thai Airways International
24/F, United Centre, Admiralty. Tel: 2876 6888 (res.); 2769 7421 (flight info.). www.thaiair.com

Virgin Atlantic Airways
27/F, Kinwick Centre, Sheung Wan. Tel: 2532 3030.
www.virgin-atlantic.com

also at the CAAC main office (Jinan Commercial Building, 300 Dongfeng Zhong Lu, Guangzhou.Tel: 950333).

Macau

Macau International Airport (for enquiries tel: 861 111) provides a convenient gateway for travellers to Macau from many points in Asia. It is on the east side of Taipa Island and is linked by bridges to the downtown area. It takes less than 30 minutes to get from the airport to anywhere in Macau. Taxi fares are about 40 Patacas (written as MOP$40).

The passenger terminal has shops, restaurants, tourist information and hotel booking counters, bank, post office and other services. For transport to and from the airport, there are authorised taxis and the regular AP1 bus, which serves major hotels, the Ferry Terminal and the border gate. The fare is MOP$6.

There are regularly scheduled flights between Macau and 22 cities in Asia – including 14 in China. Asian connections include Beijing, Shanghai, Singapore, Manila, Bangkok, Taipei and Kuala Lumpur. On departure, passengers leaving China aged 12 and above must pay a departure tax of MOP$130 (2–12s MOP$80); passengers on flights within China pay only MOP$80 (MOP$50 for children aged 2–12).

If you wish to travel by helicopter, East Asia Airways (in HK, tel: 2859 3255; in Macau, 790 7040) operates 22 or more round trips daily using helipads on the Macau Ferry Terminal in the Shun Tak Centre in Hong Kong and Macau Ferry Terminal. One-way fares are HK$1,205 on weekdays, HK$1,309 weekends and holidays. The choppers seat eight and the flight takes around 20 minutes.

BY TRAIN

Guangzhou–Hong Kong

Seven daily trains link Guangzhou's East Railway Station and Hunghom station in Kowloon, with two extra trains added during special festivals and other peak periods. Travelling time is 1½ hours. There is also a train link between Foshan and Hong Kong, with a travelling time of just over 2 hours.

In Guangzhou, away from the station itself, most hotels and the CTS office can help with train tickets. In Hong Kong, tickets can be purchased through travel agents, hotels, CTS offices and at Hunghom railway station (tel: 2947 7888). If tickets to Guangzhou are sold out, take the Kowloon-Canton Railway (KCR) to the border terminus of Lo Wu (a short 40-minute journey, with departures roughly every 10 minutes). The Shenzhen station is a few minutes walk across the border.

There are dozens of trains daily between Shenzhen and Guangzhou. Travelling time is two hours. Trains arrive in Guangzhou either at the central station or at Guangzhou East Railway Station (Guangzhou Dong), in Tianhe, a 30-minute taxi ride from the city centre.

All trains between Kowloon and Guangzhou are air-conditioned, but not all between Shenzhen and Guangzhou offer this service. Ask for the air-con class when buying a ticket – this will probably prove worth the extra money when temperatures soar in summer.

BY BOAT

Hong Kong–Guangdong

Boats travel between Hong Kong and many Guangdong cities including Guangzhou, Shekou (near Shenzhen airport) and Zhuhai. There is an overnight steamer between Hong Kong and Guangzhou, which takes 8 hours; there is also a daytime catamaran service, which takes just over 2 hours. Ferry journeys to Shantou take 14 hours; to Xiamen, 20 hours; and to Shanghai, 60 hours. All have restaurants on board.

Hong Kong is linked by hydrofoil with Guangzhou, Huangpu, Guangzhou's commercial port, and the delta cities of Lianhua Shan, Nansha, Shekou, Shunde, Zhongshan and Zhuhai. There are also services between Macau and Shekou. For information on hydrofoil schedules, call 2833 9300 or 2542 3428 in Hong Kong. Most departures are from the Hong Kong-Macau Ferry Terminal at the Shun Tak Centre (on the waterfront west of Central District, Hong Kong (Sheung Wan station on the MTR and the A2 Airbus from the airport) and from the China Ferry Terminal, Canton Road, Tsim Sha Tsui.

By day, the most impressive trip is the one between Kowloon and the port of Nansha, sited at the entrance of the Zhu Jiang (Pearl River), aboard a huge modern hydrofoil travelling at 35 knots (journey time is 1 hour 15 minutes).

From the Nansha terminal, a free bus shuttle (one hour) takes travellers to the White Swan Hotel in Guangzhou. There are five daily departures from Hong Kong (8am, 9am, 1pm, 2pm and 3.30pm) and six from Nansha (9.30am, 11am, 12pm, 3pm, 4pm and 5.30pm). Tickets can be purchased from the China Ferry Terminal (tel: 2375 0688) in Hong Kong, the Nansha Terminal (tel: 498 8312 or 8468 8963) and the basement of the White Swan Hotel.

Hong Kong–Macau

There are numerous ways to travel from Hong Kong to Macau by sea. Fares for sea crossings vary between services and the class of ticket, the time of the day, and the day of the week you travel. Generally, tickets cost between around HK$100 and HK$200. For the most up-to-date information on fares, check with the company providing the service or the Hong Kong offices of the Macau Government Tourist Office, tel: 2857 2287; www.macautourism.gov.mo

Regardless of when you go, make certain you have return tickets in your possession, since seats are always fully booked. Baggage is limited to 9 kg (20 lb), and there is not much space on board for large suitcases.

Just about all the Macau ferry sailings use the Macau Ferry Terminal in the Shun Tak Centre in Hong Kong Island's Central District, with the exception of the catamaran and hoverferries, which use the China Ferry Terminal on the Tsim Sha Tsui waterfront alongside Harbour City, on Kowloon.

Turbojets are propelled by water jets and ride above the waves at about 40 knots. They carry the largest percentage of passengers between Hong Kong and Macau in about an hour. They carry about 270 passengers, and light refreshments are provided on board, with complimentary newspapers, coffee and tea on the first-class top deck. The New World First Ferry "flying cats" are two-deck catamarans that carry 400

passengers at around 45 knots and leave every hour or so from 8am until 10pm between Tsim Sha Tsui and Macau.

Turbojets depart every 15 minutes from 7am to 5pm, then every 30 minutes to midnight, with several other sailings throughout the night. Contact the Far East Hydrofoil Co., tel: 2859 3333 or the New World First Ferry on tel: 2516 9581.

There is also a computer booking service for turbojets and flying cats called Ticketmate. Many of their 11 outlets in Hong Kong are in the major MTR stations. You can purchase a passage up to 28 days in advance. Their three outlets in Macau allow you to buy a passage up to 7 days in advance. In Hong Kong, between 9am and 8pm, holders of American Express, MasterCard or Visa cards can book by phone up to 28 days in advance by dialling 2921 6688. (This service is not offered in Macau.)

Practical Tips

Medical Services

HONG KONG

Adventist Hospital, 40 Stubbs Rd, Happy Valley. Tel: 2574 6211.
Central Medical Practice, 1501 Prince's Bldg, Central. Tel: 2521 2567.
Hong Kong Central Hospital, 1B Lower Albert Rd, Central. Tel: 2522 3141.
Prince of Wales Hospital, 30–2 Ngan Shing St, Sha Tin, New Territories. Tel: 2632 2211.
Queen Elizabeth Hospital, 30 Gascoigne Rd, Kowloon. Tel: 2958 8888.
Queen Mary Hospital, Pokfulam Rd, Hong Kong. Tel: 2816 6366.

Emergencies

For police, fire and ambulance services in Hong Kong and China, dial 999. In Macau call 999 for emergencies, or 919 for police.

GUANGZHOU

Emergencies:
Red Cross Hospital, tel: 8444 6411.
Children's Hospital, tel: 8188 6332.
Guangzhou No. 1 People's Hospital, 602 Renmin Beilu. Tel: 8399 2090.
People's No. 1 Provincial Hospital, Foreigners' Dept, 123 Huifu Xilu. Tel: 8387 0136.

Tipping

Tipping is customary in Hong Kong, especially in restaurants and hotels. A 10-percent service charge is generally added to the bill in most restaurants, but even so you will still usually receive a grumpy look if you don't add about another 5 percent of the bill in tips. This is largely because the service charge you pay often goes to the establishment rather than the staff. Taxi drivers are not generally tipped, though rounding the fare up to the nearest dollar will be appreciated.

Language

Despite the handover of Hong Kong from British to Chinese sovereignty, English remains an official language in the territory, together with Cantonese.

All street signs continue to be written in both English and Chinese characters. Street names have not been changed since the handover.

English is widely spoken, since it is the language of business and commerce, though the majority of citizens are much more comfortable with Cantonese. However, you are unlikely to encounter many difficulties with communicating in English either in hotels or with business contacts.

The majority of the population are native Cantonese speakers. The Cantonese dialect is a harsh-sounding, guttural and tonal language that is almost impossible for most visitors to attempt without considerable prior knowledge. As a general rule, most of the younger generation can speak English, while the older generation may be less fluent in it.

Since many people have been brought up in a bilingual society, they hop from one language to another almost without realising it. As more and more people are familiar with English, it has become easier to simply incorporate words into the language rather than attempting any complicated translations to Chinese.

Mandarin Chinese (also known as standard Chinese or *putonghua*) is the principal language of mainland China and is becoming more prevalent, though you will still stand more chance of being understood if you speak to a Hong Kong Chinese resident in English than in Mandarin.

At the immigration department, notices and announcements are also given in Tagalog and Thai, reflecting the increasing number of South East Asian migrant workers in the territory.

Media

NEWSPAPERS & MAGAZINES

Hong Kong has a large number of newspapers and magazines, most of which are published in Chinese. Hong Kong continues to enjoy a free press despite being part of China, and the territory is noted as a media centre for the region.

The most influential newspaper in Hong Kong is the daily English-language *South China Morning Post*. A second English daily is the *Hongkong Standard*. Two of the most popular Chinese-language dailies are the rather sensationalist *Oriental Daily News* and the *Apple Daily News*.

One magazine worth looking out for is the weekly English-language *HK Magazine*, which is published every Friday and distributed free at most popular bars, restaurants and bookshops in the territory. It is aimed at residents, but tourists who want an opinionated insider's view will find its restaurant and entertainment reviews worth a read.

RADIO & TELEVISION

Over a dozen radio stations are broadcast in Hong Kong, though there is now only one dedicated English-language channel: RTHK. Some other channels offer an element of programming in English. The BBC World Service is available 24 hours a day.

There are two English-language and two Chinese-language TV stations. The English-language stations show programmes mainly from the UK and US. At certain times of the day, these channels broadcast programming in Mandarin, Japanese and Korean. If you are staying in a major international hotel, you will also have access to international satellite TV channels and the Hong Kong Channel, a special tourist information channel broadcast to the hotels only.

Postal Services

If you are finding your trip to Hong Kong much more expensive than you had bargained for, the postal service will come as a pleasant surprise, as it is cheap and efficient. The General Post Office is located adjacent to the Star Ferry Pier in Central and is probably the best place to buy stamps. Otherwise, post offices can be hard to find, although you can always ask the hotel to post mail for you. Post offices open 8am–6pm Monday to Friday and 8am–2pm on Saturday. All post offices close on Sunday and public holidays.

Telecommunications

Hong Kong is well known for having one of the most advanced and efficient telecommunications systems in the world. Virtually the entire network consists of fibre-optic cabling with digital switching, which means a whole host of advanced telecommunications services are available to local users. Hong Kong was also the first city in the world to offer on-demand television and home-shopping services through

Useful Numbers

INTERNATIONAL AREA CODES
● **Hong Kong: 852**
● **Macau: 853**
● **Guangzhou: 86-20**

IN HONG KONG:
● **Directory Assistance:**
  1081 (in English)
● **Collect Calls: 10010**
● **Overseas IDD: 10013**

telephone lines connected to television screens.

Hong Kong has some of the highest usage of mobile phones per capita in the world. Mobiles are popular even with young children – primarily because they are inexpensive. Since most of the younger generation live with their families in small flats in housing estates, mobiles also represent a form of private communication.

Local telephone calls are free of charge, so it is perfectly acceptable to use the telephones in offices, shops or restaurants to make brief calls. It would be polite to ask first, but many locals will simply walk into a store, use the phone and leave without saying a word to the proprietor. There are public phone booths which charge HK$1 for a five-minute local call. You can also make IDD (international direct dial) calls from most public phone booths. The most convenient way is to purchase stored-value phone cards from HKTB (Hong Kong Tourism Board) Information Centres and most convenience stores and mini-marts.

International access codes:
AT&T: 800 96 1111
MCI: 800 96 1121
Sprint: 800 96 1877

Internet

Internet access is available from almost all hotels via business centres or in room computers. As so many Hong Kong people have either WAP mobile phones or access to the web at home or work, there is not much call for Internet cafes; however, the score or so branches of the Pacific Coffee Company (mainly on Hong Kong Island) cafes allow free access to their terminals for the price of a cup of coffee. Some public utilities, like libraries and post offices, also feature free on-line computers.

Consulates

Australia, Harbour Centre, 21–4/F, 25 Harbour Rd, Wan Chai. Tel: 2827 8881.

Tourist Information

The Hong Kong Tourism Board (HKTB) is the official, government-sponsored body representing the tourism industry of Hong Kong and offers many useful services and helpful publications. HKTB also hands out information at the airport during daytime hours to anyone looking like a tourist.

At the HKTB Information and Gift Centres, you'll find a wide variety of useful publications including the weekly *Hong Kong Diary*, the monthly *Official Hong Kong Map* and the highly informative *Official Sightseeing Guide, Official Shopping Guide* and *Official Dining and Entertainment Guide*.

The centres also provide a tour reservation service for selected tours, and stock a large selection of souvenirs.

HKTB Information Centres
● **International Airport:** (only accessible to arriving visitors). Open: 7am–11pm daily.
● **Kowloon:** Star Ferry Pier, Tsim Sha Tsui. Open: 8am–6pm daily.
● **Central:** Ground Floor, The Center, 99 Queen's Rd, Central. Open: 8am–6pm daily.

Other HKTB Services
● **Telephone Information Service:** Tel: 2508 1234 (multilingual). Open 8am–6pm daily.
● **Website:** A wealth of tourist information (including maps) can be obtained from the website: **www.discoverhongkong.com**

Austria, Rm 2201, Chinachem Tower, 34–7 Connaught Rd, Central. Tel: 2522 8086.
Belgium, 9/F, St. John's Bldg, 33 Garden Rd, Central (G.P.O. Box 135). Tel: 2524 3111.
Burma (Myanmar), Rm 2436, Sun Hung Kai Centre, 30 Harbour Rd, Wan Chai. Tel: 2827 7929.
Cambodia, Rm 616, Star House, Tsim Sha Tsui. Tel: 2546 0718.

Canada, One Exchange Square, 11/F, 8 Connaught Place, Central. Tel: 2810 4321.

Czech Republic, Rm 1204, Great Eagle Centre, 23 Harbour Rd, Wan Chai. Tel: 2802 2212.

Denmark, Rm 2402B, Great Eagle Centre, 23 Harbour Rd, Wan Chai. Tel: 2827 8101.

Finland, Rm 2405, Dah Shing Financial Centre, 108 Gloucester Rd. Tel: 2525 5385.

France, Admiralty Centre, Tower II, 26/F, 18 Harcourt Rd, Admiralty. Tel: 3196 6100.

Germany, 21/F, United Centre, 95 Queensway, Admiralty. Tel: 2105 8712.

Greece, Suites 2503–4, Two Pacific Place, 88 Queensway, Admiralty. Tel: 2774 1682.

India, Unit D, 26/F, United Centre, 95 Queensway, Admiralty. Tel: 2528-4028.

Indonesia, 6–8 Keswick St, Causeway Bay. Tel: 2890 4421.

Ireland, 6/F, Chung Nam Bldg 1, Lockhart Rd, Wan Chai. Tel: 2527 4897.

Israel, Rm 701, Tower 2, Admiralty Centre, 18 Harcourt Rd, Admiralty. Tel: 2529 6091.

Italy, Rm 805, Hutchison House, 10 Harcourt Rd, Admiralty. Tel: 2522 0033.

Japan, 46/F, One Exchange Square, 8 Connaught Place, Central. Tel: 2522 1184.

Korea, 5–6/F, Far East Finance Centre, 16 Harcourt Rd, Admiralty. Tel: 2529 4141.

Malaysia, 23–24/F, Malaysia Bldg, 50 Gloucester Rd, Wan Chai. Tel: 2821 0800.

Maldives, Rm 201–5, Kowloon Centre, 29–43 Ashley Rd, Kowloon. Tel: 2376 2114.

Mongolia, 3/F, Crystal Industrial Bldg, 71 How Ming St, Kwun Tong, Kowloon. Tel: 2264 6174.

Netherlands, Rm 5702, Cheung Kong Centre, 2 Queen's Rd Central, Central. Tel: 2522 5127.

New Zealand, Rm 6505, Central Plaza, 18 Harbour Rd, Wan Chai. Tel: 2877 4488.

Philippines, 14/F, United Centre, 95 Queensway, Admiralty. Tel: 2823 8500.

Russia, Rm 2932–40, 29/F, Sun Hung Kai Centre, 30 Harbour Rd, Wan Chai. Tel: 2877 7188.

Singapore, Unit 901, 9/F, Tower 1, Admiralty Centre, 18 Harcourt Rd, Admiralty. Tel: 2527 2212.

South Africa, 27/F, Great Eagle Centre, 23 Harbour Rd, Wan Chai. Tel: 2577 3279.

Spain, 8/F, Printing House, 18 Ice House St, Central. Tel: 2525 3041.

Sweden, 8/F, The Hong Kong Club Bldg, 3A Chater Rd, Central. Tel: 2521 1212.

Switzerland, 3703, Gloucester Tower, The Landmark, 11 Pedder St, Central. Tel: 2522 7147.

Thailand, Fairmont House, 8/F, 8 Cotton Tree Drive, Central. Tel: 2521 6481.

United Kingdom, 1 Supreme Court Rd, Admiralty. Tel: 2901 3000.

United States, 26 Garden Rd, Central. Tel: 2523 9011.

Vietnam, 15/F, Great Smart Tower, 230 Wan Chai Rd, Wan Chai. Tel: 2591 4510.

Getting Around

Orientation

Although the dense high-rise jungles of Hong Kong and the bright neon signs exploding in electrified Chinese may at first all look daunting to the visitor, Hong Kong is actually quite an easy city to get around. The highly efficient public transport system certainly helps matters.

Be aware, however, that since Hong Kong is an extremely crowded city, trying to navigate your way around in the rush hour may prove very unpleasant – even impossible at times – for the uninitiated. Travelling at this time of day may also make you feel less than charitable towards the local population – necessity has dictated that people push in to get onto buses, trains and trams.

If you are waiting for a taxi, don't be surprised if a nimble local resident jumps in ahead of you when one appears, even if you have been waiting on the street corner for 10 minutes. If possible, avoid taking taxis at rush hours.

Street Signs

All street signs are in both English and Chinese. Hong Kong street maps usually have both English and Chinese language sections in the back to make it easier to find your destination. Be aware that while sometimes the English name of a street or district is a transliteration of the Chinese, at other times the Chinese name is totally different and seemingly bears no relation to the English name.

Public Transport

RAIL

There are four fast and efficient rail systems – the Airport Express Line (AEL), Mass Transit Railway (MTR), Kowloon-Canton Railway (KCR) and Light Rail Transit (LRT). A fifth, the Kowloon-Canton West Rail, opened in December 2003. Each is air-conditioned and runs from early morning until late at night.

The AEL (tel: 2881 8888) links the airport with Hong Kong Island in just 23 minutes, with stops at Tsing Yi and Kowloon. Single fares cost HK$90–100, returns HK$160–180. (Free shuttle buses operate between AEL stations and nearby hotels.)

The MTR (tel: 2881 8888) network of four interlinked lines covers the north shore of Hong Kong Island, east and west Kowloon and the north shore of Lantau Island. Adult single fares range from HK$4–26.

The MTR has interchanges at Prince Edward and Kowloon Tong stations with the KCR (tel: 2602 7799), which runs from Hung Hom in Kowloon to the boundary with the Mainland at Lo Wu. Hung Hom is also the starting point for rail journeys to mainland China and beyond. KCR fares start at HK$4.50 for an adult in ordinary class.

The LRT (tel: 2468 7788) runs between Yuen Long and Tuen Mun. Fares start at HK$4.

The West Rail (tel: 2684 8833) links Sham Shui Po in north Kowloon with the western New Territories through Yuen Long and ending in Tuen Mun. There are interchange stations linking the line with the LRT and MTR. Adult single fares start from HK$4

FERRIES

The 12-strong Star Ferry fleet crosses the harbour between Central and Wan Chai on Hong Kong Island and Kowloon side from 6.30am–11.30pm every day. As fares for the upper deck are only HK$2.20 (lower HK$1.70) this ranks as one of the world's great sightseeing bargains.

Both fast and ordinary ferries to the outlying islands – Lamma, Lantau, Cheung Chau and Peng Chau – leave from the piers to the north of the Airport Express station on Hong Kong Island. Fares range from HK$10–24. The HKTB provides the fastest source of information on Hong Kong's ferries, tel: 2508 1234.

Ferries for Discovery Bay (HK$27 one-way) on Lantau, and a hoverferry for Tsim Sha Tsui East, leave from piers to the east of the Star Ferry in Central. For information, tel: 2987 7351.

Trams

A picturesque and extremely inexpensive way to get around on Hong Kong Island is by tram. Trams run across the north of Hong Kong Island west and east. Tram stops are frequent and you can simply hop on and off as you please. The flat fare is HK$2 (exact change required or use an Octopus card) and the service operates between 6am and 1am. Sit on the top deck for the best views. There are some special tourist versions with an open top that are usually chartered by tour groups. Trams can be hired for private parties.

The **Peak Tram** is actually a funicular railway and has been running since 1888. It takes just eight minutes to reach the summit of Victoria Peak.

BUSES

Six different bus companies provide services in Hong Kong, covering all the major areas as well as speedy connections to and from the airport. Routes are reduced at night. Fares range from HK$1.20 for short journeys in the city to HK$45 for longer trips into the New Territories. Final destinations are marked in English and Chinese on the front top panel. Drivers rarely speak much English, but timetables and route maps are posted at bus stops.

Enquiries: Citybus (tel: 2873 0818) and New World First Bus (tel: 2136 8888), which run on Hong Kong Island, Kowloon and the New Territories; Kowloon Motor Bus (KMB; tel: 2745 4466); Long Win Bus Co (tel: 2261 2791), which serves the airport; Discovery Bay Transportation Services (tel: 2987 0208) and the New Lantao Bus Co (tel: 2984 9848) on Lantau island.

MINIBUSES/MAXICABS

These 16-seater passenger vans, coloured cream with either a red or green sidestripe run on fixed routes but will stop anywhere except on double yellow lines. They are usually faster than regular buses, with drivers using the accelerator with gusto, but not as cheap. Destinations are written in English at the front of the van. Call out clearly when you want the driver to stop. Fares vary from HK$1.50–20.

TAXIS

Three sorts of colour-coded taxis ply for trade in Hong Kong. Red taxis can travel anywhere except for Lantau Island. Green taxis may only operate in the New Territories, and blue cabs are restricted to Lantau Island. However, all taxis may carry passengers between the airport on Lantau and their respective areas.

Flagfall in red taxis is HK$15, and HK$12.50 for other cabs. There are additional charges for heavy luggage, animals and travelling via tunnels, which are all posted inside the taxi.

Many taxi drivers can speak some English and know the main hotels and tourist spots in Hong Kong, but can at times become linguistically and geographically challenged. To avoid problems, take your destination written down in Chinese. If you encounter

Octopus Cards

Visitors staying more than a few days should buy an Octopus stored-value card, which permits travel on the rail systems and most buses, minibuses and ferries at slightly reduced fares. It can also be used at many public phones, photo booths, vending machines and an increasing number of retail outlets such as 7-Eleven, Starbucks and local supermarket chain Park'N'Shop. Octopus cards are sold at customer service counters at Airport Express and Mass Transit Railway stations. The minimum price is HK$150 which includes a refundable HK$50 deposit. Children and seniors pay reduced fares. For enquiries, tel: 2266 2266.

difficulties, all cabs are equipped with a radio telephone and somebody at the control centre should be able to translate.

Taking foreigners for a ride by a circuitous route is not unknown, and drivers will sometimes refuse a fare, usually if the journey will take them out of their way as they are about to finish work. You may call a police officer or phone the complaint hotline, tel: 2527 7177, but to save time it is probably better to walk off and find another taxi.

Where to Stay

Choosing a Hotel

Hong Kong has some of the world's best hotels, but they are also among the most expensive in the world. The majority of tourists stay either in Tsim Sha Tsui on Kowloon side, or in Wan Chai or Causeway Bay on Hong Kong Island. Business travellers tend to prefer the Central hotels or the ones in Pacific Place, near Central, or the two hotels at the Convention Centre in Wan Chai. For more information about Hong Kong hotels contact the **Hong Kong Hotels Association** at 2383 8380.

Hong Kong Island

$$$$$

Conrad International
Pacific Place
88 Queensway
Central
Tel: 2521 3838
Fax: 2521 3888
A modern luxury hotel, which forms part of the impressive Pacific Place development.

Grand Hyatt
1 Harbour Rd
Wan Chai
Tel: 2588 1234
Fax: 2802 0677
One of the glitziest hotels in Hong Kong, the Grand Hyatt is situated adjacent to the Convention Centre and is hence particularly popular with business people. The hotel charges among the highest room rates in town.

Island Shangri-La
Pacific Place
Supreme Court
Central
Tel: 2877 3838
Fax: 2521 8742

Glamourous luxury hotel in Pacific Place. Noted for its restaurants.

J W Marriott Hotel
1 Pacific Place
88 Queensway
Central
Tel: 2810 8366
Fax: 2845 0737
The Marriott is the third of the triumvirate of modern luxury hotels in Pacific Place.

Mandarin Oriental
5 Connaught Rd
Central
Tel: 2522 0111
Fax: 2810 6190
Still up there with the top hotels in town after all these years. The long-established Mandarin offers impeccable service and a grand atmosphere. Very popular with business travellers.

Renaissance Harbour View Hotel
1 Harbour Rd
Wan Chai
Tel: 2802 8888
Fax: 2802 8833
This is the other hotel that forms part of the upmarket Convention Centre complex. Those who can't afford the Grand Hyatt but still want to be seen in the complex tend to stay here.

Ritz-Carlton
3 Connaught Rd
Central
Tel: 2877 6666
Fax: 2877 6778
Stylish five-star boutique hotel in Central, with old world ambience and exquisite service.

$$$$

Novotel Century Hong Kong Hotel
238 Jaffe Rd
Wan Chai
Tel: 2598 8888
Fax: 2598 8866
A good-value choice in this price bracket. Undistinguished but convenient hotel, midway between Wan Chai and Causeway Bay.

The Excelsior
281 Gloucester Rd
Causeway Bay
Tel: 2894 8888
Fax: 2895 6459

A very popular, big hotel managed by the Mandarin Oriental group. Great location in Causeway Bay overlooking the harbour. Very popular with tourists and airline crews. The best four-star hotel in Hong Kong.

Grand Plaza
2 Kornhill Rd
Quarry Bay
Tel: 2886 0011
Fax: 2886 1738
Small but comfortable hotel on the east of Hong Kong Island.

Rosedale on the Park
8 Shelter St
Causeway Bay
Tel: 2127 8888
Fax: 2127 8833
One of Hong Kong's newest hotels, the Rosedale is thoroughly modern and overlooks Victoria Park. Rooms are on the small side, but well designed so they feel compact rather than cramped.

$$$

Empire Hotel
33 Hennessy Rd
Wan Chai
Tel: 2866 9111
Fax: 2861 3121
This is a favourite with Asian tour groups. Although the hotel is convenient and reasonably good value, don't expect five-star service.

Luk Kwok
72 Gloucester Rd
Wan Chai
Tel: 2866 2166
Fax: 2866 2622
A rather uninspiring modern hotel popular with Asian tour groups. Handy location for the Wan Chai nightlife, however.

New Harbour Hotel
41–49 Hennessy Rd
Wan Chai
Tel: 2861 1166
Fax: 2865 6111
The New Harbour is a fairly dowdy and undistinguished hotel that is popular with tour groups. But again, the location is good for Wan Chai's nightlife.

Park Lane Hotel
310 Gloucester Rd
Causeway Bay
Tel: 2293 8888
Fax: 2576 7853
Another tourist favourite – a good four-star just across from Victoria Park and right in the thick of the shopping action.

$$

Bishop Lei International House
4 Robinson Rd
Mid-Levels
Tel: 2868 0828
Fax: 2868 1551
Compact high-rise apartment-block style hotel in the Mid-Levels residential district. The facilities aren't lavish and the rooms are tiny, but it's still good value.

Emperor (Happy Valley) Hotel
1 Wang Tak St
Happy Valley
Tel: 2893 3693
Fax: 2834 6700
A boutique hotel that is handily located for horseracing fans and only a short tram-ride from Causeway Bay. They do great deals for long-term stays.

Harbour View International House
4 Harbour Rd
Wan Chai
Tel: 2802 0111
Fax: 2802 9063
Book ahead at this upscale YMCA, next door to Arts Centre and across from the Convention Centre. It's worth paying the extra HK$100 for a harbour-view room.

Newton Hotel Hong Kong
218 Electric Rd
North Point
Tel: 2807 2333
Fax: 2807 1221
Small, good-value hotel east of Causeway Bay.

Price Categories

$$$$$	=	US$200 and above
$$$$	=	US$150–200
$$$	=	US$100–150
$$	=	US$50–100
$	=	below US$50

Regal Hong Kong
88 Yee Wo St
Causeway Bay
Tel: 2890 6633
Fax: 2881 0777
Another good tourist hotel because of its convenient location in the heart of Causeway Bay.

Wesley Hotel
22 Hennessy Road
Wan Chai
Tel: 2866 6688
Fax: 2866 6633
An inexpensive hotel/serviced apartment block situated close to Pacific Place.

$

Ma Wui Hall Youth Hostel
Mt Davis Path
Victoria Rd, Kennedy Town
Tel: 2788 1638
Fax: 2788 3105
Spartan dormitory accommodation, with superb views from the mountain-top location above Kennedy Town. Beds fill up quickly.

Kowloon/Lantau/New Territories

$$$$$

The Intercontinental
Salisbury Rd
Tsim Sha Tsui
Kowloon
Tel: 2721 1211
Fax: 2739 4546
This is one of Hong Kong's grandest hotels and the choice of the international glitterati. The rooms are delightful and they offer stunning harbour views.

Peninsula Hotel
Salisbury Rd
Tsim Sha Tsui
Kowloon
Tel: 2920 2888
Fax: 2722 4170
The Pen is Hong Kong's only historic hotel and still arguably its best. It has fantastic restaurants and a spa. If money is no object, this is the ultimate choice.

$$$$

Gold Coast Hotel
1 Castle Peak Rd
Castle Park Bay
Kowloon
Tel: 2452 8888
Fax: 2440 7368
Hong Kong's only resort hotel, in an isolated area with a few shops and restaurants. Popular at weekends for residents on short getaways.

Grand Stanford Intercontinental Hotel
70 Mody Rd
Tsim Sha Tsui East
Kowloon
Tel: 2721 5161
Fax: 2732 2233
Formerly a Holiday Inn. Convenient for the shopping in Tsim Sha Tsui East.

Great Eagle Hotel
8 Peking Rd
Tsim Sha Tsui
Kowloon
Tel: 2375 1133
Fax: 2375 6611
Large hotel popular with upmarket tour groups and business people.

Holiday Inn Golden Mile
50 Nathan Rd
Tsim Sha Tsui
Kowloon
Tel: 2369 3111
Fax: 2369 8016
Nicely refurbished and popular tourist hotel right in the middle of the busy tourist stretch of Tsim Sha Tsui.

Hyatt Regency Hotel
67 Nathan Rd
Tsim Sha Tsui
Kowloon
Tel: 2311 1234
Fax: 2739 8701
Popular luxury hotel in the main tourist entertainment area.

Kowloon Hotel
19–21 Nathan Rd
Tsim Sha Tsui
Kowloon
Tel: 2929 2888
Fax: 2301 2668
Across the road from the Peninsula and run by the same company, a good hotel in an excellent location.

Kowloon Shangri-La Hotel
64 Mody Rd
Tsim Sha Tsui
Kowloon
Tel: 2721 2111
Fax: 2723 8686
A luxury hotel in a lively location.

The Marco Polo Gateway
Harbour City
Canton Rd
Tsim Sha Tsui
Kowloon
Tel: 2113 0888
Fax: 2113 0022
A good-quality tourist hotel, part of the Harbour City retail development.

The Marco Polo Hongkong Hotel
Harbour City
Canton Rd
Tsim Sha Tsui
Kowloon
Tel: 2113 0088
Fax: 2113 0011
Classy modern hotel close to the Star Ferry. Many rooms with magnificent harbour views. Located inside the enormous shopping complex at Ocean Terminal.

Marco Polo Prince Hotel
Harbour City
Canton Rd
Tsim Sha Tsui
Kowloon
Tel: 2113 1888
Fax: 2113 0066
A popular hotel, part of the huge Harbour City shopping complex.

Hotel Miramar
118–130 Nathan Rd
Tsim Sha Tsui
Kowloon
Tel: 2368 1111
Fax: 2369 1788
An unpretentious and friendly hotel with an indoor pool; a stone's throw from Tsim Sha Tsui's best bars and restaurants.

New World Renaissance Hotel
22 Salisbury Rd
Tsim Sha Tsui
Kowloon
Tel: 2369 4111
Fax: 2369 9387
A modern and efficient tourist hotel close to the Intercontinental.

Nikko Hotel
72 Mody Rd
Tsim Sha Tsui East
Kowloon
Tel: 2739 1111
Fax: 2311 3122
A four-star hotel that is especially popular with Japanese tour groups.

Panda Hotel
3 Tsuen Wah St
Tsuen Wan, N.T.
Tel: 2409 1111
Fax: 2409 1818
Part of the Mega hotel group, popular with low-budget tour groups.

Regal Airport Hotel
9 Cheong Tat Rd
Chek Lap Kok
Lantau
Tel: 2286 8888
Fax: 2286 8686
Big, superbly designed, right next to the passenger terminal – this is not at all a run-of-the-mill airport hotel.

Royal Pacific Hotel & Towers
33 Canton Rd
China Hong Kong City
Tsim Sha Tsui
Kowloon
Tel: 2736 1188
Fax: 2736 1212
Part of the China Hong Kong City building, which comprises a shopping mall and departure centre for hydrofoil services to China.

Sheraton Hong Kong
20 Nathan Rd
Tsim Sha Tsui
Kowloon
Tel: 2369 1111
Fax: 2368 1999
Business hotel near the waterfront and Nathan Road shopping areas.

$$$

Concourse Hotel
20–46 Lai Chi Kok Rd
Mong Kok
Kowloon
Tel: 2397 6683
Fax: 2381 3768
Large, moderately priced hotel in gritty, vibrant Mong Kok.

Eaton Hotel
380 Nathan Rd
Kowloon
Tel: 2782 1818
Fax: 2771 0043
Fairly new, not terribly grand, but good value nonetheless.

Imperial Hotel
30–34 Nathan Rd
Tsim Sha Tsui
Kowloon
Tel: 2366 2201
Fax: 2721 3606
Pleasant rooms, but marred by grumpy service. Good value at the bottom end of this price category. Convenient location on Tsim Sha Tsui's "Golden Mile", close to shops, restaurants and the MTR.

Nathan Hotel
378 Nathan Rd
Yau Ma Tei
Kowloon
Tel: 2388 5141
Fax: 2770 4262
Close to Temple Street night market, Yue Hwa Chinese merchandise emporium, restaurants and shops, cinema and Jordan MTR.

Newton Hotel Kowloon
58–66 Boundary St
Mong Kok
Kowloon
Tel: 2787 2338
Fax: 2789 0688
An inexpensive choice in the heart of Mong Kok.

Regal Riverside Hotel
Tai Chung Kiu Rd
Sha Tin, N.T.
Tel: 2649 7878
Fax: 2637 4748
A popular lower priced tour-group hotel in the new town of Sha Tin.

The Salisbury (YMCA)
41 Salisbury Rd
Tsim Sha Tsui
Kowloon
Tel: 2369 2211
Fax: 2739 9315
Book ahead at this very upscale YMCA. All rooms are well-equipped and many enjoy fine, panoramic views of the harbour. The centre has a large indoor pool and offers a good range of sports facilities.

Shamrock Hotel
223 Nathan Rd
Kowloon
Tel: 2735 2271
Fax: 2736 7354
The Shamrock is a budget hotel situated right in the heart of busy Nathan Road. Convenient access to Jordan MTR station.

$$

Caritas Bianchi Lodge
4 Cliff Rd
Yau Ma Tei
Kowloon
Tel: 2388 1111
Fax: 2770 6669
Clean, spacious rooms in a well-run Roman Catholic hostel between Nathan Road and the Meteorological Station. Near to Temple Street night market, shops, restaurants and Yau Ma Tei MTR.

Evergreen Hotel
42–52 Woo Sung St
Yau Ma Tei
Tel: 2780 4222
Fax: 2385 8584
Clean, tidy rooms. Triples and 4-bed rooms are good value for small groups. Situated near Temple Street night market, Yue Hwa Chinese emporium and Jordan MTR.

Price Categories

$$$$$	=	US$200 and above
$$$$	=	US$150–200
$$$	=	US$100–150
$$	=	US$50–100
$	=	below US$50

$

Anne Black Guest House (YWCA)
5 Man Fuk Rd
Ho Man Tin
Tel: 2713 9211
Fax: 2761 1269
Clean, simple rooms for women and couples. A short walk away from the Ladies' Market, Mong Kok KCR and MTR stations.

Chungking House
4–5/F, Block A Chungking Mansions
40 Nathan Rd
Kowloon
Tel: 2366 5362
Fax: 2721 3570
There are cheaper deals in the area but Chungking House is the only establishment to win the HKTD's seal of approval. Right by the MTR.

Macau

$$$$$

Hyatt Regency
2 Estrada Almirante Marques
Taipa
Tel: 831 234
Fax: 830 195
Superb facilities – especially for kids – and neatly placed for exploring the main parts of Macau and the islands.

Lisboa
2–4 Avenida de Lisboa
Tel: 377 666
Fax: 567 193
This squat orange port-holed hotel is a Macau landmark. Rooms are grand and the lobby is ornate (millionaire-owner Stanley Ho likes to show off his possessions). The hotel houses some superb restaurants and several casinos teeming with gamblers and hard-working prostitutes. There's also a nightly strip show that is billed as being tasteful If you don't stay here at least come to see the sights.

Mandarin Oriental Macau
956–110 Avenida da Amizade
Tel: 567 888
Fax: 594 589
Recently fully refurbished and augmented by an adjacent spa, pool and dining area. Macau's number one address.

Pousada de Sao Tiago
Avenida da República
Fortaleza de São Tiago da Barra
Tel: 378 111
Fax: 552 170
This Macau institution is superbly positioned at the entrance to Macau's inner harbour. The 23 rooms/suites feature traditional Portuguese decor – dark wooden furniture, tiles and white linen – and most have glorious views over the Pearl River Delta. Facilities include in-room TV and mini-bar, a swimming pool, bar and several restaurants.

Westin Resort
1918 Estrada de Hac Sa
Coloane
Tel: 871 111
Fax: 871 122
Plush rooms prettily located overlooking the sea and a golf

course, although you'll need to take a taxi or wait for the shuttle bus to get into Macau proper.

$$$

Sintra
Avenida D. João IV
Tel: 710 111
Fax: 510 527
www.macau.ctm.net/~sintra
Fairly nice hotel owned by the Lisboa. Rooms are large but basically equipped, nothing fancy here. But a good central location for the main streets in Macau.

Guangzhou

$$$$

China Hotel
Liuhua Lu
Tel: 8666 6888
Fax: 8667 7014
Five-star hotel, part of the New World Group of Hong Kong. Convenient central location just across the street from the Trade Fair grounds makes it a favourite with business people. Restaurants include the Hard Rock Café and Food Street.

Dongfang Hotel
120 Liuhua Lu
Tel: 8666 9900
Fax: 8666 2775
The Dongfang was built in the 1950s by the Soviets, with a new wing added in the 1970s, and still retains a lot of its charm. The central location is a plus.

White Swan Hotel
1 Shamian Nanlu
Tel: 8188 6968
Fax: 8186 1188
One of the finest hotels in China, the White Swan has a prime location on Shamian island and incorporates a gallery of top-class boutiques and restaurants.

$$$

Gitic Riverside Hotel
298 Yan Jiang Lu C
Tel: 8328 8888
Fax: 8328 8688

Situated on the banks of the Pearl River, this four-star hotel offers spacious rooms, full facilities and good restaurants. It's very handy for the Beijing Lu shopping area.

Guangzhou Grand Palace Hotel
148 Linhe Xi Rd
Tel: 3884 0968
Fax: 3884 0960
This recently opened hotel has 147 rooms and is close to Guangzhou's East Train Station. Popular with Hong Kong businessmen.

Landmark Hotel
8 Qiao Guang Lu
Haizhu Square
Tel: 8335 5988
Fax: 8333 6197
On the bank of the Pearl River, the Landmark Hotel is slightly run down but it still remains spacious and clean. Facilities include several Chinese restaurants and a business centre.

$$

China Merchants Hotel
8–111 Liu Hua Lu
Tel: 3622 2988
Fax: 3622 2680
240 rooms over 14 floors. The facilities here include one Western and one Chinese restaurant, a karaoke bar, business centre and laundry service.

Guangdong Hotel
309 Dongfeng Zhong Lu
Tel: 8333 9933
Fax: 8333 9723
Recently refurbished four-star monster, but rooms are well-equipped, comfortable and very good value for money, and the service is friendly.

$

Guangdong Hotel
294 The Bund
Tel: 8131 3901
Fax: 8132 4667
The two-star Guangdong hotel (not to be confused with the real Guangdong Hotel, above) has a Chinese restaurant and

Price Categories

$$$$$	=	US$200 and above
$$$$	=	US$150–200
$$$	=	US$100–150
$$	=	US$50–100
$	=	below US$50

karaoke bar. It offers inexpensive single rooms with shared bathrooms.

Guangzhou Youth Hostel
2 Shamian Sijie
Tel: 8121 8298
Cheap rooms can be found at this hostelry, which is nicknamed the "Black Duck", as it faces the luxury White Swan Hotel. It's a particular favourite with backpackers owing to its key location, although it is also very well maintained and clean.

Where to Eat

Gourmet's Paradise

Hong Kong is justifiably noted as one of the culinary capitals of the world. Its relative prosperity and the preference among its citizens for entertaining in restaurants rather than at home mean that Hong Kong has perhaps the highest number of eating places per capita in the world. Besides having the finest selection in the world of restaurants offering indigenous Cantonese cuisine, Hong Kong also has a seemingly endless supply of other Chinese, Asian and international restaurants.

Hong Kong people don't eat to live – instead, they live to eat, and meals with friends or colleagues are absolutely fundamental to social interaction. Chinese usually greet each other and foreigners by asking, "Have you eaten yet?" This is not an invitation to dine, but reflects the important connection between eating and wellbeing.

Every year, Hong Kong's passion for food culminates in a two-week festival of excess known as the Hong Kong Food Festival, generally held in March.

CANTONESE CUISINE

Most Hong Kong residents originate from the neighbouring Chinese province of Guangdong, where Guangzhou, or Canton, is located. Hence, Cantonese cuisine is the staple of Hong Kong. This is the style of food which people around the world generally know as "Chinese food", and there is nowhere better than Hong Kong to sample its endless range of taste and excellent quality. Having said

that, you're in for a big shock if you're expecting the Westernised Cantonese food found outside of Canton itself.

Cantonese food is fresh to the point of obsessiveness. The amount of time that has elapsed between a fish swimming in the tank and being on the plate is generally minimal. This type of food is oilier than most regional Chinese cuisines, although much emphasis is also placed on natural flavours, steaming and light stir-frying. Popular Cantonese dishes are too numerous to mention but include steamed fish with light soy sauce and ginger, stir-fried vegetables, roast goose or roast suckling pig and sweet-and-sour spare ribs.

Dim sum is an extremely popular form of Cantonese food consumed only in the morning and afternoon – don't embarrass yourself or your hosts by asking for dim sum in the evening. It is a series of delicious little snacks which often come in baskets. In traditional dim sum restaurants, waiters and waitresses trundle round trolleys laden with dim sum and you pick the ones you want from the selection.

In more upmarket restaurants, you are given dim sum order forms and tick off the required items. The most popular dim sum items are: *ha gau* (shrimp dumpling), *siu mai* (prawn and pork dumpling), *pai gwat* (steamed sparenbs), *chun guen* (spring rolls), *cha siu bao* (steamed barbecued pork buns) and *cheung fun* (steamed rice flour rolls with barbecue pork, beef or shrimp).

REGIONAL CHINESE CUISINES

The most popular regional Chinese cuisines besides Cantonese are: Chiu Chow, Beijing, Sichuan and Shanghainese.

Chiu Chow food is rich and prominently features goose and duck as well as seafood. Chiu Chow chefs are generally considered the masters of two of the most expensive Chinese delicacies: shark's fin and bird's nest. Tiny

cups of an extremely strong tea, *tiet kwun yum*, are generally served before and after meals in Chiu Chow restaurants.

Beijing food is extremely rich due to the Imperial court history. It makes liberal use of strongly flavoured vegetables, herbs and spices, including peppers, garlic and coriander. Noodles, dumplings and bread feature more often than rice in northern cuisines such as this.

A particular Beijing favourite with Westerners is Peking duck, in which the crispy skin is wrapped in thin pancakes together with spring onions, cucumber and plum sauce. Another popular northern dish is beggar's chicken. The bird is stuffed with vegetables and herbs, sealed with clay and slowly cooked. The guest of honour is usually invited to smash open the cooked chicken with a mallet.

Sichuan food is very spicy. Restaurants in Hong Kong often combine Beijing and Sichuan dishes together, with the result that it can be difficult to tell which is which. Popular spices include star anise, fennel seed, chilli and coriander. Smoked duck is a very popular Sichuan dish. As with Beijing food, noodles and steamed bread feature more heavily than rice, though in the Hong Kong restaurants you are almost certain to be served rice as well as noodles and bread.

Shanghai food makes much of steamed dumplings and tends to be rather heavier and oilier than other Chinese foods. One delicacy for which Shanghai is particularly renowned is hairy crab, which is available only in the autumn and

Price Categories

Prices are quoted for a three-course meal for one person. Alcohol is not included. These ranges should be taken as a guide to prices only.

$$$$	=	US$50 and above
$$$	=	US$30–50
$$	=	US$15–30
₵	=	below US$15

Chopsticks

If you want to enjoy eating Chinese food in Hong Kong, getting to grips with chopsticks should be one of your priorities. The thin ends of the chopsticks should point towards the food with the tips exactly together. Hold one chopstick firmly between the joint of your thumb and the inside tip of your index finger. Then, hold the second chopstick between the tip of your thumb and the tip of your first finger. The first chopstick remains rigid while you move the second, or upper, chopstick in a pincer motion to pick up the food.

much sought after in Hong Kong. Other Shanghainese favourites include hot-and-sour soup, drunken chicken, yellow fish and braised eel.

SOUTHEAST ASIAN CUISINE

Hong Kong also has many restaurants specialising in the hot and spicy food of other Southeast Asian countries, especially Thai food, which has become extremely popular in recent years.

Eating Etiquette

When eating Chinese food, it is a good idea – if possible – to go with a large group of people so that you can try more dishes than if you only order your own meal. If you look around in Chinese restaurants, you will see there are very few tables for two but many big round tables of boisterous colleagues, friends or families all tucking in to their food together. If you want an intimate dinner for two, avoid Chinese restaurants altogether, as they are almost without exception noisy and rarely romantic.

There are few rules as regards table manners. Chinese people tend to eat with great gusto, and slurping soup or talking at the same time as eating seems to be quite acceptable.

There are, however, some rituals that tend to be followed. The Asian style of eating is to order several dishes of food, which are put in the middle of the table and shared by all diners. Bowls of rice are separate, however. The usual way to eat rice is to pick up the bowl to your lips and scoop the rice directly into your mouth using the chopsticks.

It is considered impolite to take food from the centre of the table and put it directly into your mouth – transfer the food into your own bowl before you eat it. The superstitious also regard it as bad luck to turn a fish over to extract the flesh from the under side, as this symbolizes the capsizing of a fishing boat.

If you are hosted to dinner or lunch in formal and traditional circumstances, it is customary not to finish all the food in the centre, so as to avoid embarrassing your host, who may feel that he or she has not offered enough food.

Tea is generally served as a matter of course in restaurants, and the pot is constantly refilled throughout the meal. Note that it is considered impolite to refill your own cup without first filling the cups of fellow diners, even when their cups are not yet empty. You are often asked to choose which type of tea you would like for your table.

Hong Kong Island

CANTONESE

Dim Sum
63 Sing Woo Rd
Happy Valley
Tel: 2834 8893
Wonderful dim sum in a retro-nostalgia setting, away from the tourist circuit. **$$**

Dynasty Restaurant
3/F Renaissance Harbour View Hotel
1 Harbour Rd
Wan Chai
Tel: 2802 8888
Authentic cuisine with views of the harbour. **$$**

Fook Lam Moon Restaurant
G/F 35–45 Johnston Rd
Wan Chai
Tel: 2866 0663

One of the most famous and most expensive in town. A place to impress. **$$$$**

Fu Ho Restaurant
454–456 Lockhart Rd
Causeway Bay
Tel: 2893 6565
Extensive seafood menu with emphasis on abalone recipes. **$$$**

Golden East Lake
Shop 3
G & 1/F Eton Tower
8 Hysan Avenue
Causeway Bay
Tel: 2576 2008
Complete with running fountains and carved wooden screens. **$$$$**

The Golden Leaf
Conrad International Hotel
Pacific Place
88 Queensway
Central
Tel: 2521 3838
Palatial and sophisticated restaurant. **$$$**

Hang Fook Lau Seafood Restaurant
1/F, Hay Wah Mansion
71–85 Hennessy Rd
Wan Chai (and other locations)
Tel: 2528 2468
Popular chain; the seafood hot pots are recommended. **$$**

Jasmine Garden
Basement, Swire House
11 Chater Rd
Central
Tel: 2526 3031
Several branches in Hong Kong offering classical favourites. **$**

Jumbo Floating Restaurant
Shum Wan
Wong Chuk Hang
Aberdeen Harbour
Tel: 2553 9111
A gaudy extravaganza with seating for up to 4,000 and a seafood exhibition. Arrive by sampan from the Shum Wan pier. First-time visitors should definitely come here. **$$**

Luk Yu Tea House
24–26 Stanley St
Central
Tel: 2523 5464
Sixty-year old unofficial monument with whirring fans and brass spitoons. Great for dim sum. **$$**

Man Wah
25/F Mandarin Oriental

Price Categories

$$$$ = US$50 and above
$$$ = US$30–50
$$ = US$15–30
$ = below US$15

5 Connaught Rd
Central
Tel: 2522 0111
Top-class restaurant with superb
views and exclusive ambience. $$$

One Harbour Road
8/F Grand Hyatt Hong Kong
1 Harbour Rd
Wan Chai
Tel: 2588 1234
Exquisite split-level restaurant
accessible by private elevator.
Views of the harbour. $$$$

Steam & Stew Inn
Hing Wong Court
21–33 Tai Wong St East
Wan Chai
Tel: 2529 3913
Famous for its MSG-free dishes, a
favourite of celebrities whose
pictures are on the wall. $

Tai Woo
27 Percival St
Causeway Bay (and other locations)
Tel: 2893 0822
Seafood is the forte of this highly
rated Cantonese restaurant. Set
menus are a boon to the
uninitiated. $$–$$$

Tsui Hang Village
2/F New World Tower
16–18 Queen's Rd
Central
Tel: 2524 2012
Another MSG-free restaurant with
speedy service. $$

Yung Kee
32–40 Wellington St
Central
Tel: 2522 1624/2343
Cheap, cheerful, brash and noisy,
this multi-level restaurant is famous
for its roast goose and is popular
with visitors. $$

Zen Chinese Cuisine
LG1 The Mall
Pacific Place Phase 1
88 Queensway
Central
Tel: 2845 4555
Stylish, modern restaurant. $$

CHIU CHOW

Chiuchow Garden Restaurant
Basement, Jardine House
1 Connaught Place
Central
Tel: 2525 8246
This well-known restaurant has
several other branches including
one on the ground floor of the Lippo
Centre in Admiralty. It is big,
popular and does all the Chiu Chow
favourites well. $$

Harbour Chuichow
2/F Allied Kajima Bldg
138 Gloucester Rd
Wan Chai
Tel: 2877 7728
Bright cheery restaurant with good
shark's fin specialities. $$

BEIJING & SICHUAN

China Lan Kwai Fong
17–22 Lan Kwai Fong
Central
Tel: 2536 0968
Dramatic interior and menu. The all-
you-can-eat weekend dim sum
brunch is superb. $$

Hong Kong Chung Chuk Lau
30 Leighton Rd
Causeway Bay
Tel: 2577 4914
Specialises in Beijing food and
Mongolian hotpot. $

Imperial Kitchen
3/F Caroline Centre
28 Yun Ping Rd
Causeway Bay
Tel: 2577 2018
A rich diversity of northern cuisine.
The Peking duck is especially good
here. $$

Peking Garden Restaurant
1st & 2nd Basements
Alexandra House
6 Ice House St, Central
Tel: 2526 6456;
also at The Mall
Pacific Place
Central
Tel: 2845 8452
Classy and rather theatrical Peking
restaurants, featuring set meals,
noodle-making displays and
beggar's chicken clay-breaking
ceremonies. $$

Red Pepper Restaurant
7 Lan Fong Rd
Causeway Bay
Tel: 2577 3811
Atmospheric family-run restaurant
with traditional Chinese decoration
serving fiery Sichuan and Beijing
foods. $$

SHANGHAI

**Kung Tak Lam Shanghai
Vegetarian Restaurant**
31 Yee Wo St
Causeway Bay
Tel: 2881 9966
Imaginative and, if requested, MSG-
free vegetarian fare from this family
enterprise established *circa* 1900.
$$

Liu Yuan Pavilion
3/F, The Broadway
54–62 Lockhart Rd
Wan Chai
Tel: 2804 2000.
Well-established restaurant for
Shanghainese fare. $$

Shanghai Garden Restaurant
3/F Hutchison House
10 Harcourt Rd
Central
Tel: 2524 8181
Cocktails downstairs in the lobby
lounge, followed by dinner (or lunch)
in the elegant upstairs dining room.
An unusually sophisticated
Shanghainese restaurant. $$

Snow Garden Restaurant
2/F Eight Plaza
8 Sunning Rd
Causeway Bay
Tel: 2881 6837
Popular and grand Shanghainese
restaurant with more than 300
items listed on the menu. Worth a
visit. $$$

Yè Shanghai
Shop 332, Pacific Place
Admiralty
Tel: 2918 9833
An atmospheric place, with an
interior designed to mimic a
1920s Shanghai restaurant and
old-style Chinese music on
weekends. The menu features
Shanghai, Zhejiang and Jiangsu
dishes. $$$

"Face"

The concept of "face" is particularly important in Hong Kong, as it is in most Asian societies. It is very important to avoid trying to make people "lose face", which will gain you an enemy. To prevent people, especially business partners, from losing face, you should take particular care not to argue with them or correct them publicly. Direct conflict should be avoided, especially with superiors. Most people would rather give gifts than receive them, or host a meal rather than be hosted, as they gain a great deal of face by doing so. If a business colleague invites you to lunch or dinner, you should allow them to pay the bill – it would be a loss of face for them to invite someone and then let the other party pay.

OTHER ASIAN

Banana Leaf Curry House
440 Jaffe Rd
Causeway Bay
(and other locations)
Tel: 2573 8187
Cheap and cheerful but extremely popular restaurant with Asian favourites from several countries. Food is served on banana leaves instead of plates, together with big dollops of steamed rice. **$$**

Cafe Deco Bar & Grill
Levels 1 & 2, Peak Galleria
118 Peak Rd
The Peak
Tel: 2849 5111
Eclectic menu strong on pizza, tandoori and Thai. Spectacular city views and live jazz each evening. Dinner reservations are advised, especially for a window table. **$$**

Chilli Club Thai Restaurant
1/F 88 Lockhart Rd
Wan Chai
Tel: 2527 2872
Small, cheap, popular Thai restaurant. Always packed. **$**

Cinta Restaurant
10 Fenwick St
Wan Chai
Tel: 2527 1199
Popular hangout with Filipinos that serves inexpensive Indonesian and Malay food. Live music in the evenings. **$$**

Good Luck Thai
13 Wing Wah Lane
Lan Kwai Fong
Central
Tel: 2877 2971
Inexpensive Thai dishes out on the street amid the lively goings-on in nearby bars. Its popularity is proof of its good, unpretentious food. **$**

Green Cottage
32 Cannon St
Causeway Bay
Tel: 2832 2863
Very popular, very crowded and very simple canteen-style seating, but the food is good authentic Vietnamese and inexpensive. Wash it down with bottles of 333 beer. **$**

Gu Gu Jang Korean Barbecue
3/F Caroline Centre
28 Yun Ping Rd
Causeway Bay
Tel: 2577 2021
Nibble on spring onion pancakes while you watch marinated meat and fish sizzle to perfection on a table-top hotplate. **$$**

Kat+Man+Du
11 Old Bailey St
SoHo
Central
Tel: 2869 1298
Upmarket Nepalese cuisine in this long-standing (for this area) restaurant. The menu also features a few Tibetan staples. **$$$**

Indochine 1929
2/F California Tower
Lan Kwai Fong
30–32D D'Aguilar St
Central
Tel: 2869 7399
Chic, designer Vietnamese restaurant that attempts to recreate French colonial Vietnam. Expensive. **$$$$**

Koh-I-Noor
California Entertainment Bldg
34 D'Aguilar St
Central
Tel: 2877 9706
Delicately spiced Mughlai, tandoori and other delicious fare from northern India. **$$–$$$**

Kublai's
3/F, 1 Capital Place
18 Luard Rd
Wan Chai
Tel: 2529 9117
Good-value all-you-can-eat Mongolian barbecue place. **$$**

Lotus Thai Restaurant
Shop C & D
93–107 Lockhart Rd
Wan Chai
Tel: 2866 0228
Great value, friendly Thai restaurant with huge portions and speedy service. Always busy. **$$**

Nadaman Island Shangri-La Hotel
Pacific Place
88 Queensway
Admiralty
Tel: 2820 8570
Gracious service and elegant surroundings heighten the gastronomic pleasure of fine Japanese cuisine. **$$$**

Patong Thai
1/F, JP Plaza
22–36 Paterson St
Causeway Bay (and other locations)
Tel: 2972 2954
Table-side aquariums and Thai beach scenes decorate this affordable restaurant with cheery service. **$$**

Spices
G/F The Arcade
109 Repulse Bay Rd
Repulse Bay
Tel: 2812 2711
Semi al-fresco restaurant just across from Repulse Bay Beach with delicious pan-Asian menu. Expensive. **$$$$**

Wasabisabi
13/F Food Forum
Times Square
1 Matheson St
Tel: 2506 0009
Chic, sleek and patronised by Hong Kong's jet set. The décor is certainly something to stare at. Slightly on the expensive side, but the Japanese dishes are very fine indeed. **$$$**

Thai Basil
Shop 5–6, Lg-1 The Mall
One Pacific Place
88 Queensway
Central
Tel: 2537 4682
Pan-South East Asian restaurant.

Mild but exquisitely cooked food and a lengthy and inventive list of ice creams and sorbets. Subdued decor and pleasant atmosphere allow you to forget you're in a shopping centre. **$$**

Tokio Joe
16 Lan Kwai Fong
Central
Tel: 2525 1889
Pleasantly avant-garde sushi bar and Japanese restaurant in the heart of Lan Kwai Fong, with good-value set lunches. **$$**

TOTT's Asian Grill
34/F The Excelsior Hotel
281 Gloucester Rd
Causeway Bay
Tel: 2894 8888
This place offers excellent pan-Asian food with an emphasis on tandoori in an opulent lounge on the top floor of the Excelsior Hotel. Recommended. **$$–$$$**

Viceroy Restaurant and Bar
2/F Sun Hung Kai Centre
30 Harbour Rd
Wan Chai
Tel: 2827 7777
Popular Indian restaurant which offers al fresco and indoor dining. The verandah has fountains, fine views and Parisian street lamps. Indian and South East Asian cuisine. **$$–$$$**

Wyndham Thai
Shop 3
G/F, The Centrium
60 Wyndham St
Central
Tel: 2869 6216
The most outrageously expensive Thai restaurant in Hong Kong, possibly in the world. Trendy design and ambience, food is more experimental Thai-based than classical Thai. Hip crowd. **$$$$**

WESTERN

Alibi
73 Wyndham St
Central
Tel: 2167 8989
Very trendy French-style brasserie plus light and healthy fare. Reservations vital. **$$$$**

Baci
2F/1 Lan Kwai Fong
Central
Tel: 2801 5885
Contemporary Italian with a touch of New York chic. **$$$$**

Boca
65 Peel St
Central
Tel: 2548 1717
Tremendous tapas with an atmosphere to match. A true SoHo eatery. **$$$$**

California
G/F California Tower
24–26 Lan Kwai Fong
Central
Tel: 2521 1345
The one that started off the whole Lan Kwai Fong phenomenon. Still trendy and fun. Californian cuisine, of course. **$$$**

Price Categories

$$$$	=	US$50 and above
$$$	=	US$30–50
$$	=	US$15–30
$	=	below US$15

Café Deco Bar & Grill
Peak Galleria
118 Peak Road
The Peak
Tel: 2849 5111
Absurdly fantastic views of Hong Kong and a wide selection of international cuisine including an oyster bar, Japanese sushi, pizza and tandoori from this art deco-style restaurant. **$$$**

Coyote Bar & Grill
114–120 Lockhart Rd
Wan Chai
Tel: 2861 2221
All your Mexican favourites served along with optional tequila shots in an open-fronted bar in rowdy Wan Chai. **$$**

Dan Ryan's Chicago Grill
114 The Mall
Pacific Place
88 Queensway
Central
Tel: 2845 4600
Big, popular and friendly joint with above-average ribs and burgers. Big American portions. **$$**

El Cid Spanish Restaurant
9–11 Cleveland St
Causeway Bay
(and other locations)
Tel: 2576 8650
Pleasant if a little kitsch; plenty of tapas and other Spanish favourites. Al fresco seating allows strumming guitarists to roam the tables at night. **$$**

Fat Angelo's
49 Elgin Street
SoHo
Central
(and other locations)
Tel: 2973 6808
Big, friendly American-Italian restaurant with massive helpings. Great for families. **$$**

Grissini
2/F The Grand Hyatt Hotel
1 Harbour Rd
Wan Chai
Tel: 2588 1234
Legendary chic Italian where the glitterati and top corporates spend huge sums to impress. **$$$$**

Habibi
112–114 Wellington St
Central
Tel: 2544 9298
Classic Egyptian food; portions are smallish but tasty. Interior is designed to recreate a Cairo of the 1930s with weekend belly dancers, hookah pipes and cushioned cubby holes. **$$**

Jimmy's Kitchen
Basement, South China Bldg
1 Wyndham St
Central
Tel: 2526 5293
An institution, serving western food for longer than any westerner has ever been in Hong Kong. A formal clubby atmosphere prevails and the elderly Chinese waiters are usually endearingly grumpy. Well worth a visit. **$$**

La Bohème
3–5 Old Bailey St
SoHo
Central
Tel: 2526 6099
This bistro/piano bar serves great French-Moroccan food. Order a filling platter of couscous and a pot of mint tea to share. **$$$.**

Le Rendez-vous
5 Staunton St
SoHo
Central
Tel: 2905 1808
Cosy candle-lit cafe with sweet and savoury French crepes and cheery Nepalese staff. **$$**

M at the Fringe
1/F, 2 Lower Albert Rd
Central
Tel: 2877 4000
This trendy spot is for special occasions. Excellent Continental menu, well-chosen wine list, pleasant service, very arty dining room and an aura of romantic intimacy. Expensive. **$$$$**

Mandarin Grill
Mandarin Oriental
5 Connaught Rd
Central
Tel: 2522 0111
Traditional, opulent, reliable and expensive. The place for a serious business lunch. **$$$**

Pasta E Pizza
Basement, 11 Lyndhurst Terrace
Central
Tel: 2545 1675
Simple but tasty Italian cuisine at comparatively low prices. A nice romantic evening choice. **$**

Post 97
9–11 Lan Kwai Fong
Central
Tel: 2810 9333
A European cafe-restaurant with a welcoming ambience and imaginative menu. Tasty vegetarian options and herb teas for the health-conscious. **$$**

Va Bene
58–62 D'Aguilar St
Central
Tel: 2845 5577
Excellent Italian restaurant in Lan Kwai Fong. Perfect for a social lunch, or dinner combined with people watching. **$$$$**

Verandah Restaurant
1/F South Wing
The Arcade
109 Repulse Bay Rd
Repulse Bay
Tel: 2812 2722
Delightful colonial-style restaurant of the utmost sophistication and style. Recreates the original

Price Categories

$$$$ = US$50 and above
$$$ = US$30–50
$$ = US$15–30
$ = below US$15

ambience of the former Repulse Bay Hotel. **$$$$**

Vong
24/F Mandarin Oriental Hotel
Central
Tel: 2522 0111
On the top floor of the Mandarin, a place to be seen and to enjoy superb, expensive Thai- and Vietnamese-influenced French cuisine. Reservations are always essential. **$$$$**

W's Entrecôte
6/F Sharp St East
Causeway Bay
Tel: 2506 0133
Well established French steakhouse that serves its own homemade chocolate. **$$$**

Kowloon/ New Territories

CANTONESE

The Chinese Restaurant
2/F Hyatt Regency Hong Kong
67 Nathan Rd
Tsim Sha Tsui
Tel: 2311 1234
1920s Shanghai teahouse style, with high ceilings and great food. **$$$**

Dong
L/2, Miramar Hotel
118–130 Nathan Rd
Tsim Sha Tsui
Tel: 2368 1111
Dong (east in Chinese) serves dim sum and modernised Cantonese dishes. Its partner restaurant, Xi, (West in Chinese), offers western food, Both in fairly standard hotel-style surroundings. **$$–$$$**

Dynasty Restaurant
4/F New World Renaissance Hotel
22 Salisbury Rd
Tsim Sha Tsui
Tel: 2734 6600
Features rich rosewood furnishings and traditional home-style cuisine. **$$$**

Fook Lam Moon Restaurant
Shop 8
1/F, 53–9 Kimberley Rd
Tsim Sha Tsui
Tel: 2366 0286
The Kowloon version of the exclusive Wan Chai favourite. **$$$$**

Golden Jade
1/F, 71–77 Peking Rd
Tsim Sha Tsui
Tel: 2311 2888
Specialises in seafood. **$$**

Heichinrou Restaurant
2/F Lippo Sun Plaza
28 Canton Rd
Tsim Sha Tsui
Tel: 2375 7123
Chic dining salon with a cocktail area and light background music – rare for a Chinese restaurant. Try the roast pigeon with Chinese "cheese" sauce. **$$**

Kau Kee (Beverley) Restaurant
Basement, Beverley Commercial Centre
87–105 Chatham Rd South
Tsim Sha Tsui
Tel: 2722 1663
Dim sum and a wide range of Cantonese dishes opposite the Science Museum. **$$**

Loong Yuen
Holiday Inn Golden Mile
50 Nathan Rd
Tsim Sha Tsui
Tel: 2315 1006
An elegant Cantonese dining experience. **$$$**

Ocean Palace Restaurant
4/F Ocean Centre
Harbour City
Canton Rd
Tsim Sha Tsui
Tel: 2730 7111
A huge traditional restaurant where you can feast on an Imperial Banquet for 12 in an Imperial Court setting. (Note that three days advance booking is required.) **$$**

Royal Garden
B2 The Royal Garden
69 Mody Rd
Tsim Sha Tsui East
Tel: 2724 2666
Gourmet food served in a delightful water-garden setting. Popular. **$$$**

Shang Palace
B1 Kowloon Shangri-La Hotel
64 Mody Rd

Tsim Sha Tsui
Tel: 2733 8754
The Shang Palace features glitzy decor and it's a gourmet's heaven. Has a special trolley service offering a memorable choice of teas. **$$$**

Spring Moon
1/F The Peninsula
Salisbury Rd
Tsim Sha Tsui
Tel: 2920 2888
Pink-and-grey plush Art Deco decor. Exquisite, top-quality cuisine. Highly recommended. **$$$$**

Super Star Seafood Restaurant,
1/F Tsim Sha Tsui Mansion
83–97 Nathan Rd
Tsim Sha Tsui
Tel: 2366 0878
The menu has photographs to help you order. Popular. **$$**

Yan Toh Heen
G/F Intercontinental Hotel
18 Salisbury Rd
Tsim Sha Tsui
Tel: 2721 1211
The Intercontinental's classy Chinese restaurant with superb views is rated by many as the best in town. **$$$$**

BEIJING & SICHUAN

Kam Kong Restaurant
53–63 Peking Rd
Tsim Sha Tsui
Tel: 2367 3434
Good variety of spicy Sichuan dishes; try the chicken slice sauté with lemon. **$$**

Heaven on Earth
6 Knutsford Terrace
Tsim Sha Tsui
Tel: 2367 8428
The restaurant, decked out like a traditional Chinese teahouse, sits atop a bar, both open to the street. A range of regional cuisines from Beijing through to Taiwanese is on offer. **$$$**

Spring Deer Restaurant
2/F 42 Mody Rd
Tsim Sha Tsui
Tel: 2723 3673
An excellent authentic place popular with locals and tourists for Peking

duck and beggars' chicken. Order a day in advance. **$$**

Yunyan Szechuan Restaurant
4/F Miramar Shopping Centre
132–134 Nathan Rd
Tsim Sha Tsui
Tel: 2375 0800
Offers a range of cuisine with spicy signature Sichuan dishes and tamer Hunanese food. **$$**

SHANGHAI

Great Shanghai Restaurant
26 Prat Avenue
Tsim Sha Tsui
Tel: 2366 8158
This great-value restaurant has been open for more than 25 years. Vast menu. **$**

Kung Tak Lam
1/F 45–47 Carnarvon Rd
Tsim Sha Tsui
Tel: 2367 7881
MSG-free and vegetarian Shanghai dishes and dim sum. Good value for money. **$$**

Snow Garden Restaurant
10/F London Plaza
219 Nathan Rd
Yau Ma Tei
Tel: 2736 9188
Very popular and grand Shanghainese restaurant with huge menu. Well worth a visit. **$$$**

Wu Kong Shanghai Restaurant
Basement, Alpha House
27 Nathan Rd
Tsim Sha Tsui
Tel: 2366 7244
Art-deco restaurant with a wide range of menu items. **$$–$$$**

Yap Pan Hong Restaurant
G/F 35 Kimberley Rd
Tsim Sha Tsui
Tel: 2721 1663
Over 350 items on the menu and tempting displays of traditional appetisers as you enter. **$**

OTHER ASIAN

Bali Restaurant
10 Nanking Rd
Jordan
Tel: 2780 2902
Red plastic booths make for a very

kitsch, 1960s-style canteen. The menu offers inexpensive Indonesian fare including nasi goreng and coconut curries. **$**

Banana Leaf Curry House
3/F Golden Crown Court
68 Nathan Rd
Tsim Sha Tsui
Tel: 2721 4821
Cheap, cheerful and popular restaurant with Asian favourites from several countries. Food is served on banana leaves, together with large portions of rice. **$**

Golden Bull Vietnamese Cuisine
101 Ocean Centre
Harbour City
5 Canton Rd
Tsim Sha Tsui
Tel: 2730 4866
Stylish restaurant offering a wide range Vietnamese dishes. **$$$**

Her Thai
Tower 1
China Hong Kong City
Canton Rd
Tsim Sha Tsui
Tel: 2735 8898
Excellent Thai food with added bonus of panoramic views. **$$**

Spice Market
3/F The Marco Polo Prince Hotel
Harbour City
Canton Rd
Tsim Sha Tsui
Tel: 2113 6046
Decorative stalls present the authentic cuisines of Asia. Delicious and fun. **$**

Wong Chun Chun Thai
8/F Causeway Bay Plaza Two
463–83 Lockhart Road
Tel: 2721 0099
This is a sister branch to one of Hong Kong's original Thai restaurants located in Kowloon City. Pleasant, fast service, relaxing décor in a gaudy, faux Thai way, and good fiery dishes. **$$**

Woodlands International
Mirador Tower
61 Mody Rd
Tsim Sha Tsui East
Tel: 2369 3718
Woodlands offers good Indian vegetarian food in a relaxed environment. Try the crispy *dosai* pancakes and the delicious *thali* appetisers. **$–$$**

Outlying Islands

The following is a selection of the best seafood restaurants on the outlying islands.

Baccarat Restaurant
G/F, 9A Pak She Praya Rd
Cheung Chau
Tel: 2981 5567

Han Lok Yuen Restaurant
16–17 Hung Shing Ye
Yung Shue Wan
Lamma Island
Tel: 2982 0608

Hong Kee Restaurant
G/F, 11A Pak She Praya Rd
Cheung Chau
Tel: 2981 9916

Lancombe Seafood
47 Main St
Yung Shue Wan
Lamma Island
Tel: 2982 0881

Lamma Mandarin Seafood
G/F, 8 First St
Sok Kwu Wan
Lamma Island
Tel: 2982 8128

Man Feng Seafood Restaurant
5 Main St
Yung Shue Wan
Lamma Island
Tel: 2982 1112

Peach Garden Seafood Restaurant
D.D. 10, Lot 583
Sok Kwu Wan
Lamma Island
Tel: 2982 8581

Rainbow Seafood Restaurant
G/F, 16–9 First St
Sok Kwu Wan
Lamma Island
Tel: 2982 8100

WESTERN

Fat Angelo's
33 Ashley Rd
Tsim Sha Tsui
Tel: 2730 4788
The Tsim Sha Tsui branch of this friendly American-Italian pizza and pasta house. $$

Felix
28/F The Peninsula
Salisbury Rd
Tsim Sha Tsui
Tel: 2366 6251
Stylish Philippe Starck-designed restaurant atop the Peninsula Tower. Dine amid an exclusive international glitterati with unrivalled panoramic views of Hong Kong and Kowloon. $$$$

Gaddi's
1/F The Peninsula Hotel
Salisbury Rd
Tsim Sha Tsui
Tel: 2366 6251 ext. 3171
Superlatively classy restaurant that deserves every one of the accolades it receives for its classic French cooking, fine wines, impeccable service and elegant setting. Reservations are necessary and the dress code is smart. $$$$

Jimmy's Kitchen
1/F Kowloon Centre
29 Ashley Rd
Tsim Sha Tsui
Tel: 2376 0327
Western food is served in a formal clubby atmosphere. The elderly Chinese waiters are endearingly grumpy. Worth a visit. $$

The Mistral
Grand Standford Intercontinental
70 Mody Rd
Tsim Sha Tsui East
Tel: 2731 2870
This hotel restaurant is a member of the Italian Buon Ricordo organisation and serves fine Italian food in a warm setting. $$$

Verandah
1/F The Peninsula
Salisbury Rd
Tsim Sha Tsui
Tel: 2366 6251
A marvellous evocation of the colonial era, especially the curry tiffin lunches. Stylish, yet not too expensive. Recommended. $$$

Yu, The Seafood Restaurant
Mezz. Level
Hotel Intercontinental
18 Salisbury Rd
Tsim Sha Tsui
Tel: 2721 1211
The Intercontinental's excellent seafood restaurant whose centrepiece, perhaps tastelessly, is a giant central aquarium. $$$

Macau

CHINESE

456
Lisboa Hotel
New Wing
Avenida do Infante D. Henrique
Tel: 715 667
One of the region's best Shanghainese food restaurants. $$$

Canton Tea House
Hyatt Regency Hotel
Taipa
Tel: 831 234 ext. 1937
Cantonese style restaurant, serving dim sum at lunch time. $$

Chan Chan Kun
22 Rua da Cunha
Tel: 827 168
Cantonese dishes with a heavy emphasis on snake and eel. $$

Federal
5/F, 19–21 Avenida do Dr. Rodrigo Rodrigues
Tel: 313 313
Another of Macau's favourite eateries. $$

Kapok Cantonese Restaurant
60 Rua de Hong Chai
Hoi Yee Garden
Taipa
Tel: 833 333
Just behind the Hyatt Regency. An extensive and imaginative range of Cantonese dishes. $$

Long Kei
7B Largo do Senado
Tel: 573 970
This "shabby grand" Chinese restaurant, with its high ceilings, chandeliers and canteen-style tables, has a huge menu. It sits right in the main square. $

Nga Tim Café
8 Rua Caetano
Coloane Village
Coloane
Tel: 882 086
Simple outdoor seating in the square fronting the pretty St Francis Xavier chapel and facing the South China Sea. Lots of Chinese seafood dishes and a few Macanese ones too. A good place to watch the sun set with a glass of wine. For the brave, the restaurant opposite serves roasted worm omelette. $

Tung Yee Heen
2/F, Mandarin Oriental Hotel
Avenida de Amizade
Tel: 567 888 ext. 3821
A very upmarket Cantonese
restaurant, serving dim sum at
lunch time. **$$$–$$$$**

Vila Porto de Macau
Level One
Macau Tower Convention and
Entertainment Centre
Tel: 968 899
Sister restaurant to Café Madeira,
also sporting good views of the
harbour. Main cuisine on offer is
fiery Sichuan. **$$**

MACANESE/PORTUGUESE

Afonso's
Hyatt Regency Hotel
Taipa
Tel: 831 234 ext. 1921 or 1922
One of the best Portuguese
restaurants in Macau. Great
seafood, lovely breads and buffet
on Sundays. **$$$**

A Lorcha
G/F, 289A Rua Almirante Sergio
Tel: 313 193
A small unpretentious eatery
on the Inner Harbour specialising
in Portuguese food. Its Chinese
dishes are good too, as they
have a distinct Portuguese flavour.
$$

Barra Nova
287 Rua do Almirante Sergio
Tel: 965 118
Small restaurant featuring
Portuguese and Macanese cuisine
on the Inner Harbour, located just
near the A-Ma Temple. **$$**

Bee Vee
Rotunda de Leonel da Sousa
Praca da Portagem
Taipa
Tel: 812 288
A great spot for Portuguese and
Macanese specialities. **$$**

Café Madeira
Level One
Macau Tower Convention and
Entertainment Centre
Tel: 963 399
Outdoor seating with great views of
the harbour and nightly live music. A
good selection of Portuguese

seafood; try the braised chicken
with port wine. **$$**

Espaco Lisboa
8 Rua das Gaivotas
Coloane Village
Coloane
Tel: 882 226
Bright and cosy, and located in an
older Mediterranean-style house,
this popular local restaurant serves
Portuguese food in large portions.
Try the rabbit stew. **$$**

Fernando's
9 Praia Hac Sa
Hac Sa Beach
Coloane
Tel: 882 264
Large menu with both Portuguese
and Chinese dishes. Seafood,
especially clams, and rabbit
specialities. Wonderful place to
while away an afternoon when you
are tired of the beach. **$$**

Flamingo
Hyatt Regency
Taipa
Tel: 831 234 ext. 1834 or 1874
Authentic Portuguese and
Macanese food served in the open
air in a pavilion over a man-made
lake. Marvellous atmosphere. **$$**

Galo
G/F and 1/F, 45 Rua dos Clerigos
Taipa
Tel: 827 318
This is the place to go for African
Chicken, though other Portuguese
and Macanese dishes are also on
the menu. **$$**

Henri's Galley
4 Avenida da República
Tel: 556 251
A long-standing favourite in central
Macau; African chicken and giant
spicy prawns are their showpiece
dishes. **$$**

Litoral
261a Rua do Almirante Sergio
Tel: 967 878
Opposite the Maritime museum,
this busy Portuguese restaurant

has all the favourites including a
fine selection of crab dishes and
good wines. **$$**

O Santos
20 Rua do Cunha
Taipa
Tel: 825 594
A small restaurant with a gritty,
authentic feel. Often overlooked
(and it seems the owner and
customers prefer it that way), this
restaurant has excellent fish
dishes and is great for a cosy
lunch. **$$**

Os Gatos
Avenida da República
Fortaleza de São Tiago de Barra
Tel: 378 111
Fancy restaurant tucked into the
Barra fort serving fine Macanese
cuisine along with beautifully
prepared international dishes.
$$$

Platão
3 Travessa São Domingos
Tel: 331 818
Turn right into a side alley past a
McDonalds in the main square.
Great Portuguese food in elegant
surroundings; on fine days tables
are set out on the small terrace.
Closed Monday. **$$**

Pinocchio's
4 Rua do Sol
Taipa
Tel: 827 128
Spicy fish and fowl served in a tree-
shaded courtyard. **$$**

Praia Grande
G/F, 10A Praca de Lobo de Avila
Tel: 973 022
One of Macau's older and better
restaurants. **$$$**

Safari
14 Patio do Cotovelo
Tel: 574 313
Small and cosy, serving inexpensive
Portuguese food with a few
French dishes in a 1970s-style
eatery. **$**

Price Categories

$$$$	=	US$50 and above
$$$	=	US$30–50
$$	=	US$15–30
$	=	below US$15

OTHER ASIAN

Aruna Indian Curry House
779B Avenida da Amizade
Tel: 701 850
A long list of curries from royal lamb
to cheese. **$**

Indian Garden Restaurant
6 Rua de Seng Tou
Nova Taipa Gardens
Taipa
Tel: 837 088
Saturday buffets and free limo service to premises, call in advance. **$$**

Thai
27E Rua Abreu Nunes
Tel: 573 288
For the unsuspecting, the Thai cuisine here is some of the hottest in Asia. The *tom yam* is a good test of your endurance. **$$**

Guangzhou

CHINESE

Banxi
151 Longjin Xilu
Tel: 8181 5718
Established in the late 19th century, this is one of the oldest restaurants in Guangzhou. Located on the shore of Liwan Lake, it has an old pavilion where the dining room is entirely wood-panelled and decorated with antique porcelain. **$$$**

Dansanyuan
260 Changdi Lu
Tel: 8101 3277
A popular restaurant that has been open for 30 years, Dansanyuan is known for its stewed shark's fin soup, chicken's feet and tea chicken. A very noisy and energetic spot. **$$**

Datong Restaurant
63 Yanjiangxi Lu
Tel: 8188 8441
Serving over a thousand dishes, with crispy skin chicken, roast suckling pig, Xi Shi duck and cactus with chicken wings as the favourites. Eight floors overlooking the Pearl River. **$$**

Flora City Restaurant
China Merchant's Hotel
8/111 Liu Hua Lu
Tel: 8650 3188
Busy Cantonese dining hall. **$$**

Food Street
G/F, China Hotel Liuhua Lu
Tel: 8666 3888
The concept of Food Street was so successful, it has been copied by

other hotels. A variety of open kitchens serve dim sum, hot pot, Cantonese and a combination of regional foods. Good *xiao long bao* buns. **$$**

Fu Si Jie
Niunai Changjie, off Tongfu Zhonglu
Tel: 8424 3590
Located south of the Pearl River near the small Hai Tong Si temple, this is one of the few restaurants in Guangzhou that serves Buddhist vegetarian food. **$**

Guangzhou Restaurant
2 Wenchang Lu
Tel: 8138 9840
The largest in Guangzhou, serving 10,000 a day, with branches south of the city and also in Hong Kong and Los Angeles. The restaurant is famous for its shark's fin soup and abalone sprinkled with 24K-gold flakes. **$$**

Imperial Garden
Gitic Plaza Hotel
339 Huanshi Lu
Tel: 8335 0909
Specialising in seafood dishes and Cantonese favourites. Designed like a garden with pavilions around an artificial pond. **$$$**

Jade River
3/F White Swan Hotel
Shamian Island
Tel: 8188 6968
A luxurious restaurant with superb Cantonese dining and seafood specialities. **$$$$**

Muslim Food Restaurant
82 Heng Fu Lu
Tel: 8358 9625
Inexpensive and hearty Xinjiang food from Guangzhou's Muslim community, open 24 hours. **$**

Ruby Seafood Restaurant
3/F Lidu Hotel
182 Beijing Lu
Tel: 8332 1988
Cantonese seafood in the heart of Guangzhou's shopping district. **$$**

Jiang Nan Zhi Chun (Spring of Jiang Nan)
8 Tian He Bei Lu
Tel: 3881 9320
Dodgy service but some tasty Cantonese and Hangzhou dishes. Try the zesty fried pearl and fingered citron (squeezed lemon). **$$**

Tai Woo Seafood Restaurant
617 Dongfeng Dong Lu
Clattering dim sum dining hall, very popular. **$$**

Tao Ran Ju
4/F Du Shi Hua Ting
368 Tian He Bei Lu
Tel: 3881 5762
Sichuan hot pots with a punch served by waiters clad in Sun Yatsen garb. **$**

OTHER ASIAN

Banana Leaf
8 Lu Hu Lu
Tel: 8359 1288
A popular Thai restaurant, large portions at reasonable prices. Spicy noodle dishes and seafood soups, accompanied by live music; be warned, you may be forced to dance! **$$**

Hirata
Mezzanine Fl, White Swan Hotel
1 Shamian Nanlu
Tel: 8188 6968
The only genuine Japanese restaurant in Guangzhou, according to local Japanese residents. Food prepared by well-trained Cantonese cooks and supervised by a Japanese. **$$$**

Maharaja Indian Kebab Corner
2/F China Hotel
Liu Hua Lu
Tel: 8666 6888 ext. 2217
One of Guangzhou's few Indian restaurants, the name says it all; no credit cards. **$$**

Culture

Museums

Museum of Tea Ware, Flagstaff House. Originally the home of the commander-in-chief of the British forces, Flagstaff House is now devoted to a collection of Chinese tea ware. The museum is in Hong Kong Park, and admission is free. Open daily except Tuesday 10am–5pm. Tel: 2869 0690.
Hong Kong Museum of Art. A vast exhibition space within the Hong Kong Cultural Centre Complex in Tsim Sha Tsui. Chinese fine arts and antiquities as well as contemporary Hong Kong art. Open daily except Thursday 10am–6pm. Entrance fee, free on Wednesday. Tel: 2721 0116.
Hong Kong History Museum. The museum presents "The Story of Hong Kong", not just since the colonial era but drawing on relics from 6,000 years ago. Open daily except Tuesday 10am–6pm, Sunday 10am–7pm. Entrance fee, free on Wednesday. Tel: 2724 9042.
Hong Kong Racing Museum, Happy Valley Racecourse. This museum highlights the phenomenal popularity of horse-racing in Hong Kong since its introduction in the 1840s. It is

Visitors' Passes

A visitors' pass allows unlimited entry to four museums run by the Urban Council: the Hong Kong Museum of Art, the Science Museum, the Space Museum and the Museum of History. The HK$30 pass is valid for a week and is available from these four museums and HKTB information centres *(see page 288.)*

located on the second floor of the Happy Valley Stand of the Happy Valley Racecourse. Open daily except Monday 10am–5pm. Admission free. Tel: 2966 8065.
Hong Kong Railway Museum. A small picturesque homage to Hong Kong's railway history located at the 1913 former Tai Po Market railway station. Open daily except Tuesday 9am–5pm. Admission free. Tel: 2966 8065.
Hong Kong Science Museum. Interactive exhibits covering science and technology areas such as robotics, virtual reality and transport. Cheong Wan Road, Tsim Sha Tsui. Open Monday–Wednesday and Friday, 1–9pm, Saturday and Sunday 10am–9pm. Closed Thursday. Entrance fee, but free on Wednesday. Tel: 2732 3232.
Hong Kong Space Museum. A planetarium and space technology exhibition with screenings several times a day. Open Monday, Wednesday–Friday 1–9pm, Saturday, Sunday and most public holidays 10am–9pm. Closed Tuesday. Entrance fee, but free on Wednesday. Tel: 2721 0226.
Police Museum. The former Wan Chai Gap Police Station showcases the history of Asia's finest and includes exhibitions on narcotics and the notorious triad societies. Open Wednesday–Sunday 9am–5pm, Tuesday, 2–5pm. Closed Monday and public holidays. Admission free. Tel: 2849 7019.
Heritage Museum. A Chinese art gallery, a permanent expo on the New Territories and the history of Chinese Opera. 1 Man Lam Road, Sha Tin. Open Monday, Wednesday–Saturday 10am–6pm, Sunday 10am–7pm. Closed Tuesday. Entrance fee. Tel: 2180 8188.

MACAU

Macau Cultural Centre/Art Museum. The focal point of the development on reclaimed land by the Outer Harbour. Galleries, exhibitions, conferences etc are all held in the Auditoria Building. Next

For information on cultural events and museums, visit the following tourist office websites:

Useful Websites

For information on cultural events and museums, visit the following tourist office websites:
Hong Kong
www.discoverhongkong.com
Macau
www.macautourism.gov.mo

door is the Art Museum, home to over 3,000 artworks and a notable collection of Chinese calligraphy. Open daily except Monday 10am–5pm. Entrance fee. For details, visit www.artmuseum.gov.mo
Maritime Museum. Presents a collection of boat building, Chinese and Portuguese maritime traditions and fishing techniques. Open daily except Tuesday 10am–5.30pm. Entrance fee, half price on Sunday.
Museum of Macau. Built on the remains of Macau's fortress and overlooking the fabulous facade of São Paulo church, this three-storey museum documents the unique and colourful history of the ex-Portuguese colony, concentrating on its ethnography and anthropology.
Open daily except Monday 10am–6pm. Entrance fee.

GUANGZHOU

Guangdong Folk Arts Museum. Housed in the Chen Family Temple, this museum is more a gallery of arts and crafts from various regions in China. Pottery, porcelain from Shiwan, stone and wood carvings, embroidery and stitchwork are displayed in the halls of the temple. Zhongshan Qi Lu. Tel: 8881 4559.
Museum of the Western Han (Nanyue Wangmu). The emperor Wen Di, who ruled southern China from 137 to 122 BC, was buried here. Today a museum houses the skeletons of the emperor and fifteen courtiers who were buried alive with him. Funerary objects from jade armour to bronze chimes are displayed. 807 Jiefang Dei Lu. Open daily 8am–6pm.

Nightlife

Where to Party

Hong Kong has an extremely lively nightlife scene, and you won't be short of places to party. There are plenty of western-style bars and discos, some of which attract a mainly western clientele, while others cater to a mix of locals and expats.

There are three districts in which most bars and clubs likely to appeal to visitors are located: Central, Wan Chai (including Causeway Bay) and Tsim Sha Tsui. Central is where most expats and trendy locals go after work, especially Lan Kwai Fong, SoHo and Boho. All are packed with chic bars and restaurants. Wan Chai, including nearby Causeway Bay, has a grittier nightlife scene, with many bars and discos that are in full swing in the small hours. On Kowloon side, Tsim Sha Tsui's nightlife tends to be split between bars that are exclusively for locals and those aimed mainly at tourists.

CENTRAL

Captain's Bar, Mandarin Oriental Hotel. Tel: 2522 0111. Where the captains of industry congregate after work.
Club 97, 9 Lan Kwai Fong. Tel: 2810 9333. One of the longest-running but still one of the hippest clubs in town.
Club Feather Boa, 38 Staunton St. Tel: 2857 7156. Like a regency drawing room; amazing, eclectic and so SoHo.
Drop, 39–43 Hollywood Rd. Tel: 2543 8856. The ultimate groovy BoHo bar and disco. Entrance opposite Tun Wo Lane.
Dublin Jack, 37–43 Cochrane St. Tel: 2543 0081. Compulsory rowdy

Irish bar. Big screen sports and comedy tapes in the toilet. The first bar in Hong Kong to go completely smoke-free.
Fringe Club, 2 Lower Albert Rd. Tel: 2521 7485. Live bands downstairs, or a relaxing beer garden on the roof. Along with reasonable drinks prices, this place is a rare gem.
La Dolce Vita, 9 Lan Kwai Fong. Tel: 2810 9333. The people-watchers' eyrie in Lan Kwai Fong. Pity about the offhand staff.
Le Jardin, 1/F, 10 Wing Wah Lane, Central. Tel: 2526 2717. The best outdoor bar in Central/Lan Kwai Fong. Laid back atmosphere with a good mix of people.
Post 97, 9 Lan Kwai Fong. Tel: 2810 9333. Comfy all-night restaurant and hang-out above Club 97.
Staunton's Bar & Cafe, 10 Staunton St. Tel: 2973 6611. Top cappuccino and people-watching.
Vodka Bar, 13 Old Bailey St. Tel: 9803 6650. Hip bar and gallery on the fringe of SoHo. Open late.
Yumla, Lower Basement, Harilela House, 79 Wyndham St, Central. Tel: 2147 2382. Trendy place with top notch music and a lively crowd.

WAN CHAI/ CAUSEWAY BAY

Carnegie's, 53–65 Lockhart Rd, Wan Chai. Tel: 2866 6289. A rowdy, rocky two-tier bar that is packed and boisterous at weekends and fun most nights. Hosts live-music events.
Champagne Bar, Grand Hyatt, Wan Chai. Tel: 2588 1234. Intimate, opulent bar for expensive after-work entertaining.
Club ING, 4/F Convention Plaza, Renaissance Harbour View Hotel. Tel: 2824 0523. American-style club with R&B most nights, but rambunctious salsa nights on Wednesdays. Come early for free lessons.
Delaney's, One Capital Place, 18 Luard Road, Wan Chai. Tel: 2804 2880. Very popular Irish theme pub with good food.
Klong Bar and Grill, The Broadway, 54–62 Lockhart Rd, Wan Chai. Tel:

2217 8330. Named after Bangkok's network of tiny canals. There's optional pole dancing, zebra-patterned pool tables, and niches hiding faux opium dens.
JJ's, The Grand Hyatt, Wan Chai. Tel: 2588 1234. The Grand Hyatt's huge disco has been going for over 10 years but is still the party choice of local and visiting glitterati.
Joe Banana's, 23 Luard Rd, Wan Chai. Tel: 2529 1811. This bar/club has been running for years and has a reputation as somewhat of a meat market for expatriates.
La Vie, 39 Yiu Wa St, Causeway Bay. Tel: 2881 8367. Themed bar south of Times Square. Relaxed wine and sake bar with a very chilled-out atmosphere.
TOTT's Asian Grill and Bar, 281 Gloucester Rd, Causeway Bay. Tel: 2894 8888. This chic restaurant at the top of the Excelsior turns into a popular night spot after dinner.

KOWLOON

48th Street Chicago Blues, 2A Hart Avenue, Tsim Sha Tsui. Tel: 2723 7633. Small friendly bar with nightly live jazz and blues.
Bahama Mama's, 4–5 Knutsford Terrace. Tel: 2368 2121.

Karaoke

Many bars and even restaurants have private rooms where groups get together to sing Chinese songs. There are TV screens showing music videos and the words to the song in Chinese. Words are highlighted when you are supposed to sing them. Some karaoke bars also employ "hostesses" to sing together with the customers, who are usually rowdy groups of Asian businessmen. A night out in one of these establishments will prove extremely expensive. Westerners unaccompanied by local Chinese will probably not be made very welcome.

Caribbean-themed bar that spills out onto the street.

Chemical Suzy, 2 Austin Avenue, Tsim Sha Tsui. Tel: 2736 0087. For the young and groovy wannabes. Thursday is ragga night.

Club Bboss, New Mandarin Plaza, Tsim Sha Tsui East. Tel: 2369 2883. Japanese-style glitzy hostess bar, with dance bands and karaoke rooms and over 1,000 hostesses. For gentlemen with plenty of cash to burn.

Rick's Café, 4 Hart Avenue, Tsim Sha Tsui. Tel: 2367 2939. Loud basement bar/club, usually packed.

Someplace Else, Sheraton Hotel and Towers, Tsim Sha Tsui. Tel: 2369 1111. Popular, comfortable rendezvous point with live music late at night.

Gay/Lesbian Nightlife

Hong Kong has a small but thriving gay scene, though lesbians are stuck with a few local-style karaoke bars in Causeway Bay office blocks. The bars and clubs that are most welcoming to foreigners are located in Central.

New Wally Matt Lounge, 5A Humphrey's Avenue, Tsim Sha Tsui. Tel: 2721 2568. Laid back simple bar for men.

Propaganda, 1 Hollywood Rd, Central. Tel: 2868 1316. A big, packed dance club open 10pm till late every day except Sunday; there's also a restaurant, open 7–10pm.

Works, 30–32 Wyndham St, Central. Tel: 2868 6102. This hot and sweaty club decked out in black is a serious cruising joint for men.

Shopping

Shopper's Paradise

Hong Kong has frequently been called a shopper's paradise and it is certainly true that most Hong Kong citizens are insatiable shoppers. Shopping places range from colourful night markets and glitzy malls, to multi-storey department stores and bustling narrow streets full of antiques and bric-a-brac. These days, Hong Kong may not be the bargain basement it once was, but shopping may nonetheless prove one of the most compelling activities of any trip to the territory for many visitors.

Shopping Advice

The Hong Kong Tourism Board offers two golden rules for shoppers:
● Shop around and compare prices before you make any decision to buy, particularly for an expensive purchase.
● Always deal with reputable establishments, such as members of the Hong Kong Tourism Board's Quality Tourism Services Scheme (identifiable by the logo of a red junk set next to a big golden Q with the Chinese character for quality written in black inside. The sign should be displayed prominently on the premises).

Make sure when buying electrical goods that you get an international guarantee and not just a local Hong Kong guarantee. Sometimes goods that seem suspiciously cheap may not have this guarantee. It is rare for local retailers to accept responsibility for faulty goods. Instead, you will have to return them to the manufacturer for repair.

The problem of retailers cheating tourists was rife a few years ago,

but has been brought much more under control. However, if you do have a problem you should contact the HKTB or the **Consumer Council** (Tel: 2929 2222). Both organisations are keen to protect Hong Kong's shopping reputation and will offer whatever assistance they can. Calling in a police officer in a case of very obvious cheating can also be helpful, as shopkeepers do not wish to waste their time getting into disputes and do not like to have their reputation publicly damaged by the appearance of the police.

Shopkeepers may often appear to be rather rude and impatient. It's partly just the way that Hong Kong English sounds and partly the pace of life in Hong Kong. There is a fine line to be drawn between rude and unhelpful shopkeepers and those who just practise the normal Hong Kong behaviour of trying to do things quickly. Shopkeepers rely on fast turnover to make profits, so you may find them unwilling to devote much time to ponderous tourists who are taking a lot of time over a relatively small purchase.

Where to Shop

The "prime" shopping centres are Central, Admiralty and Causeway Bay on Hong Kong Island, and Tsim Sha Tsui and Mong Kok in Kowloon. Shopping hours vary, but the good news is that shopping basically goes on until late seven days a week. Even during public holidays, shops are almost always open, except during the annual Lunar New Year holiday. As a guide, shops in Central close around 7pm, but the other main areas tend to stay open till 9.30pm, sometimes even later.

MALLS

The best-known shopping malls on Hong Kong Island are Landmark in Central, Pacific Place in Admiralty, Times Square in Causeway Bay and City Plaza in Taikoo Shing. In Kowloon, the linked Ocean Terminal

Watches

Note that if you are not buying from a reputable outlet, and if the price of the watch seems to be a bargain, it's extremely likely that it will be a fake.

and Harbour Centre complexes plus Festival Walk in Kowloon Tong can keep you busy. The newest additions to Hong Kong's trademark malls are IFC 1 and IFC 2 – a vast selection of swanky shops and snack bars wrapped in a cocoon of shiny steel and glass just above the Hong Kong Airport Express station. Hong Kong's most luxurious cinema, the Palace, is here too with its comfy armchair seats.

MARKETS

Hong Kong has a number of lively and interesting shopping markets.

Cat Street off Hollywood Road in Central is a flea market offering inexpensive trinkets and bric-a-brac. The surrounding area is famous for fine arts and antiques.

Stanley Market, on the south side of the island, is famous for sports and casualwear, linen, tableware, silk, and leather garments. Open 10am–7pm daily.

Temple Street, Hong Kong's most popular night market, runs from Jordan to Yau Ma Tei in Kowloon. Cheap clothing, watches, pens, sunglasses, CDs, electronic gadgets and luggage abound in its colourfully lit stalls. There are also Chinese fortune-tellers and Chinese

opera singers practising. Open 8pm to midnight.

Tung Choi Street is a busy street market in Mong Kok and is less tourist oriented than Temple Street. Specialities include local women's fashions, jewellery and accessories. Open 3–10pm.

Jewellery fans may like to check out the **Jade Market**, located under the flyover near Kansau Street in Yau Ma Tei. Open daily 10am–6pm.

What to Buy

ANTIQUES & WORKS OF ART

The network of antique shops located around Hollywood Road and Cat Street offers an extraordinary range of Asian antiquities and artworks at a very wide range of prices. The Chinese department stores scattered around Hong Kong also offer many inexpensive antiques and handicrafts from mainland China.

Ivory

For many years, Hong Kong was the international centre of carved ivory. However, the ban imposed by the Convention on International Trade in Endangered Species (CITES) means that you now have to obtain an import licence from your country of residence in order to take any ivory out of Hong Kong.

COMPUTERS

Hong Kong is a major exporter of computers, components and

accessories, and you will find the most up-to-date models at great prices. There are a number of arcades solely devoted to selling computers and accessories. If you are buying a computer, make sure that the keyboard is in English and not English with Cantonese symbols. Ask to see it before you buy. The best retailers are found in Star House in Tsim Sha Tsui near the Star Ferry, Windsor House in Causeway Bay, and Whampoa Gardens in Hung Hom, Kowloon.

CLOTHING

Hong Kong has a superb range of clothing to suit all ages, tastes and budgets. Although many visitors from South East Asia flock to Hong Kong for the latest names in international fashion, most Western visitors will find they get much better buys on the big names at home. The factory outlets in Wan Chai, Tsim Sha Tsui and Mong Kok, however, are extremely popular with tourists. These are essentially seconds and over-runs from Hong Kong's export industry and are available at a fraction of the selling price overseas. The Chinese Products emporia such as the CRC Department Stores have great bargains on Chinese-made silks.

CUSTOM TAILORS

Having your own suit made to measure is still a popular luxury for visitors to Hong Kong. The territory has some of the legendary tailors

Bargaining

Contrary to popular belief, the practice of bargaining for goods in Hong Kong is a dying art. Price differences are usually so marginal that it is hardly worthwhile trying to bargain. Shopkeepers who are not used to bargaining will probably react rather impatiently to your efforts. If you settle by cash you may get a slightly better deal than

if you use a credit card – in many cases, shops will add an extra few percent to the price if you pay by credit card.

Don't waste time trying to bargain in department stores or modern shops. They frequently offer marked discounts to induce sales but are not amenable to any bargaining. Small family-run stores

may do so, and in markets you should certainly attempt to use your bargaining skills. Remember, though, that if you buy from a market there are no guarantees and there's no possibility of exchanging goods. Even in street markets, it is highly unlikely that you'll be able to reduce the asking price by much more than about 10 to 20 percent.

Cameras & Electricals

Cameras and electrical wares are still good buys in Hong Kong, but pay particular attention in camera shops that you are not being conned. Most camera and electronics stores are in Causeway Bay, Tsim Sha Tsui and Mong Kok. They seldom have price tags on the items, so bargain, compare prices and beware. Most resident expatriates prefer the camera stores in Stanley Street, Central. There is not such an extensive range there, but the shopkeepers are friendly, the goods are reasonably priced and there are few reports of cheating. With electronic goods, remember to check for correct voltage, adaptors etc. Hand-held electronic games are particularly advanced in Hong Kong and make great gifts for teenagers. Hong Kong is also one of the best places in the world to buy cheap CDs.

of old Shanghai who have passed on their skills to the next generation. The speed and quality of craftsmanship and the range of fabrics here are all excellent. Such personal tailoring is no longer a massive bargain, but still worthwhile. A few places can produce your suit within 24 hours, but you won't usually see the best-quality results. Expect your tailor to take about a week if you want a high-quality garment. There are a lot of tailors in Tsim Sha Tsui and a few in Wan Chai and Causeway Bay. The Shanghai Tang store in Central also offers a Shanghainese tailoring service for either Western- or Mandarin-style suits.

JEWELLERY

Hong Kong is the world's fourth largest exporter of jewellery, and there is a wide range of designs available in retail outlets throughout the territory. Because Hong Kong is a free port and there is no tax on the import or export of precious metals, prices are good. Particularly popular jewellery includes jade items (though you should avoid buying expensive pieces without expert advice) and bright yellow 24-carat gold, called *chuk kam* in Cantonese. Jewellery stores specialising in *chuk kam* are usually very crowded and the atmosphere is more akin to that of a betting shop than an exclusive store. These items are sold by the weight of the gold only, so you pay no premium for the design. There are many fine jewellery stores selling a vast range of gem-set designs – here, you pay for the craftsmanship as well as the materials. Another good buy in Hong Kong are pearls, which come in all shapes, sizes and colours. The practice of bargaining is much less common in jewellery stores now, but you can certainly try your luck by asking for a discount.

LEATHER GOODS

Many shops stock a wide range of leather shoes, bags, wallets and luggage. There are top-quality, brand-name goods as well as very inexpensive wallets and bags from discount stores in the main shopping areas of Tsim Sha Tsui and Causeway Bay.

SPORTSWEAR

Hong Kong has many chain stores selling inexpensive sportswear and sports shoes (try Marathon Sports or Royal Sporting House). In Mong Kok the streets east of Tung Choi street market are devoted to sports stores.

Macau

Macau is a good place to buy Chinese antiques and artefacts, and an excellent place to buy well-crafted Asian furniture in wood or wicker. Many Hong Kong expats buy their furniture here and have it delivered to Hong Kong, often free of charge. Shipping prices may be lower than expected.

The majority of the antique stores are clustered in Rua de São Paula, the busy lane which leads up to the facade of São Paulo. You are free to bargain hard here. Otherwise, Macau is rarely thought of as a shopping mart, except for its magnificently priced wines, brandies and ports, which are restricted upon return to Hong Kong. Though it is a duty-free port like Hong Kong, the array of goods available is not nearly as extensive. Some items, such as cameras or stereo systems, are more costly in Macau because of the smaller number sold. Like Hong Kong, Macau is a clothing manufacturing centre.

Guangzhou

Don't expect the glitz and variety of goods available in Hong Kong to be on offer here, although Guangzhou does still have interesting shopping and good bargains. Among Chinese cities, Guangzhou is considered to have the widest range of goods, many of which are imported from other parts of the country.

The main shopping areas are Zhongshan Wulu, Beijing Lu, Renmin Nanlu, Zhongshan Silu and Xiajiu Lu-Shangjiu Lu. The main open-air market is at Qingping Lu, near Shamian Island.

There are several large department stores worth a visit for their wide array of foreign merchandise, at prices lower than in Hong Kong. Nanfang Dasha (49 Yanjiang Xilu) offers a good choice of local products. Xihu Lu Baihuo Dasha, on Xihu Lu, has a huge choice, especially foreign goods, at amazing prices. Xin Da Xin, at the corner of Beijing Lu and Zhongshan Wulu, offers a good range of Chinese goods, including silk (and the rare Guangdong black-mud silk), and a large musical instrument department. The Guangzhou Foreign Trade Centre at the Guangzhou Fair Building, on Renmin Beilu, has a large arts and crafts department and a good choice of silk merchandise.

Pearls

For centuries, pearls have been the indispensable ornament of the nobility, especially emperors. Most of the pearls on sale in Guangzhou are saltwater southern pearls called *hepu*, cultured in silver-lipped oysters. The largest of these lustrous pearls can have a diameter of 12–16 mm (0.47–0.63 in). Recommended shops include the following: Guangzhou Gold and Silver Jewellery Centre (109 Dade Lu) and Sun Moon Hall (Equatorial Hotel, Renmin Beilu).

The government-owned Friendship Store, on the ground floor of the China Hotel, and the Kwangchow Friendship Store, at 369 Huanshi Donglu, opposite the Garden Hotel, offer a wide selection of goods.

ANTIQUES

The largest private market for antiques is the Daihe Lu Market, which sprawls over several lanes. Access the market by the first lane on the right after entering Daihe Lu from Changshou Xilu. There are smaller antique markets nearby; one at the middle lane of the Qingping Market and the other at the Jade Market.

Antiques that date from before 1795 may not be legally exported. Any antique over a century old must carry a small red wax seal or have one affixed by the Cultural Relics Bureau before it can be taken out of China. All other antiques are the property of the Peoples' Republic of China and, without the seal, will be confiscated without compensation.

Beware of fakes, as the production of new "antiques" complete with "official" seal is a thriving industry in China. Despite the pitfalls, there is still much to buy: *kam muk* (gilded sculptured wood panels), vintage watches, tiny embroidered shoes for Chinese women with bound feet and beautiful Shiwan porcelain.

If you are a serious collector, antiques with authentic red-wax seals authorising export can be purchased from government shops. Try the Guangzhou Antique Shop (146/162/170 Wende Beilu. Tel: 8333 0175, fax: 8335 0085) for *kam muk*, calligraphy works, jewellery boxes, paintings, porcelain and silver jewellery.

CLOTHING & TEXTILES

Guangdong Province is a major production centre for ready-to-wear clothes and shoes. The biggest variety of shops is to be found at the government-owned Friendship Stores. These stores are your best bet for down jackets (typically costing only one-fifth the price you would pay elsewhere) and cashmere sweaters and scarves. The Bingfen Fashion Market on Haizhu Square, Gong Lu Fashion Market on Zhongshan Erlu in Dongshan District, the night market under the Quzhuang Overbridge and the Xihu Lu night market are also good hunting grounds for apparel.

Of special interest is Guangdong black-mud silk, which is hand-made by means of a painstakingly lengthy process and dyed as many as 30 times, using the red extract of the

Jade

Jade holds a greater fascination for the Chinese than any other stone. Traditionally, it is worn for good luck, as a protection against sickness and as an amulet for travellers. There are several types of jade: nephrite, jadeite and a local variety, *nanyu* jade. Do not buy from open-air private markets, as there are plenty of imitations in the market. Buy from established shops such as the Jade Shop (12–14 Zhongshan Wulu), Baoli Yuqi Hang (220 Zhongshan Silu), Guangzhou Antique Shop (696 Wende Lu), and the jewellery shops of the China, Garden and White Swan hotels.

gambier root and the iron-rich river mud from the Pearl River. The material stays cool and dry in humid weather. The silk is available from the Xin Da Xin department store, at the corner of Beijing Lu and Zhongshan Wulu.

HANDICRAFTS

Bird cages

The Chinese are renowned for their love of songbirds and their tendency to show such birds off in splendidly decorated cages at public parks. Antique cages cost from 100 to 700 yuan; newer ones can be bought at the Bird Market, located at the Dongfeng Lu entrance of Liuhua Park.

Mao Memorabilia

The Daihe Lu antique market has a reasonable variety of Mao artefacts, while the Friendship Stores sell 24-carat, diamond-studded medals. For badges, the stamp market in People's Park has the best pieces. Prices can be steep.

Paper Cuts

The Renshou Temple in Foshan, previously famous for its paper cuts of scenes from the Cultural Revolution, has remained the major production centre for this delicate craft. However, its production nowadays focuses on farm scenes.

Seals

You can have your name engraved in Chinese characters on a seal, called a chop, at the basement floor of the White Swan Hotel. When selecting your Chinese name, limit yourself to two or three characters. If you need help, the staff at the shop will help you to choose the right combination. The material used can be hard wood, soapstone, crystal or agate. The shop also sells special red ink *(hong yau)* for the seal. Do not buy from side street sellers, as the seals they sell are made of bakelite and resin imitations of stone.

Further Reading

Fiction

Clavell, James. *Taipan*. Antheneum & Dell, New York, 1966. The rise of an influential 19th-century British merchant family in Hong Kong.
Elegant, Robert. *Dynasty*. William Collins & Sons, Glasgow, 1977. Written by a foreign correspondent based in Hong Kong, this is the tale of a powerful Eurasian family in the colony from 1900 to 1970.
Feign, Larry and Nury Vittachi. *The Lillygate Letters/Execute Yourself Tonight*. Hambalan, Hong Kong, 1993. An amusing look at the 1997 issue through the eyes of popular local cartoon heroine, Lily Wong.
Mason, Richard. *The World of Suzie Wong*. 1957, new edition Pegasus Books, Hong Kong, 1994. An English artist falls in love with a local lass in this, the book that made Wan Chai famous.
Xi Xi. *Marvels of a Floating City*. Renditions Paperbacks, 1997 and *A Girl Like Me and Other Stories*. Renditions Paperbacks, enlarged edition, 1996. Short stories from Hong Kong's most prominent female fiction writer Zhang Yan, aka Xi Xi.

History/Geography

Endacott, G.B. *A History of Hong Kong*. Hong Kong, Oxford University Press, 1958 and 1973. The established "Bible" of Hong Kong history, this is an extensive study of the former British colony, from ancient to modern times.
Hong Kong Government. *Hong Kong 2002*. A detailed review of contemporary Hong Kong. *Updated annually*.
Stokes, Edward. *Across Hong Kong Island* (HKCP Foundation, 1998) and *Hong Kong's Wild Places: An Environmental Exploration*. Oxford University Press, 1995. Both books explore the scenic beauty of Hong Kong Island and her countryside.

Other Insight Guides

Insight Guides

Celebrated for their stunning photojournalism, the *Insight Guides* series brings to life the history, culture, politics and people of almost 200 destinations around the world. Guides in the China series include Beijing, Shanghai and China.

Pocket Guides

Insight Pocket Guides replace the need for a tour guide, advising on the best things to see in a short time. Each guide includes itineraries exploring the main attractions, plus expert practical advice and a detailed pull-out map. There are *Insight Pocket Guides* to Beijing, Hong Kong and Macau.

Compact Guides

Insight Compact Guides – handy, informative quick-reference books – are ideal for on-the-spot use. Guides in the China series include Beijing, Shanghai and Hong Kong.

FlexiMaps

Insight FlexiMaps are essential travel maps. Highly durable, with detailed cartography, plus expert travel tips and information on major tourist attractions. Titles include Beijing, Shanghai and Hong Kong.

Feedback

We do our best to ensure the information in our books is as accurate and up-to-date as possible. The books are updated on a regular basis, using local contacts, who painstakingly add, amend and correct as required. However, some mistakes and omissions are inevitable and we are ultimately reliant on our readers to put us in the picture.

We would welcome your feedback on any details related to your experiences using the book "on the road". Maybe we recommended a hotel that you liked (or another that you didn't), as well as interesting new attractions, or facts and figures you have found out about the country itself. The more details you can give us (particularly with regard to addresses, e-mails and telephone numbers), the better.

We will acknowledge all contributions, and we'll offer an Insight Guide to the best letters received.

Please write to us at:
Insight Guides
PO Box 7910
London SE1 1WE
United Kingdom
Or send e-mail to:
insight@apaguide.co.uk

ART & PHOTO CREDITS

Apa 72
David Bowden 111, 256, 269, 272L/R, 275
Ray Cranbourne 44R
Gertrud & Helmut Denzau 89
Richard Dobson 97, 103, 104, 214/215, 216
Jean-Léo Dugast 79L, 178/179
Alain Evrard 46L/R, 47, 68, 77, 78, 120/121, 167, 169, 203, 237, 238R
Government Information Services 38, 260
Dallas & John Heaton 105
Peter Hessel 258
Jack Hollingsworth 10/11, 60, 62, 64, 70/71, 75, 87R, 90/91, 119, 137, 148, 156, 161, 174/175, 198/199, 202, 211, 218, 250, 265, 271
Hong Kong Museum of Art Collection (Auguste Borget) 27, 29, 30/31, 230/231
Gerhard Jörén 42, 59, 98R, 118
Catherine Karnow 8/9, 12/13, 40/41, 48, 49, 51, 52/53, 54/55, 56, 58, 61, 63, 69, 84, 92, 102, 112, 115, 126/127, 136, 145, 154, 163, 164/165, 171, 173, 186L, 188, 193, 224, 239, 240, 241, 245, 264, 268, 274
Taras Kovaliv/Apa 2T, 2B, 6/7, 65, 67, 76, 85, 94, 95, 107, 110, 113, 114, 132, 138L/R, 140R, 141, 142L/R, 143, 144, 149, 150, 152, 153, 155, 157, 160, 166, 168, 170, 180, 181, 182L/R, 183, 184, 185, 186R, 187, 189, 190,

191, 194/195, 200, 201, 204, 206, 207, 213, 219, 220L/R, 222, 223, 226, 227, 270L/R, 273, all small cover pictures except back flap bottom
Earl Kowall 44L, 96, 98L, 209, 229
Olivier Laude 246/247, 248/249, 262
Max Lawrence 81, 116, 128
Leo Haks Collection 32, 37, 79R
Ian Lloyd 80, 117
Pat Lucero 254, 255, 259, 261, 263R, 267
Keith McGregor 57, 124/125, 205
Mainichi Shimbun/Tokyo 35L
Manfred Morgenstern 28L/R, 33, 34L/R, 35R, 36, 45
National Palace Museum 73, 74, 86
Photobank/Singapore 22/23, 263L
Public Record Office, London 24/25
G.P. Reichelt 88
Liau Chung Ren/Globe Press Agency back flap bottom
Frank Salmoiraghi 99
Shanghai Banking Corporation 26
South China Morning Post 39, 43
Chris Stowers/Panos Pictures 108/109
Rick Strange 93
The Travel Libary/John Lawrence 14
Bill Wassman 1, 17, 18/19, 66, 87L, 122/123, 140L, 142T, 208, 210, 234, 242, 243, 244, 276
Joseph Yogerst 232/233, 238L

INSIGHT GUIDE
HONG KONG

Cartographic Editor **Zoë Goodwin**
Production **Linton Donaldson, Caroline Low**
Design Consultants **Klaus Geisler, Graham Mitchener**
Picture Researchers **Hilary Genin, Britta Jaschinski**

Picture Spreads

Pages 82/83:
Left to right from top: Impact Photos/Dave Young; Impact Photos/Alain Evrard; Impact Photos/Alain Evrard; Impact Photos/Alain Evrard; The Image Bank/Derek Berwin; Impact Photos/Caroline Penn; Impact Photos/Alain Evrard; James Davis Worldwide Travel Library.

Pages 100/101:
Left to right from top: The Anthony Blake Photo Library/Peter Williams; The Anthony Blake Photo Library; The Anthony Blake Photo Library; The Anthony Blake Photo Library; The Anthony Blake Photo Library; Cephas/Wine Magazine; Panos Pictures/Wang Gang Feng; Cephas/Wine Magazine.

Pages 146/147:
Left to right from top: Impact Photos/Mark Henley; Impact Photos/Mark Henley; Catherine Karnow; Catherine Karnow; Catherine Karnow; Catherine Karnow.

Map Production Polyglott Kartographie

© 2004 Apa Publications GmbH & Co. Verlag KG (Singapore branch)

Index

A
B
C
D
F
G
H
I
J
a
b
c
d
e
f
g
h
j
k
l